PACIFIC
NORTHWEST
TRAIL
GUIDE

PACIFIC NORTHWEST TRAIL GUIDE

Ron Strickland

The Writing Works
Seattle, Washington

The section on Hypothermia, written by Jeffrey P. Shaffer,
is reprinted from *Pacific Crest Trail,* © 1979 by
Wilderness Press. Used by permission.

Library of Congress Cataloging in Publication Data
Strickland, Ron.
Pacific Northwest trail guide.
(Northwest collection)
Bibliography: p.
Includes index.
1. Hiking—Pacific Northwest Trail—Guide-books.
2. Pacific Northwest Trail—Guide-books. I. Title.
II. Series.
GV199.42.P33S77 1984   917.95   84-15304
ISBN 0-916076-62-8

This is a Northwest Collection book
published by The Writing Works
P.O. Box 24947
Seattle, Washington 98124
THE WRITING WORKS IS A MEMBER OF THE CONE-HEIDEN GROUP

CONTENTS

Acknowledgments   iv
A Word About Maps   vii

Part One: Before You Go   1
1. The Romance and Challenge of the Pacific Northwest Trail   2
2. Pacific Northwest Trail Realities   8
3. Planning Your Trip   12
4. The Responsible Trail User   20

Part Two: Route Descriptions   25
1. The Rocky Mountains   28
2. The Purcell Mountains   56
3. The Inland Empire   80
4. The Kettle River Range   112
5. The Okanogan   131
6. The Pasayten   149
7. North Cascades to Salt Water   173
8. Dikes and Islands   202
9. The Olympic Mountains   220
10. Pacific Ocean Wilderness Beach   246

Bibliography   262
Index   266

ACKNOWLEDGMENTS

Because of the volunteer nature of the Pacific Northwest Trail Association, it is very difficult for me to thank all of the people who have helped to make the Trail a success. Hundreds deserve recognition, but I can list only a few.

The many helpers and friends out along our thousand-mile pathway include: Jim Beisel (Great Falls); John Frederick (Polebridge); Ralph Thayer (Columbia Falls); Bert Wilke (Fortine); Bill and Clara Fewkes (Rexford); Linda Stehlik and Crash Pringle-Kruse (Yaak); Nan Flannigan (Moyie Springs); Bill Tilley (the Purcells); Ellen Dietel, Will Venard, Bob Crooks, and Jerry Pavia (Bonners Ferry); David Boswell and Ralph Fulp (Priest River); Bill Fisher (Leadpoint); Ollie Mae Wilson (Northport); Leonard Merkel (Orient); Dean Fischer and Anne Lawson (Kettle Range); Bob and Denise Zipperer (Malo); Helen and Dick Slagle (Republic); Dick Thayer and Stan and Syd Porter (Oroville); Vic Barnes and Willard Newton (Loomis); Deke Smith, Dave Stone and Vicki Nordness (Carlton); Glee Davis and Les Hilde (Sedro Woolley); Mary Hilliard (Bow); Greg Aanes (Bellingham); Mark Gilkey and Bob Rose (Anacortes); Merle Segault (Oak Harbor); Bill and Gwen Howard (Port Townsend); and "Chiggers" (Forks).

I would like to mention the leadership of Robert C. Randolph and Kelby Fletcher, past treasurer and president, respectively, of the Association. And the long term help of: Chris Kounkel (Spokane, WA); Zhang Ke (Peking, P.R.C.); Jean-Louis Dethier (Liege, Belgium); Mandy ("Camper") Kent (Bennington, VT); Harvey Manning (Issaquah, WA); Rick ("Mr. Risk") Russin (Monaca, PA); Elise ("Blossom") duPont (Wilmington, DE); Margie Albertson (Portland, OR); and Jill ("Siwash") Kern (Washington, D.C.). Eighty-year-old Paris Walters of Newark, Delaware, was the man who first fascinated me with tales of Northwest long-distance hiking back in 1962; that I went on to found this great trail in 1970 was largely due to his influence and example.

The officers and board members of this Association deserve special thanks from all who love the Pacific Northwest Trail. President Larry Reed has inspired all of us through his long dedication to the project. Trail locator Max Eckenberg has earned my lasting gratitude for his constant reminders about the difficulties Clinton C. Clark overcame in creating the Pacific Crest Trail a half century ago. Randolph W. Urmston, our first president, has contributed his good humor, his house, and his time when those things were invaluable to our cause. Carol Little has coaxed prodigious feats out of our trail crew. Ome Daiber has contributed his long experience from mountain rescue and scouting. And Pat Cummins has provided invaluable liaison with the forest industry.

Although most use of long-distance trails consists of local hikes, the romantic lure of such a trail lies in its highly extended length. In our case, the lucky few who have successfully struggled to become "end-to-enders" have had a unique part to play in the creation of the PNWT. Part of our difficult task as volunteers has been getting word about the Trail out to the hiking/horse-riding public. So far, we have been very fortunate in the dedication, humor, and diplomacy of our end-to-enders. Our two dozen long-distance laureates have gone out of their way to recruit new members and to publicize our work. Janet Garner and Rex Bakel, for instance, had a cover article in *Backpacker* magazine about their historic 1977 Divide-to-Pacific walk. Col. Pete Langstaff and John Molohon visited local newspaper offices, and Linnea Carlson published a fascinating diary of her travels. Nick Gelesko enthusiastically recruited six end-to-enders after his own trek.

PNWT END-TO-ENDERS

1977:	Janet Garner		Jim Koegle
	Rex Bakel		Paul Dillon
	Jerry Smith	1983:	Ted Hitzroth
	Scott Shuey		Ronald Strickland
	Heath Hibbard		Kathie Smyth
1979:	Linnea Carlson		John Spiess
	Barb Wesser		Laura Messick
	John Molohon		Leonard Adkins
	Pete Langstaff		Jan Collins
1981:	David Brill		Stu Kane
	Nick Gelesko		

Janet Garner and Rex Bakel completing PNWT on Olympic Coast

I want especially to thank my 1983 guidebook-expedition partner, Ted Hitzroth, for making both that memorable 3½-month hike and this book possible. I very much appreciate his patience and quiet humor across more than a thousand miles of backcountry and his hard work to create the best possible maps of the Trail for you.

We have borrowed the section on hypothermia from Jeff Schaeffer's *The Pacific Crest Trail*. Mark Albright of the University of Washington Geography Department contributed the PNWT temperature chart. Howard Burd at Metsker Maps Of Seattle was very helpful in obtaining the several hundred dollars worth of maps we needed to put this book together. Janet Garner and Rex Bakel prepared the equipment and low-impact-camping suggestions.

My long-ago dream of creating America's finest "national scenic trail" has touched and enriched many lives. But as you will see in this guidebook, completion of that vision cannot be taken for granted. There is an enormous, mind-boggling amount of work to be done. That, of course, is part of the fun. I am confident about the future. I am happy for those who will be enjoying the Trail for the first time, whether on a day trip, a circuit hike, or a more extended trek. I am excited for those who will be returning to some favorite spot, making lasting friendships along the route, or contributing toward completion of our blazed and signed pathway.

Backpacking is a totally absorbing experience, which a book such as this can only suggest. If possible, abandon your armchair, put this guidebook in your pack, and head out the door. Backpacking is not a spectator sport. The pleasures of putting one foot in front of the other, of blending into the countryside, and of feeling its rhythms—these must be experienced firsthand.

Adventure, the boundless possibilities at camp-breaking, the satisfactions of full days, the subtle and grand impressions of nature—these will be the elements of our new Pacific Northwest National Scenic Trail.

This book is dedicated to all who share that great dream.

A WORD ABOUT MAPS

The topographic maps in this book are black and white reproductions of the U.S. Geological Survey's popular 7½ and 15 minute series quadrangles. All the maps have been printed at a scale of 1:50,000. This means that approximately 1.27 inches on the maps equals one mile on the ground. The land net, superimposed on many of the maps, can be helpful in judging map distance. An average section is one mile across.

The PNWT Practical Route is marked on the maps in two ways. When the route follows existing roads or trails it is marked with a heavy dashed line. In the few instances where the route strikes off cross-country, it is indicated by a dotted line.

The maps for each chapter are organized in chronological order at the end of each chapter. Since the text describes the trail from east to west, the maps are numbered and arranged the same way. To aid in orienting the maps with one another we have provided margin notes indicating how the maps tie together. For example, the note in the left hand margin of map 4E, SEE MAP 4F, tells us that the trail continues on Map 4F.

Below is a legend showing some of the most common symbols used in the route maps. To get the most out of the maps it is important to have a good knowledge of these symbols and what they represent on the ground.

PNWT ROUTE	— — —	PNWT ROUTE (Cross Country)	– – – – –
PRIMARY HIGHWAY	▬▬▬▬	BUILDINGS	
LIGHT DUTY ROAD	════════	CAMPGROUNDS	×
UNIMPROVED ROAD	=========	SCHOOL AND CHURCH	‖‖‖‖‖‖‖‖‖
TRAIL	– – – – –	TOWER	⌐o
RAILROAD	┼─┼─┼─┼	MINE TUNNEL	
PERENNIAL STREAM	～～	GLACIER	⊱
INTERMITTENT STREAM	‥‥‥	SPRING	⊙
INDEX CONTOUR	～ —	LEVEE	⫶
INTERMEDIATE CONTOUR	～ —	SPOT ELEVATION	✗
TOWNSHIP AND RANGE LINE	▬▬▬	SECTION LINE W/ FOUND CONTOUR	
SECTION LINE	– – – – –	FENCE	● ● ●

Scale 1:50,000 approx. 1 inch = .79 miles

1	0	1 MILE

1000 0 1000 2000 3000 4000 5000 6000 7000 FEET

1 5 0 1 KILOMETER

One of the most important features of a topographic map is the contour lines. Each contour represents a hypothetical line which follows the terrain at a specific elevation. Every fifth contour is a bolder *index contour* labeled with its elevation. The difference in elevation between contours, *the contour interval,* can be found by taking the difference between consecutive index contours and dividing by five, the number of intermediate intervals between index contours.

The land net is another helpful feature included on many of the maps. These lines represent the surveyed division of the land into townships and sections. A township contains 36 one-mile-square sections. Section corners are often physically marked on the ground, enabling an experienced traveler to locate his exact position on his map.

For more information on USGS map symbols, you can write to Branch of Distribution, U.S. Geological Survey, Box 25286, Federal Center, Denver CO 80225.

Since the maps in this book cover only a limited area on either side of the trail route, we suggest the user purchase national forest road maps for the area being walked. These can be invaluable to the hiker if weather or emergency require an alternate route back to civilization. The national forests crossed on the PNWT are, from east to west: Flathead National Forest, Kootenai National Forest, Panhandle National Forest, Colville National Forest, Okanogan National Forest, Mt. Baker-Snoqualmie National Forest, and Olympic National Forest. These maps can be obtained from local national forest ranger stations.

Part One:

BEFORE YOU GO

Olympic National Park

THE ROMANCE AND CHALLENGE OF THE PACIFIC NORTHWEST TRAIL

Pacific Ocean Wilderness Beach

Walking is beautifully simple. Long-distance walking has the purity and economy of well-lived days. Trekking is both esthetically pleasing and physically fulfilling. For many of us, walking is a must, a passion.

The quality of every romance is colored by its circumstances. In walking, too, the finest experience will be found in the most inspiring surroundings. The walks described in this book are for passionate walkers.

The Pacific Northwest Trail offers more than a thousand miles of the most varied, most magnificent country in North America: subtle deserts, grand Rockies, tide pools, alpine gardens, rain forests, and saltwater coasts.

How to explain the lure of the Pacific Northwest Trail? The word "recreation" suggests the beginning of an answer, but "freedom" is closer to the mystique and romance that motivates our hikers, horsemen, and local volunteers. And even the stay-at-homes. How many armchair adventurers have said, "Someday I'm going to do that PNWT." Even just saying it makes you feel better.

The frontier shaped American character in ways that we are beginning to forget. Our old safety valve of "lighting out for the territory" has largely disappeared. In its place is a more static, highly developed, bureaucratized society. The lesson of personal independence is less easy to learn. The Trail is in a real way a counterbalance to all that.

The non-romantic 1980s are, we hear, a time to concentrate on "the bottom line." But I believe that much of the population hungers for something more. Long-distance trekking offers an exciting alternative to the expected, settled, practical life. On the PNWT, every day is an adventure; every camp, a triumph; and every mountain crossed, an inspiring passage.

However challenging our trail may be, it is easy compared with planning and building the PNWT. The philosophy of this Association is that volunteers—especially local volunteers—can do the best job for the least money.

Only sixteen years remain of this century. The Association's goal is to locate, mark, and protect a continuous route across the whole region by the year 2000. Important progress toward reaching that not-so-distant goal has already been made by the Association's volunteers:

1970–1976 Initial exploration of alternative routes for a new recreation trail using existing trails, cattle driveways, Indian paths, and primitive roads.

1976 Passage of P.L. 94-527 requiring a federal report to Congress on "the desirability and feasibility" of adding the Pacific Northwest Trail to the National Trails System.

1977 Incorporation of the non-profit Pacific Northwest Trail Association in Seattle, Washington.

1977 First PNWT trail sign erected at Copeland, Idaho, by local volunteers.

1977 Trail hiked by five hikers in one season.

1978 "National Scenic Trail" status for the PNWT favored at public hearings in seven Northwest towns.

1979 Publication of the PNWTA's first *Guide.*

1979 Release of joint National Park Service/Forest Service PNWT Study Team official report recommending against inclusion of the PNWT in the National Trails System because of: (1) no recreational need; (2) $100-million estimated cost; and (3) alleged extreme environmental impact. PNWTA countered with a 30-page indictment of the government report's biases and inaccuracies.

1980 Publication of a revised edition of the *Guide.*

1980 Brushing out and reconstruction of the Long Canyon section begun by Boundary County, Idaho, volunteers.

1981 Data about current Trail conditions gathered by four-man PNWTA expedition.

1982   Unanimous resolution by Washington State's House and Senate in favor of the PNWT.

1982   Blazing with the PNWTA's standardized 6-by-2-inch white paint blaze begun in every county.

1982   Introduction of the PNWT bill in Congress.

1983   Location and construction of the first new, volunteer-built link in the PNWT.

Long-distance trails are as old as the seasonal migrations of herders and their livestock in ancient times. In the United States the nineteenth-century emigrant routes, such as the Oregon Trail, populated the vast West. But long-distance recreational trails are a distinctly twentieth-century phenomenon. Vermont's Long Trail dates from 1910, and the Appalachian Trail from 1921.

The Pacific Northwest Trail began to take shape after my first trip from the East Coast to Washington State in 1968 to hike the famous, north-south Pacific Crest Trail. I wondered about a route that would link wilderness areas across the whole northern part of the region. An east-west route from the Continental Divide to the Pacific Ocean would have enormous variety: desert and rain forest, glaciers and seastacks. Such a Pacific Northwest Trail would be a path through paradise.

For over twenty years I have been captivated by the idea of long-distance trails, and it was natural that eventually I would try to create one.

I began to explore my new route in the summer of 1970 by following existing trails created by the Indians and the early explorers, trappers, miners, herders, and foresters. Maps (often contradictory), the advice of local outdoorsmen, and intuition were my guides. While I was walking, constructive bewilderment often led me in rewarding directions.

Most of the time during those early years I walked alone. This was partly by choice and partly by necessity; good companions were scarce. Today if you wish to find a partner for a major PNWT trip, our Association can help you locate one.

Unlike the Northwest's existing network of Forest Service administrative pathways of the 1930s, the PNWT is being developed in the volunteer tradition of the Appalachian Trail. About sixty years ago an architect and land-use planner named Benton MacKaye worried about the frightening pace of development of the Appalachian Mountains. He proposed creation of a Maine-to-Georgia trail that would provide both needed nature contact for city people and a method of backcountry zoning. He envisioned a 20-mile-wide corridor of preserved rural land, an Appalachian "greenway." In the 1930s Benton MacKaye further refined his preservation ideas and with several friends founded the Wilderness Society.

From the beginning the Appalachian Trail was a nongovernmental effort. In addition to visionaries like Benton MacKaye and Myron Avery, the Appalachian Trail became a reality through the grass-roots dedication of thousands of enthusiasts over many decades. This pattern changed somewhat after 1975 as the National Park Service began to play a larger

PNWTA Trail Crew

Mt. Baker's Deming Glacier

planning, acquisition, and development role under the 1968 National Trails System Act. However, as federal trail budgets evaporate, the Appalachian Trail and the other great volunteer trails will once again become entirely dependent upon their own resources. In the long run that is probably best for the "national scenic trails," which have already received statutory protection. Government support brings the danger of govermental control.

Several Western examples illustrate the dangers of too great governmental direction of long-distance-trail planning. First, the Pacific Crest Trail (now almost entirely a Forest Service project) has been reconstructed to inappropriate roadlike standards. Second, the bureaucrats in charge of the PNWT study, despite spending at least $100,000, never produced an inch of treadway or a single new PNWT sign or blaze. They never even left their offices to hike the route. They concentrated on map-room research on three 6-mile-wide "corridors" for their cost estimates. Imagine what would have happened if, instead, the $100,000 had been given directly to the local volunteers for use in planning, construction, and signing.

The bedrock of our philosophy is that local volunteers are the key to developing and maintaining the Trail. Only they have the grass-roots contacts and knowledge to do the job right. Oroville civic leader Dick Thayer, for instance, was a Boy Scout at Blue Diamond Lake forty years ago and was able to recommend it for inclusion in the Okanogan County route. Or take Max Eckenburg. His grandfather was a timber cruiser in the Whatcom County area where Max has been so successful in designing our route. Max himself worked right there for the Civilian Conservation Corps and the U.S. Forest Service, developing a wealth of knowledge and experience, which he now applies to the PNWT.

This book is intended not only as a where-to-go book, but also as an inspiration to potential trailbuilders. Come join us, it says, in helping to improve and link together existing sections of the PNWT.

Consider volunteering for a work trip. (No, you don't have to be a muscleman.) Or adopt a section of the route as your personal project.

(Back East, clubs often have waiting lists for such trail sections; here there's no waiting.) If you live too far away to become a grass-roots activist, sign up for one of our excellent summer work trips. (Write to the PNWTA's local coordinator for the area in which you would like to help.) Work trips are not work at all in the usual sense. They are fun shared with your new friends. And at a time when most people's employment consists of paperwork, the personal satisfaction is immediate and concrete when you install a water bar, repair washed-out tread, and open up a brushy pathway. Please help us. Helping the Trail is a good way to help yourself.

How do trails get built? First and most importantly, we must have the permission of whoever owns the land. After our Trail corridor has been decided upon, our local clubs and volunteers carefully work out easement agreements with the landowner. On the PNWT that usually means the U.S. Forest Service.

Next we must go over every square foot of ground in the area where the Trail is to be built. This time-consuming reconnaissance is essential if we are to pick out the key points that will add up to the best possible trail. We must squeeze the area like a sponge for its outstanding features and scenic vistas. We must build in south exposures wherever possible because they are the last spots to be snowed in, and in spring the first to open. Also, they have fewer bugs, are more open, and require fewer trail-building hours. Reconnaissance is the most time-consuming and important part of Trail location.

After we select the route, we ribbon it with marking tapes at regular intervals and at eye level. This allows us to design in grade of 10 percent or less (with only occasional steeper exceptions). A 10-percent-or-less grade allows greater daily travel distances, and it reduces tread deterioration from feet and hooves. Ribboning the route also involves brushing out a line-of-sight right-of-way, the visible beginning of the new trail.

Now we are ready to stake the route. A wooden stake is hammered in every 5 feet on ground that needs to be dug out and every 25 feet or so on flat ground. At this point we also chainsaw out the small trees in the right-of-way. We leave very large trees and roots.

Finally, the digging volunteers come with their earthmoving tools. Each person is responsible for the space between at least three stakes. Where it is necessary to cut into a hillside, the stake is considered the outer edge of our 18-inch tread. On flat ground the stake is considered the center of the tread. In each area the physical development of the PNWT tread is a compromise between keeping the Trail as low profile as possible and building it strongly enough to withstand erosion and other wear and tear.

Building or maintaining the Trail is a fascinating process. We welcome your help.

There are as many ways to enjoy the Pacific Northwest Trail as there are people travelling it. As readers of my *Going the Distance—The Pacific Northwest Trail* know, my own trailside view sometimes narrows alarmingly to bakeries, bakeries, and more bakeries.

You, for instance, may have studied geology and have a special feeling for rock and glacial record, which everywhere begs to be read along the PNWT. Or you may decide to keep lists of the wildflowers and birds you encounter.

The romance and challenge of the PNWT is ultimately very personal. Experience it for yourself. The first pleasure comes from the country itself—the mountains, rivers, coasts. But another delight is the feeling of personal accomplishment you get from navigating unknown country or helping with some aspect of the Association's work. Probably the richest experience of all is that of making lasting friendships among people with whom you have shared a special love.

PACIFIC NORTHWEST TRAIL REALITIES

When you opened this book, you were probably asking yourself, What is this trail really like? The answer—expect many types of trail conditions and always be prepared for the worst.

As of this writing, the PNWT is an informally linked-together skein of existing trails, backcountry roads, Indian routes, stock driveways, and cross-country travel. These 1100 + miles have been chosen as the best combination of scenic beauty, environmental protection, educational interest, land ownership, and practical movement. Often features already in place, such as an existing bridge crossing, have dictated our choice. In other places we follow the old Forest Service trails—but only for a temporary lack of better-designed pathways. Often we are concerned with environmental factors such as fragile alpine areas or grizzly bear denning sites. Amenities are important, too; we try to design natural campsites and water sources and viewpoints into the PNWT. And, as much as possible, we try to keep to the high country and its far horizons, where a traveller can reflect upon challenges already overcome and delights ahead.

The conditions you will encounter range from luxury trails (perfectly built and groomed) to totally faded tracks to sections where even a deer trail would offer unspeakable relief. The most difficult sections of the PNWT are in Montana and Idaho. There the Forest Service neglect of the old trail network has been the most saddening.

Why, you ask, are so many trails abandoned by the U.S. Forest Service? The answer is both a matter of changing needs and changing congressional appropriations. The Northwest's original trails were Indian, trapper, game, and mining routes. After the great forest fire outbreaks of the teens and twenties, the Forest Service built a very impressive web of pack trails, lookouts, primitive airstrips, guard stations, and roads in all of our backcountry areas. Imagine what an enormous task that was! The logging roads of the last two or so decades had not yet penetrated vast regions of unknown country. Even today, the federal government owns large amounts of Montana, Idaho, and Washington, respectively. The challenge of administering this vast area was effectively met with thousands of miles of new trails, especially during the 1930s Depression, when the CCC, WPA, and other "make work" projects provided a needed source of manpower. However, the technology of fighting fire shifted to airplanes after World War II, and the old trail and fire-lookout systems became obsolete.

Beginning in the late sixties, the backcountry experienced an explosion of recreational use, primarily the new/old sport of walking for pleasure. The government's changing backcountry management priorities and the new backcountry recreation movement met head on. The result was constantly increasing pressure on the relatively few popular trails maintained for outdoor recreation. The budget situation for trail maintenance worsened during the 1980s depression, so you can begin to understand why many old trails need a kind of Sherlock Holmes to decipher them.

There are two kinds of route-finding challenges on the PNWT: (1) how to follow obscure, overgrown sections and (2) how to navigate cross-country where the PNWT follows no existing trail at all. (We offer alternate routes for horsemen or hikers who wish to avoid all bushwhacking.)

Following abandoned trails is actually more difficult than having no trail because it is so much more frustrating. Parts of our route appear as finely built trail on the current Forest Service maps. However, when you actually begin your search, you learn that you may be the first person (other than PNWT hikers) to go that way in years. In fact, the agency drops more old trails each time it revises its maps. But the old paths rarely disappear entirely. You *can* find them.

PNWT long-distance hikers quickly begin to develop an intuitive sense for old-trail direction finding. But even so, going astray is extremely easy and quick. The best advice is always to remain very sure of your last, certain reference point before proceeding too far ahead. If you are at all unsure, go back. Don't worry about lost time or your pride. Go back and be certain that you are following the true trail.

What to look for? First, the most obvious indication that you are on an old Forest Service trail is a blaze. In the Northwest the agency's standard trail blaze was, and is, a long, vertical chop mark topped by a much smaller cut (as in an upside-down exclamation mark). Because this blaze was almost always hatcheted into both sides of a tree, an indication that a tree scar is really a blaze is that it appears going and coming. Old blazes are excellent indicators that you are on a trail. But such blazes are not perfect. They only indicate that you are on *a* trail, maybe not the one you want. And the blazed tree may have died and fallen to the ground, where you overlook it as you zip by. Or the blaze may be so old that heavy layers of pitch and overgrown bark obscure it. In that case, look carefully for little cuts typical of hatchet work and for a similar mark on the obverse side of the tree. Some natural tree scars are easily mistaken for old blazes.

The most obvious sign that you are on a lost trail is that you can make out the tread, often a distinct rut in the earth, where generations of mule and horse strings have passed. Be certain that you are not following a game trail; those canny deer and elk sometimes make a better path than the men who were paid to do the job. (A game trail is likely to be steeper and inconsistent and, of course, will never be blazed.)

A very reassuring symbol of the trail crew's long-ago passage is one or more cut logs. These may be hoary with age, yet they are a sign of man in otherwise untouched country. Sometimes you can follow the trail by these alone, reconstructing the route from the places where the crew cleared away deadfalls. Lettered signs are a valuable resource, but do not expect too much from them. Often they have fallen to the ground, have

Crossing Long Canyon Creek

been partially devoured by porcupines, or have been mutilated by bears or vandals. Or they may be so old that their wood and paint have totally weathered away. And sometimes even if you can read them, their directions are unclear.

A variety of other.clues may help you, such as a rusty nail on a tree where once there was an old sign. Stumps deep in the woods are an ambiguous sign. Cairns in open stretches are invaluable, especially in fogs or storms. (In some places vertical stakes or poles substitute for cairns.) In cattle country there may be so many "trails" that you will be better off following Chinese tea leaves.

Whatever kind of country you are travelling across, you can have fun by trying to discern the style of the local, long-ago trail locator. Guess which way he was likely to turn next. Did he prefer direct, straight-line approaches? Was he a contour-around-it man or a straight-up-and-over-it man?

The key to following old trails is the same for cross-country navigation —know the general lay of the land and the direction of your march and of the major landmarks. Trust your compass; it never lies. This is not the place to give a complete course on orienteering, but if you want to become a PNWT hiker, especially in Montana and Idaho, be sure to carry an excellent compass and the correct topographic maps. Practice map and compass direction finding *before you begin* your PNWT trek. Each year the PNWT Association gives this advice to would-be end-to-enders, even to people who have hiked the entire 2000 miles of the Appalachian Trail, and each year at the end of the season we hear reports about how difficult certain PNWT sections were because of the traveller's unfamiliarity with map and compass.

I like the Swedish-made Silva Ranger compass for use with USGS topographic maps. Its combination of base plate, sighting mirror, magnetic needle, and declination adjustment is excellent. The Silva Ranger costs over $30; it's not cheap. But do not consider skimping on your compass any more than you would consider economizing by carrying too little food.

Cross-country travel is not for all hikers, and it is often not a good idea for pack stock. So wherever the PNWT involves bushwhacking, this guidebook offers an easier alternate route. Consider carefully whether you really want to cross those stormy ridges or buck that brush down in that trailless valley. Chances are that if you get lost, you will have only yourself to get you unlost.

But do not become unduly fearful of cross-country. Everyone who has travelled far on the PNWT has complained about the navigational difficulties but has also concluded that that part of the PNWT challenge was one of the rewards of the Trail.

One of our primary goals as a volunteer trail club is to preserve that frontier challenge, which everyone of us has enjoyed so much (at least in retrospect). So although we have begun PNWTA blazing in every county along the Trail, we are trying to develop the route lightly. We do not want to overblaze, to have a blaze every 10 feet, as sometimes seems the case back East. Nor do we want the physical character of our path to conform to the freeway standards of the Forest Service's great show trails. We plan the PNWT to be a low-impact, high-enjoyment, primitive path through a great variety of natural and human habitats. Because its development is largely up to local volunteers and because it uses quite a hodgepodge of existing routes, the PNWT will not be totally standardized from one end to the other.

Except in the matter of our 6-by-2-inch white paint blazes. When you see one, you will know that you are OK. Unfortunately, as of this writing our white paint blazes are far and few between. For several more years you will not be able to guide yourself over the PNWT following the white blazes alone.

Why a white paint blaze? Long experience elsewhere has shown that metal markers are too attractive to souvenir hunters and vandals. Wooden signs suffer the same fate and are also attractive to chewing, gnawing, and scratching wild critters. Traditional hatchet blazes in our part of the world could easily be confused with the standard Forest Service markings. Plus, the white paint is cheap, easily visible, and highly distinctive.

One further note. Where the PNWT changes direction, we place two white blazes, one over the other. A double white paint blaze means, "caution, slow down and look for the new bearing."

PLANNING YOUR TRIP   ‖ 3

To plan your trip, first decide what kind of trek you really want. Most people, of course, cannot get away for the 2½ to 3½ months necessary to complete the entire PNWT in a single season. Most people, in fact, can manage only day trips or short, overnight jaunts. Such outings, however, provide an intense experience of one particular place and can often be arranged as loop or circuit trips. (This guidebook describes outstanding loop trips wherever possible.)

Some people will want to hit highlights of the PNWT over a number of years. Maybe someday they will decide to link those sections together and become "end-to-enders."

A tiny minority of PNWT enthusiasts—people of all ages, by the way, and not just the 20-year-olds—will arrange their lives so that their ultra-trek dream of a thousand-mile summer becomes a reality. A very long trip accentuates to the maximum degree all of the PNWT's feelings of freedom and adventure. It has twin disadvantages. The trip is so long that there may not be enough time to appreciate the country; it all begins to go by in a blur. And if the trip is not extremely well planned, its burdens may be too much even for the strongest backs and legs.

That brings up the important subject of your purpose in undertaking a difficult, extended march across wild country. If slogging away at it is all you're after, stay home. Long-distance hikers too easily fall prey to "mileage mentality." "If I don't make my 20 miles today . . ." Think about how crazy that is. It's far better to get to know one trail or area well—perhaps over a period of years—than to sacrifice seeing for speed. Don't hike so fast that you are oblivious to the daily miracles around you.

The most important preparation for a successful distance hike is psychological. We are attracted to trekking (foot or horse) because of its frontier adventure, the satisfactions of full days, and the subtle and grand impressions of nature. But let's face the fact that interspersed with those memorable times will be severe trials, storms, for instance, which make your way a path of sorrows. Long-distance hiking can also be lonely and stressful. Meeting these psychological challenges may mean the difference between your trip's success or failure.

Beyond that, proper equipment is a must! For instance, your choice of clothing can make an enormous difference in on-the-trail comfort and safety. Many fine new fabrics and designs have appeared during the last ten years, but the best approach is still the layer method. If you get hot, take something off.

Be sure to carry your first aid information around in your head—not in a book or pamphlet deep in your pack. Take care of your feet; check them regularly for blisters, overheating, and infection. Many hikes have come to a screeching halt because of foot problems. (Need I add that you should break in your boots *before* your expedition?) From my own "end-to-end" experience, I advocate the heavier, traditional mountain boots for our snow, rock, and cross-country sections and the new lightweight boots for our road and trail walking.

By all means carry extra food, sunglasses, knife, fire starter, matches, first aid kit, canteen, flashlight, map, compass, soap, insect repellent, signaling device, cook kit, and a pack large enough for all of these. Not too large, however, or you will lug along more stuff than you really need. If there is extra room in your pack, you will fill it with something. Go light!

One or more companions can be a help or a hindrance, depending upon your relationship, capacity for loneliness, and individual resourcefulness. The solo hiker is his own boss and can often see wildlife, which a noisy group cannot. He is also a potential accident and loneliness victim.

Another precaution concerns nutrition. Be prepared to eat ravenously and nutritiously; otherwise your body may not be able to withstand the grueling Olympic challenge of day-in, day-out backpacking. And don't forget to eat an ample amount of fats—especially in cold weather (of which you will encounter plenty during an end-to-end trip).

PNWT 1000-milers have always begun at Waterton-Glacier and set off westward toward the setting sun. But whether you journey toward the ocean or toward the Rockies, you will encounter cold weather *and snow* somewhere during your $100 \pm$ days on the Trail. At Glacier National Park, areas such as Boulder Pass may not melt out until midsummer. In years of heavy snowpack (e.g., 1982) even the Olympic National Park's Low Divide is snowbound well into July. If you are not trying to hike all of the Trail in one season but are seeking the extra solitude of the "off season," beware of April, May, June, September, and October high-country snowstorms. Indeed, in a place like the Pasayten Wilderness you can encounter snow and hail any day of the summer! Yet August daytime temperatures in the Okanogan regularly exceed 100°F. Be prepared to alter your gear as conditions change. For instance, after leaving Glacier National Park, send home your ice axe. When you approach the Okanogan, break out your bathing suit.

Unlike the Appalachian Trail, the PNWT does not have periodic shelters along its length. Hikers must carry their own tarps or tents, preferably very lightweight ones with good insect protection.

This is not the place for specific guidance about brand names of camping gear. That information changes very quickly and, anyway, a serious hiker is likely to be only slightly less loyal to a wife or husband than to long-held opinions on equipment. Just be sure that your gear suits *you*. Don't become a slave to the mystique of gadgetry. Remember that what you take with you is only a means to enjoy the PNWT, not an end in itself.

CHECKLIST OF GEAR

GENERAL EQUIPMENT
- ☐ Backpack
- ☐ Pack cover
- ☐ Accessory straps
- ☐ Lightweight tent
- ☐ Sleeping bag
- ☐ Sleeping pad
- ☐ Flashlight/batteries, bulbs
- ☐ Compass
- ☐ Maps
- ☐ Boot waterproofing
- ☐ Nylon cord, 25 ft.
- ☐ First aid kit
- ☐ Clips and pins
- ☐ Cloth tape
- ☐ Needle, thread
- ☐ Patches, button
- ☐ Safety pins
- ☐ Eyeglasses
- ☐ Screwdriver
- ☐ Stove parts
- ☐ Repair kit
- ☐ PNWT guidebook
- ☐ Snowshoes*
- ☐ Ice axe*

CLOTHING
- ☐ Boots
- ☐ Thongs or tennis shoes
- ☐ Socks (3 or 4 changes)
- ☐ Long pants (wool or quallofil pile)
- ☐ Shorts (2 nylon gym trunks)
- ☐ Underwear (2)
- ☐ T-shirts (2)
- ☐ Long-sleeved shirt (wool or quallofil pile)
- ☐ Vest or parka
- ☐ Rain parka
- ☐ Rain pants
- ☐ Watch cap and broad-brimmed hat
- ☐ Bandana
- ☐ Gloves*
- ☐ Gaiters

COOKING
- ☐ Stove
- ☐ Fuel bottle/fuel
- ☐ Cook pot/lid
- ☐ Plate
- ☐ Eating utensils
- ☐ Quart water bottle
- ☐ Cup
- ☐ Pocketknife
- ☐ Matches/Bic lighter
- ☐ Fire starter
- ☐ Water purifier
- ☐ Litterbag

TOILETRIES
- ☐ Toilet paper
- ☐ Biodegradable soap
- ☐ Small towel
- ☐ Toothbrush/paste
- ☐ Comb
- ☐ Sunscreen
- ☐ Insect repellent

OPTIONAL
- ☐ Day pack
- ☐ Journal
- ☐ Field references
- ☐ Pen/pencil
- ☐ Writing paper/stamps
- ☐ Whistle
- ☐ Sunglasses
- ☐ Watch
- ☐ Candles
- ☐ Swimsuit
- ☐ Lip balm
- ☐ Photo Equipment
  - Camera/case
  - Film
  - Prepaid processing mailers
  - Lenses
  - Tripod
  - Lens paper/cleaner
  - Photo log

*—Denotes items needed for snow travel only

You will probably find that bears are the number-one concern of hikers along the Pacific Northwest Trail. However, if you take the standard precautions, you are unlikely to experience that kind of trouble. Hypothermia is a much more serious concern because it can creep up on you much more silently than any bear. Hypothermia is a killer, and all backpackers and horsemen are potential victims.

HYPOTHERMIA

Every year you can read accounts of hikers freezing to death in the mountains. They die of hypothermia, the #1 killer of outdoor recreationists. You too may be exposed to it, particularly if you start hiking the PNWT in April in order to do all 3 states. Because it is so easy to die from hypothermia, we are including the following information, which is endorsed by the Forest Service and by mountain-rescue groups. Read it. It may save your life.

Hypothermia is subnormal body temperature, which is caused outdoors by exposure to cold, usually aggravated by wetness, wind and exhaustion. The moment your body begins to lose heat faster than it produces it, your body makes involuntary adjustments to preserve the normal temperature in its vital organs. Uncontrolled shivering is one way your body attempts to maintain its vital temperature. *If you've begun uncontrolled shivering, you must consider yourself a prime candidate for hypothermia and act accordingly.* Shivering will eventually consume your energy reserves until they are exhausted. When this happens, cold reaches your brain, depriving you of judgment and reasoning power. You will not realize this is happening. You will lose control of your hands. Your internal body temperature is sliding downward. Without treatment, this slide leads to stupor, collapse and death. Learn the four lines of defense against hypothermia.

Your first line of defense: avoid exposure.

1. *Stay dry.* When clothes get wet, they lose about 90% of their insulating value. Wool loses less; cotton, down and synthetics lose more.

2. *Beware of the wind.* A slight breeze carries heat away from bare skin much faster than still air does. Wind drives cold air under and through clothing. Wind refrigerates wet clothes by evaporating moisture from the surface.

3. *Understand cold.* Most hypothermia cases develop in air temperatures between 30 and 50 degrees. Most outdoorsmen simply can't believe such temperatures can be dangerous. They fatally underestimate the danger of being wet at such temperatures. But just jump in a cold lakelet and you'll agree that 50° water is unbearably cold. The cold that kills is cold water running down neck and legs, cold water held against the body by sopping clothes, cold water flushing body heat from the surface of the clothes.

Your second line of defense: terminate exposure.

If you cannot stay dry and warm under existing weather conditions, using the clothes you have with you, *terminate exposure.*

1. *Be brave enough* to give up reaching your destination or whatever you had in mind. That one extra mile might be your last.

2. *Get out of the wind and rain.* Build a fire. Concentrate on making your camp or bivouac as secure and comfortable as possible.

3. *Never ignore shivering.* Persistent or violent shivering is clear warning that you are on the verge of hypothermia. *Make camp.*

4. *Forestall exhaustion.* Make camp while you still have a reserve of energy. Allow for the fact that exposure greatly reduces your normal endurance. You may think you are doing fine when the fact that you are exercising is the only thing preventing your going into hypothermia. If exhaustion forces you to stop, however briefly, your rate of body heat production instantly drops by 50% or more; violent, incapacitating shivering may begin immediately; you may slip into hypothermia *in a matter of minutes.*

5. *Appoint a foul-weather leader.* Make the best-protected member of your party responsible for calling a halt before the least protected member becomes exhausted or goes into violent shivering.

Your third line of defense: detect hypothermia.

If your party is exposed to wind, cold and wetness, *think hypothermia.* Watch yourself and others for hypothermia's symptoms:
1. Uncontrollable fits of shivering.
2. Vague, slow, slurred speech.
3. Memory lapses; incoherence.
4. Immobile, fumbling hands.
5. Frequent stumbling; lurching gait.
6. Drowsiness—to sleep is to die.
7. Apparent exhaustion, such as inability to get up after a rest.

Your fourth and last line of defense: treatment.

The victim may deny he's in trouble. Believe the symptoms, *not* the patient. Even mild symptoms demand immediate, drastic treatment.
1. Get the victim out of the wind and rain.
2. Strip off *all* wet clothes.
3. If the patient is only mildly impaired:
   a. Give him warm drinks.
   b. Get him into dry clothes and a warm sleeping bag. Well-wrapped, warm (not hot) rocks or canteens will hasten recovery.
4. If the patient is semiconscious or worse:
   a. Try to keep him awake. Give warm drinks.
   b. Leave him stripped. Put him in a sleeping bag with another person (also stripped). If you have a double bag or can zip two together, put the victim between two warmth donors. *Skin to skin contact* is the most effective treatment. Never leave the victim as long as he is alive. To do so is to kill him—it's just that simple!
5. Build a fire to warm the camp.

Other notes on avoiding hypothermia.
1. Choose rainclothes that are effective against *wind-driven* rain and

cover head, neck, body and legs. Polyurethane-coated nylon is best. The coatings won't last forever, so check them periodically.

2. Take woolen clothing for possible hypothermia weather, such as a 2-piece woolen underwear set or long wool pants and sweater or shirt. Include a knit wool cap that can protect neck and chin. Cotton underwear is *worse than useless* when wet, as are cotton shirts and pants. As native Americans long ago discovered, one stays warmer in a cold rain when he is stark naked than when he is bundled up in wet clothes.

3. Carry a stormproof tent with a good rain fly and set it up *before* you need it.

4. Carry trail food rich in calories, such as nuts, jerky and candy, and keep nibbling during hypothermia weather.

5. Take a gas stove or a plumber's candle, flammable paste or other reliable fire starter.

6. Never abandon survival gear under any circumstances. If you didn't bring along the above items, stay put and make the best of it. An all-too-common fatal mistake is for victims to abandon everything so that, unburdened, they can run for help.

7. "It never happens to me. I'm Joe athlete." Not always is it the other guy on the trail. It can be you even if you are in fantastic shape and are carrying the proper equipment. Be alert for hypothermia conditions and hypothermia symptoms.

AVERAGE CLIMATIC CONDITIONS
ALONG THE PACIFIC NORTHWEST TRAIL
(Compiled by Mark Albright)

	April	May	June	July	Aug.	Sept.	Oct.
West Glacier Elev. 3154'	53	65	71	80	79	70	53
	30	37	43	46	45	36	33
	1.9	2.4	3.0	1.3	1.5	1.9	2.6
Eureka R.S. Elev. 2532'	59	69	75	83	82	73	55
	32	40	42	46	45	36	33
	1.2	1.8	2.4	1.1	1.3	1.3	1.6
Bonners Ferry Elev. 1860'	60	69	75	85	82	73	57
	34	41	47	51	48	43	35
	1.1	1.4	1.6	0.8	0.8	1.3	2.4
Northport Elev. 1320'	65	74	79	90	87	77	61
	35	42	48	51	49	43	37
	1.3	1.7	2.2	0.8	0.8	1.2	2.0

	April	May	June	July	Aug.	Sept.	Oct.
Republic Elev. 2610'	58	68	74	84	82	74	59
	30	36	42	44	42	37	31
	1.1	1.5	1.7	0.8	0.8	0.8	1.3
Mazama Elev. 2150'	57	66	74	82	79	72	59
	32	40	46	52	51	42	30
	0.8	1.1	1.4	0.5	0.6	0.7	1.4
Stevens Pass Elev. 4070'	46	52	59	69	67	62	49
	29	34	39	45	45	41	35
	4.2	3.4	3.1	1.2	1.4	4.2	7.7
Diablo Dam Elev. 891'	57	66	70	78	77	71	58
	37	43	48	52	52	48	41
	4.4	2.5	2.1	1.2	1.3	3.5	8.0
Bellingham Elev. 149'	57	64	67	72	72	68	59
	37	41	47	48	48	44	39
	2.3	1.8	1.9	1.0	1.1	2.0	3.6
Port Townsend Elev. 100'	57	63	67	71	71	67	59
	41	46	49	51	51	49	45
	1.1	1.4	1.4	0.7	0.7	1.1	1.7
Elwha Elev. 360'	57	65	69	76	74	70	58
	37	42	46	49	50	47	41
	3.4	1.4	1.2	0.8	0.8	1.9	5.6
Quillayute Elev. 179'	55	61	65	69	68	65	61
	37	41	46	49	50	48	40
	8.2	4.7	3.5	2.4	2.8	5.2	11.6

First row across—Average daily maximum temperatures (Fahrenheit).
Second row across—Average daily minimum temperatures.
Shaded row—Average daily precipitation.

The most enjoyable part of planning a PNWT excursion for me has always been researching the natural and human history of the area I am about to visit. The Pacific Northwest Trail Association's brochure contains the following two sentences. "Every day on the Trail is an education in the region's natural and human environments. Bears, cowboys, elk, sasquatches, Indians, dippers, prospectors, conies, steelheaders, and cougars are all part of the Pacific Northwest Trail's hearty hiking." People all over the United States have asked me to explain the meaning of "steelheader." "And what the heck is a dipper?"

When you really understand the Pacific Northwest Trail, you will know the answers to these and many more fascinating questions.

The bibliography at the end of this guidebook is a good place to begin your PNWT reading fun. And once you are out along the route, local libraries and museums are very enjoyable places to visit—and will also keep you warm and dry.

LOCAL HISTORICAL AND EDUCATIONAL RESOURCE CENTERS
Museum of the Plains Indian, Browning, MT
Tobacco Valley Historic Village, Eureka, MT
Historical Society Museum (in basement of public library),
    Bonners Ferry, ID
Ferry County Museum, Republic, WA
Oroville Public Library, Oroville, WA
Okanogan County Historical Society, Okanogan, WA
Seattle City Light Museum at Gorge Power Plant (near Newhalem, WA)
Skagit County Historical Museum, La Conner, WA
Breazeale-Padilla Bay Interpretive Center, Bay View, WA
Port Townsend Museum (in city hall), Port Townsend, WA
Makah Museum, Neah Bay, WA

THE RESPONSIBLE TRAIL USER

4

Because the Pacific Northwest Trail is being developed in each area by hometown volunteers, PNWT visitors have a special responsibility to conduct themselves in a way that will do credit to our local members.

Good PNWT manners are primarily a matter of attitude. If someone approaches the Trail experience with a willingness to help—even by a little gesture such as clearing the pathway while travelling it—he or she will be attuned to the type of low-impact, everyone-pitch-in project we are trying to create. And make no mistake about it, the Pacific Northwest Trail will always be the sum total of all the people who are travelling and working on it at any one time. Your help *is* important.

At the possible expense of sounding preachy, I want to share our perspective on how you can each enjoy the Trail as much as possible without overstepping the boundaries of someone else's pleasure.

The most important common-sense no-no concerns private land. Be doubly careful and considerate there. One bad incident could force the owner to evict us. Follow any regulations posted by owners. Build no fires on private land without the owner's written permission. Leave no sign of your passage.

Because you will meet very few people along most of the PNWT, stop to talk and learn and make friends and spread the word about the PNWT when you do encounter someone. In the fast-urbanizing West the tradition of the palaver is a dying art. So take time to talk about the weather, trail conditions, wildlife, and food. PNWTA distance hikers always say, "The people make the Trail." Contrary to popular opinion, there is no room for misanthropes in the mountains. And if you see someone in trouble, go out of your way to help. The next time the boot could be on the other foot.

Or the horseshoe. Sometimes city backpackers do not know how to behave around stock when they meet horsemen or cattlemen in the back-country. Riders have the right of way. Hikers should stand off the trail (on the downhill side) to let a rider and/or pack string pass. Horses may spook at the strange sight of a backpacker's hunchbacked form, so take off your pack and make reassuring conversational sounds that will calm the animal(s).

An all too common attitude among hikers is a wish that the four-legged barnyard set—the pack strings and the herds of cattle and sheep—be eliminated from the national forests. "We don't like to step in their horse manure," say some dainty walkers. Or "We don't think cows are compatible with wilderness," say the sophisticates over their steak dinners. Naturally, horsemen respond with distrust of backpackers. This division is extremely unfortunate. The Pacific Northwest Trail Association is an alliance of hikers and horsemen which is dedicated to bridging this totally unnecessary gap. Horse groups and hiking groups are allies in developing the PNWT—so whichever side of this fence you are on, try to understand the other person's point of view. Especially if you are a backpacker. Almost all of the Forest Service trails used by the PNWT were developed originally for pack stock. Until about 1940 much of the region's logging was ox and horse logging. East of the Cascades much of the route has been sheep and cattle country for a century. Read Owen Wister's *The Virginian* (written about Winthrop, Washington) for a bit of this atmosphere. Part of the direct pleasure of experiencing the PNWT is the chance to dwell in the rawhide West of legend.

Please consider this book your appointment from us to be a Pacific Northwest Trail ambassador.

Our travelling ambassadors are courteous, discreet, and cooperative. They follow rules, obtain necessary permits, and, in general, reflect credit upon the Pacific Northwest Trail Association. Plenty of misconceptions already exist out there about backpackers. One rural county commissioner I knew opposed the Trail because he believed that all hikers were hippies and that as soon as the PNWT hippies saw how beautiful his county was, they would immediately settle there and go on welfare. Any confirmation of that stereotype on our part reinforces such harmful opinions. If you come from distant cities or suburbs, you may not realize how people in the PNWT counties are reacting to you. Believe me, each local person will probably remember your visit for a long time to come and judge the entire PNWTA by the impression that you personally have made.

What about our responsibility to the natural environment? No doubt as the PNWT becomes more widely known, an increasing number of people will be attracted to the beauty, isolation, and challenge it offers. And rightly so, for only as more people discover the healing that wilderness has on body and soul, will these places and trails be preserved from irreparable exploitation.

This increase in use puts an increasing responsibility on each trail user to travel lightly and respectfully, leaving no trace of his or her passing. Obviously, this is most critical in areas receiving heavier or more concentrated use, such as Glacier National Park or the North Cascades. In other places, northwestern Montana for example, where brush is eye-level, dense and deadly, one may be less concerned with minimum impact on the land and more concerned with minimum impact on one's own body.

In regard to no-trace camping, the two crucial concerns of the PNWT hiker are the use of fire and the preservation of pure drinking water. During the summer months most areas along the route are extremely prone to forest fires, and indeed, in many areas fires will be restricted altogether. The well-equipped distance traveler should have no need for a campfire. Backpacking stoves eliminate the need for time-consuming wood gathering and fire building. Stoves create no smelly smoke or blackened pots and leave no ugly fire rings.

If a campfire becomes necessary, consider these guidelines: Use an existing fire ring if possible, and use only dead wood lying on the ground. If no fire ring is available, don't create one, Simply scoop out a fire hole in mineral soil, away from burnable vegetation and fragile areas like lakeshores. Keep the fire small and never leave it unattended. To put the fire out, drown it thoroughly with water, mixing the water, soil and ashes. Be sure it is cold to the touch before leaving. Make every effort to return the area to its natural appearance.

When selecting a campsite, choose a spot away from the trail and at least 100 feet away from sensitive lakeshores, streams, and other water sources (regulations in some parks and wilderness areas along the PNWT may require that this distance be increased to 200 feet). This common-sense rule protects essential water sources and also cuts back on "visual pollution" in more popular areas. Campsites tucked away in the forest are less noticeable than those lined up along the lakeshore. The use of tents, packs, and clothing in earth-tone colors also makes camps less visible.

Soap, even biodegradable soap, pollutes lakes and streams. If you must use soap to wash, put some water in a container and wash well away from the water source. To clean clothes, simply rinse them out and save soap use for the laundromat. Likewise, dirty dishes can soak overnight or be scrubbed out with sand or a pinecone. Keep in mind that clean, drinkable water is a necessity to the distance traveler, and it's up to the trail users to keep it uncontaminated.

Proper sanitation habits protect both water sources and the visual appearance of wild areas. Nothing is more disgusting than seeing a wad of soiled toilet paper behind every tree and bush. To dispose of human waste, dig a hole 6–8 inches deep, away from the trail and at least 100 feet from water. After use, cover the hole with loose soil and tamp it down. Nature will take care of the rest. Toilet paper may be buried or burned, but always use extreme caution with fire. Tampons and sanitary napkins should be burned or packed out. Always burn them in grizzly bear country, however, for their odors may attract bears.

When traveling along the Trail, don't cut switchbacks. It erodes the trails and may cause you to miss an important sign or trail junction. Travel quietly, respecting not only other humans, but also the needs of birds and animals for undisturbed territory.

Always follow the basic rule, pack out what you pack in. Nobody wants to look at trails littered with cigarette butts and candy wrappers, or fire pits filled with cans and aluminum foil. Pack out everything that won't burn, including the foil packaging often used on freeze-dried foods. Then, maybe go a step further and carry out the litter left by less-responsible hikers and horse riders. Horseback riders have an added responsibility toward the environment as saddle horses and pack animals can cause severe damage if not well supervised. Pack in a good supply of feed pellets, especially in the more heavily used wilderness areas and where forage is scarce. Don't tie animals to live trees; rather, use hobbles or string a line between two trees. Never tether an animal in wet, easily damaged meadows or within 200 feet of a water source.

No-trace hiking is really just common sense combined with caring and a little bit of effort. There are no set rules as each situation is different. Most people who choose to travel a long trail already have a deep respect for the natural environment. They realize that to mar the land would take away the very qualities that drew them to the PNWT in the first place. After weeks of walking along the Trail, one's belief in the value of wilderness grows. The contrast between man's creation and nature sharpens, and we realize the pricelessness of a racing alpine stream, a grove of virgin cedars, or a trail where one can walk freely for hundreds of miles.

NOTE

This book gives no one the right to cross private property without permission. Where the PNWT Practical Route crosses private property, that route is at publication time still only a goal and not, for the most part, a legal achievement of the PNWT Association. Landowners have legitimate concerns about unwelcome outside use of their property—problems such as fire, vandalism, and livestock enclosure.

Dear PNWT ambassadors, please remember that this book is only a guide and not a passport.

Part Two:

ROUTE DESCRIPTIONS

Copper Ridge View

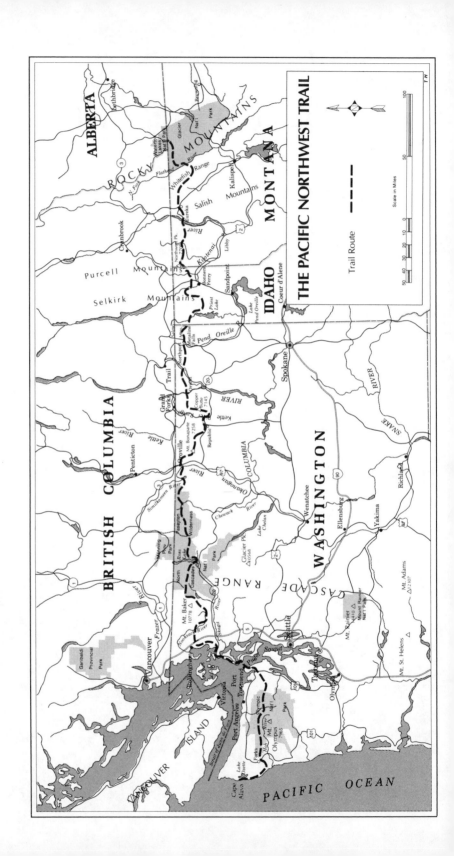

The lands and waters of a region are a seamless design not easily divided into chapters for a guidebook. The ten geographic headings that I have chosen represent a compromise between the landscape's natural breaks and the traveller's needs.

Each chapter provides useful information about the highlights, supply points, problems, mileages, and elevations that you will encounter. I have described both our Practical Route, which can be travelled on foot or horseback immediately, and our Ideal Route, which volunteers will gradually develop. Thus, this book is not only a map of present PNWT opportunities but also a blueprint for our future progress.

Actually, the Ideal Route is usually quite feasible to hike now, too, if you do not mind plenty of time-consuming bushwhacking. Both the Practical and the Ideal route descriptions will give you an idea of the relative difficulty to expect. In general, horse riders should keep to the Practical Route.

Because most PNWT travellers will be out for short periods of time, I have tried to indicate the best circuit hikes along the route. Think of the PNWT as merely an introduction to the region that you can use to acquaint yourself with the whole skein of mountains and valleys over many years. Don't be content with *one* Pacific Northwest Trail when you can create many versions of your own.

The Pacific Northwest—the historic 1840s Oregon Territory of Oregon, Washington, Idaho, British Columbia, and west-of-the-Divide Montana—was late to be explored and exploited. Much of its interior was not settled until the second half of the nineteenth century and even the beginning of the twentieth. Within living memory the search for ore and timber fertilized the growth of boom towns, railroads, stage roads, and other evidences of civilization. Would-be Northwesterners flooded in from everywhere, almost wiping out the highly developed Indian cultures. Civilization spread farther and farther, but much of the Northwest somehow escaped development. The great mountain ranges, especially, have remained to this day as wilderness sanctuaries. The PNWT's free-flowing mountain rivers, alpine tundra, violent storms, and wild animals all evoke a time not so many years ago when all of the region was pristine, unknown.

To me the Northwest has always meant adventure, the American frontier, untrammeled nature, and peace of mind. The following chapters explain how you, too, can experience this amazing heritage.

THE ROCKY MOUNTAINS

(Waterton, Alberta, to the Tobacco Plains, Montana)

Bowman Lake from Boulder Pass Trail

INTRODUCTION

How could you better it? A trail across the Continental Divide in the midst of some of North America's finest scenery. A jumping-off place on a mountainous fiord complete with a fairybook-castle hotel and a junction of three notable long-distance trails. A chance to see major species of wildlife in the wilds. A link with prehistoric, pioneer, and contemporary Western history. A look at rapidly changing rural America. A route-finding adventure across remote ridges and forests. All this and more await you on the easternmost section of the Pacific Northwest Trail.

PROBLEMS

First to the most serious problem—the fact that you are going to get lost. Maybe "lost" is too strong a word. Try thinking of it as temporary bewilderment. Whatever the name, the reality is that you may sometimes not know exactly where you are. This is part of the charm of the Pacific Northwest Trail. Trust your map and compass and your ability to work out eventually every route-finding problem. Never be afraid to ask directions (but always take the directions with a grain of salt). And if you are in a great rush, don't be. The purpose of having come to the Rockies is to enjoy each day for its own pleasures. Slow down and let these wonders sink in. If this is the beginning of a long trip (especially a Divide-to-Ocean trip), get into a daily rhythm that suits you. And adjust your pace realistically to the demands of the part of the trail you happen to be on each day. Your pace will vary a lot as conditions change.

David Brill of Cincinnati, Ohio, had this to say about his 1981 PNWT experiences: "Back at home before we began the hike, it was impossible to imagine the adventure in other than purely logistical terms. We all walked by the route maps pasted on our refrigerators and saw only cumulative mileage joining one supply point to the next. There was no way to accurately anticipate the real quality of each section or the difficulty it would pose. We learned early in the trip just how deluded our pretrip projections had been; mileage as the sole means of charting our progress was simply inadequate. It took us three days to hike the 35 miles through Glacier and over the Divide on clean trail. It took us two days to bushwhack only ten miles in the exhausting section that followed."

For early season (June and July) visits to Glacier Park's high country, take an ice axe (which you can mail home at Polebridge). A pair of light-weight snowshoes might also be helpful.

The long tradition along the international border, especially during the Dry Squad years, of informal or illegal entry is not encouraged today. If you take the boat south from Waterton, reporting into the United States is very convenient at the Goat Haunt Ranger Station.

Water is sometimes scarce in the Whitefish Range. Plan ahead there for springs, off-trail seeps, shortcuts to creeks and ponds, and seasonal snowbanks on north slopes. If in doubt about the availability of water, by all means ask people whom you meet in Polebridge and elsewhere. However, remember that the route you will be travelling is very little travelled, even by locals and Forest Service personnel. You will soon know more about it than most people who live in the area.

Sometimes the Park Service's quota of campsite permits for back-country campsites is filled. In that case, consider an alternate route. Sometimes the Kintla Lakes and/or Bowman Lake trails are closed because of bear incidents; choose an alternate route.

And don't become a bear incident yourself. Read the description in this book and in Canadian and U.S. government brochures about how to conduct yourself in bear country.

SUPPLIES

Resupply is not difficult in this section. The longest hop between supply points is 65.3 miles (Polebridge to Eureka). The tiny Polebridge Mercantile usually has a better-than-expected selection of groceries and camping supplies. (The Northern Lights Saloon next door offers home-cooked meals.) The post office is in back, behind the granola, etc. Send your cache drop box to yourself, c/o General Delivery, Polebridge, MT 59928. Mark it "Hold For PNWT Hiker." (Incoming mail arrives Tuesdays and Fridays only.) The Mercantile also has a pay phone, a rarity in the North Fork's unpaved, non-electric valley. And the North Fork Hostel, just down the road, has hot showers.

Once you cross the Whitefish Divide into Lincoln County, the Grave Creek Road is a potential route out of the mountains for supplies. In any case, after the Ten Lakes Scenic Area the PNWT descends into downtown Eureka, MT 59917, where all services are available.

DECLINATION   20½° E

Canadian Maps

Waterton Lakes Park map— 1:63360 scale; Map Distribution Office, Dept. of Mines and Tech. Surveys, Ottawa, Ontario, Canada.

Flathead, British Columbia— 1:125000; Map Production Division, British Columbia Lands Service, Parliament Buildings, Victoria, B.C. (Ask for Flathead, B.C. Map 82 G/SE)

USGS TOPOGRAPHIC MAPS

Porcupine Ridge	Red Meadow Lake
Mount Carter	Trailcreek
Kintla Peak	Mount Hefty
Kintla Lake	Mount Thompson-Seton
Polebridge	Tuchuck Mountain
Cyclone Lake	Stahl Peak
Moose Peak	Ksanka Peak
Upper Whitefish Lake	Eureka North

MILEAGES   (total 119.6)

		Total
Waterton Townsite (4196)	0.0	0.0
Goat Haunt Ranger Station (by boat)	7.0	7.0
Lake Janet (4950)	3.5	10.5
Lake Frances (5255)	2.8	13.3
Brown Pass, the Continental Divide (6255)	2.3	15.6
Hole-in-the-Wall (6400)	2.0	17.6
Boulder Pass (7470)	3.1	20.7
Kintla Lake, upper end (4371)	11.1	31.8
Kintla Lake car campground	6.6	38.4
Polebridge by road (3532)	15.0	53.4
Forest Service Road 376 (Hay Creek)	1.5	54.9

Forest Service Road 909	1.3	56.2
Trail No. 4	3.0	59.2
Coal Ridge via Trail No. 4	4.5	63.7
Whitefish Divide via Trail No. 14	8.2	71.9
Lewis Creek Road via Trail No. 26	22.5	94.4
Grave Creek Road 319 (4519)	2.7	97.1
Near Mount Wam via a trailless ridge (Mount Wam is 7203)	3.7	100.8
Stahl Peak Trail No. 81 (6775 at junction and 7430 if you make the summit side trip)	3.0	103.8
Trail No. 88 (6600) via Highline Trail No. 339	3.5	107.3
Lower dirt road (3400) via Trail No. 88	5.0	112.3
St. Clair Creek Road 7125	1.3	113.6
Eureka City Park (2566)	6.0	119.6

ROUTE DESCRIPTION

Waterton Park, Alberta, is the best starting place for walking or horse riding westward on the Pacific Northwest Trail.

From the United States, Waterton Park is reached through Glacier National Park. Daily Amtrak trains are the only public transportation to the park. Get off the train at East Glacier, at the southeast end of Glacier National Park. From there a Glacier Park, Inc., bus goes to Waterton Park (80 miles by road), but its departure time may just miss the arrival of the train. Write to Glacier Park, Inc., 1735 East Fort Lowell, Tucson, AZ 85719.

If you approach Waterton Park from a point in Canada, Lethbridge is only 77 miles away and has daily bus service. For more information write to Glacier National Park, West Glacier, MT 59936 (406/888-5441) and Waterton Lakes National Park, Waterton Park, Alberta T0K 2M0 (403/859-2262).

Waterton Park is located at the head of Waterton Lake and is the headquarters town for this unit of Parks Canada. The American park was created by Congress in 1910. In 1895 Canada had designated its own Kootenay Lakes Forest Reserve, which became Waterton Lakes National Park in 1911. In 1932 these two parks became the world's first international peace park, a symbol of the amazing record of friendship and cooperation between Canada and the United States. Waterton Park is an incredible mecca for long-distance-trail enthusiasts because three major routes begin here: the Pacific Northwest Trail, the Continental Divide Trail, and the Great Divide Trail (a route being developed by Canadian volunteers along the boundary between Alberta and British Columbia). For more information about the CDT and the GDT, write to the Continental Divide Trail Society, P.O. Box 30002, Bethesda, MD 20814, and the Great Divide Trail Assn., P.O. Box 5322, Station "A", Calgary, Alberta T2H 1X6.

Waterton Park is a miniature city with a full range of services. For park information visit the park headquarters, on the main street opposite the Emerald Bay Wharf. If you are beginning an end-to-end PNWT adventure, I hope that you will inaugurate your journey with appropriate ceremony at the classic Prince of Wales Hotel. (You may want to bring your own champagne.) Please toast the many PNWT volunteers who have made your trip possible.

The best way to begin the Pacific Northwest Trail is to take the excursion boat International down Upper Waterton Lake (4196) across the frontier to the Goat Haunt Ranger Station. (The 11.7-mile lakeshore trail is an up-and-down, often-unmaintained affair.) This 7-mile-long lake is 317 feet deep, a classic glacial valley. Mt. Cleveland's spectacular 6000' face is the most prominent natural landmark and the highest mountain in the two parks. Notice the avalanche chutes on Mt. Bertha and also the cleared strip of the border, which parallels the PNWT westward all the way to salt water.

Check in at the ranger station (.2 mile from the excursion boat dock). Obtain your backcountry use permit and campground reservation—something that cannot be done more than one day in advance. There are six backcountry campsites along the PNWT's Brown Pass/Boulder Pass route: Lake Janet; Brown Pass; Hole-in-the-Wall; Boulder Pass, west side; Upper Kintla Lake, head; and Kintla Lake, head. (Beyond is the car campground at the foot of Kintla Lake.) At the height of the July/August season, permits to camp at these highly desirable and very limited sites may be difficult to obtain. Be ready to camp wherever you can obtain a permit. Goat Haunt itself—in addition to its nature trail, exhibits, and ranger's talks—has overnight shelter facilities for trekkers.

From the ranger station go .5 mile on the Waterton Lake Trail (No. 135) southwest across Cleveland Creek and across Waterton River to a campground. Here leave Trail No. 135 for Trail No. 6, switchbacking up through spruce-fir forest for 2 miles to Lake Janet (4950). This trail roughly parallels Olson Creek.

The PNWT ambles west across forest and brush 2.8 miles to Lake Frances (5255), hemmed in by Shaheeya Peak to the north and prickly looking Porcupine Ridge to the south. This lake is spectacularly enclosed by the rock walls of the Sentinel (8835) and its Dixon Glacier and the Hawksbill. A mile later, Thunderbird Pond is a great place to strip off your sweaty clothes on a hot day and splash off a great rock into the instant refreshment of Thunderbird Glacier meltwater.

Brown Pass (6255) is 2.3 miles farther across mostly open, brushy, wildflower-sprinkled terrain. (The tall, spiky blooms are bear grass.) This col hangs almost suspended between Chapman Peak (9406) and Thunderbird Mountain (8790). Seen from farther west, it appears as the top of a great drop-off down to Bowman Creek. Bowman Lake, visible soon along the trail, a mile of astoundingly scenic altitude, is 5400' lower than Chapman Peak. But the up-and-down variation is not the only thing that makes this spot on the Continental Divide so stunning. Everywhere you look you see the layer-cake geological record of sediments and overthrusts, synclines and anticlines. Geology also speaks to us in colors—the reds, greens, grays, and purples of the different epochs.

A tiny campsite at Brown Pass has a sure source of water .4 mile down the Bowman Lake trail. Between Brown Pass and Boulder Pass the trail hugs the Divide walls and slopes to the great cirque called Hole-in-the-Wall (named for the way Bowman Creek's headwaters spurt out of Hole-in-the-Wall Falls). The Hole-in-the-Wall campsite on the flat bottom of the mammoth cirque's upper basin is likely to be quite snowy early in the season. That should not discourage you from camping there; it certainly will not discourage the tame mule deer, who will gobble up any slightest scent of salt you drop—including your boots if you leave them out at night.

Here the trail is close to several notable lakes, including Lake Wurdeman, Lake Nooney, Cameron Lake, and Pocket Lake. However, the mountains hide them unless you climb high. A good vantage point is the summit of Boulder Peak (8528), from which Pocket Lake (6613) looks so wild that you imagine that you are the first person ever to discover it. By the way, while you're up on this flattish summit of odd reddish slates, look closely at the many peculiar round patterns—stromatolites—in the stone. This airy heaven, from which Brown Pass and all the rest of the Continental Divide heights are visible, was once a sea bottom where large algal masses grew in the sunny warmth of shallow, lapping waters. Those extremely early life forms are now some of the world's oldest fossils.

Brown Pass commemorates one of the greatest characters who ever lived in the Pacific Northwest Trail country, John George "Kootenai" Brown, probably the first white man to cross this pass. He first entered the Waterton area in 1865 and spent about forty years trapping and hunting the region.

Glacier National Park received its name from the lingering evidence of the great ice ages. Boulder Pass is an excellent place to observe this phenomenon—both in the primeval, flat valley north of the campsite and in Boulder Glacier itself. Although we can accept the theory that the mountains and valleys here look the way they do partially because of the irresistible sculpting power of slowly flowing frozen snow, the time and force involved are difficult to comprehend. At spectacular Boulder Pass the position of the trail gives a hint of this alpine country's impermanence and malleability. Notice that 1.2 miles beyond the Hole-in-the-Wall camp trail, a side trail, which was the original trail, crosses a moraine and beautiful flowered benches up to Boulder Pass. This moraine was actually the edge of the Boulder Glacier when the trail was built a few decades ago. Since then the glacier has shrunk drastically, permitting construction of a new, mile-shorter, cairn-marked route across the ice-scoured, pond-dotted former glacier floor at 7200' and up to the pass at 7470'. Notice, too, Agassiz Glacier as you continue west. In 1910 it was one of the new park's largest glaciers; since then it has receded at least ¼ mile.

From Boulder Pass the PNWT follows a glacial trough westward to the North Fork of the Flathead River, losing 3600' in elevation in 20 miles.

Unfortunately for your knees or your horse's knees, most of that drop occurs on the long switchbacks down the slopes of Gardner Point to the lake. At first Upper Kintla Lake (4371) appears impossibly distant and small in the rugged landscape of the Boundary Mountains and Kinnerly Peak (9944). Finally, after a long descent on good trail across open slopes and through lush summer brush and fir/spruce copses, we reach the campsite at the eastern end of the lake beyond Kintla Creek.

A pleasant shoreline trail brings us to a campsite at the lower end of the lake. Then 3 miles of woods walking parallel to Kintla Creek take us to a campsite at the east end of the lower lake, beyond a ranger cabin.

The 6.5-mile trail to the west end of Kintla Lake should be relocated to avoid the viewless ups and downs in its middle section. Do you agree?

From the car campground at the south end we follow the auto road out 3 miles to the North Fork, mostly through even-aged, spindly lodgepole-pine stands. About .2 mile before the road from Kintla Lake crosses the little gorge of Kintla Creek (close to the North Fork), a pack trail heads northwest up the river, crossing Starvation Creek and Kishenehn Creek to the old ford at Abbotts Flats. The PNWT Ideal Route will someday go this way. However, as far as we know, the fordability of the old crossing was destroyed by a big flood twenty years ago. We would like to revive this Indian and pioneer crossing-place with a cable car or, better yet, a hiker's suspension bridge. (Any volunteers?) However, for now the Practical Route continues south along the river road to Polebridge, affording fine views of the meandering, Dolly Varden–filled waters, picturesque gravel bars and sharply cut riverbanks. It crosses open pastures called prairies where the Indians, and later the pioneers, flourished. The North Fork

Bowman Lake

Valley, too, was sculpted by the ice, and the best places to view it are either here, close up along the river banks, or from high ridges where the big picture comes into focus.

The PNWT's Waterton/Goat Haunt/Brown Pass/Kintla Lake route is both a hiking and stock tour, though horses are not permitted overnight at Boulder Pass. Water is readily available along this section except in the woods part (middle) of the Kintla Lake trail. Be prepared to follow an alternate route if this one is closed for fire, bear, weather, or other reasons.

Glacier National Park's policy is to issue campsite reservations no earlier than the day before a party or person wishes to begin. That means that even if the Boulder Pass trail is open, you may not be able to beat the other peak-season hikers and horsemen to a reservation. In that case, try the Bowman Lake route from Brown Pass to Polebridge. It also has superb mountain vistas of Hole-in-the-Wall Falls and of Bowman Lake's Cerulean Ridge. A backcountry campground is available at the upper end of the lake, and an automobile campground and ranger station at the lower end.

The last half of the lake trail jogs up and down through the woods more than you will like, but the final mile is very pleasing to us because it was built by Eagle Scout volunteers from all over the United States. (As you may have guessed by now, we are trying to encourage this volunteer spirit everywhere along the Pacific Northwest Trail.) The Bowman Lake route to Polebridge ends with 6 miles of dreary road walking. But overall from Bowman Pass this way is attractive and 18 miles shorter than the Boulder Pass/Kintla Lake route.

Of course, the same problems of permits and fire and bear closure apply to the Bowman Lake trail. A second alternate begins at Waterton, but instead of entering the United States via Waterton Lake, it crosses the Continental Divide in Canada at South Kootenay Pass and descends the Kishinena Creek Valley through British Columbia provincial-forest lands and through the upper northwest corner of the American park to the ford at Abbotts Flats. In terms of the Ideal Route's crossing there, too, this alternate is the most direct link between the Divide and the North Fork.

Go 9.4 miles via the Red Rock Canyon Highway from Waterton Park to the Red Rock Warden Station. From there take the South Kootenay Pass Trail 3.2 miles, crossing Bauerman Brook, passing Blakiston Falls and Anderson Peak, and ascending forested Lone Brook Canyon to a junction with the Twin Lakes Trail. Not far to the left is another junction, where the Lone Lake Trail takes off to the left. (Lone Lake 2 miles south is a good campsite at 6700'.) However, instead of going to Lone Lake, continue 1 mile up to South Kootenay Pass (6903).

South Kootenay Pass is rich in history, and it makes a very fitting beginning to a PNWT journey. I once visited this rather unprepossessing pass with Canadian paleo-ecologist Wayne Choquette, the ultimate expert on the prehistoric Kootenai Indians who inhabited this region. Wayne first found an ancient lithic skin scraper and then spotted a broken lance point. By the design and flaking he could tell that the lance point was a Scott's

Bluff type—7,000 years old—and one of the earliest he had ever found.

The trail continues west and down Kishinena Creek, with excellent views of Mt. Yarrel and Starvation Peak and of the distant North Fork. The area is an ecological extension of Glacier National Park and is favored by grizzlies, wolves, goats, eagles, cougars, and other wilderness animals.

Just down from South Kootenay Pass you will be following the old Akamina Pass jeep road on the north side of Kishinena Creek, then on the south side. Where the road again crosses to the north side, the old trail instead continues downstream on the south side. From the pass to the American border is 13.5 miles, with an additional 4 miles via the American end of the trail.

A third alternate, and one suitable for stock use, crosses the Divide at Akamina Pass. Take the Akamina Highway from Waterton Park 9.5 miles along Cameron Creek's scenic canyon to Cameron Lake. Cameron Lake has excellent campgrounds and a bungalow camp. But .2 mile before the lake, follow the old jeep road .5 mile up to Akamina Pass (5835). Continue along Akamina Creek and Kishinena Creek 22 miles to the North Fork. The old bridge close to the border is out, so a detour is necessary to the next bridge 4 miles upstream. (There is a cable car near the old bridge but it may be inoperable or locked.) Cross the international border at the checkpoint, and continue 6 miles south to Trail Creek and the Ideal Route over the Cleft Rock Mountain trail or the stock-use route up the Trail Creek road to the Whitefish Divide.

Polebridge is the supply, communication, and gossip center for the North Fork on the American side. Change is the primary topic of conversation when people gather in the Mercantile or the Northern Lights Saloon or up the river at the community center. Although the valley probably has fewer winter residents than it did in 1924 at the end of the open-entry homesteading era, there is constant agitation for completing the paving of the road. And with that, electricity will certainly come. The new order is apparent when you walk across the plotted subdivision on your way to the North Fork Hostel.

Although the North Fork is rapidly being pushed and pulled into the 1980s, the next, long, ridgehop part of the Pacific Northwest Trail is, if anything, wilder than it was fifty years ago because its trails are so rarely travelled. If you close your eyes to the peripheral clearcuts, you are in very remote country indeed. From Glacier National Park the Practical Route goes west from Polebridge, then follows the Whitefish Divide north. The Ideal Route is much more northerly, beginning at Abbott's Flats and going west via Cleft Rock Mountain, Seemo Pass, Mount Thompson-Seton, and the Whitefish Divide. From Polebridge the Practical and the Ideal are about equal in length, but the former avoids about 16 dusty road miles.

To follow the Practical Route, go due west from the Polebridge Mercantile .3 mile to the North Fork Road 210. Turn left at the ranch buildings and go south 1.2 miles to a junction with Forest Service Road 376 (shortly after the bridge over Hay Creek). Turn right (northwest) and go up the Hay Creek Road 1.3 miles to a left onto Forest Service Road 909. Road

909 follows the divide between Cyclone Peak and the ridge north of it along the route of an old trail. In 3 miles we reach the sign for Trail No. 4. (For an interesting side trip to the manned 6000' Cyclone Peak Lookout, continue up the road until you reach the lookout trail.)

Follow Trail No. 4 northwest and then southwest 4.5 very steep miles along the 6000' ridge immediately north of Cyclone Creek, an outlier ridge from Coal Ridge, our next destination. Though the upper end of this trail may be menziesia choked, you will not have real difficulty finding your way. At this height we can look northwest to 7404' Moran Peak and back east to the fabulous mountains of the Continental Divide.

Coal Ridge averages 7000' in elevation, one of the longest stretches of high-elevation walking on the entire PNWT. These 8.2 miles on Trail No. 14 and the next, even better, 22.5 miles on Whitefish Divide Trail No. 26 make up one of the PNWT's longest, continuous alpine delights.

Coal Ridge Trail No. 14 meanders more or less due west 8.2 miles to the Divide. From its junction (7069) with Trail No. 4, we climb quickly to the Coal Ridge Lookout Tower (7105). Actually, there are two towers and a separate cabin spaced out along a half-mile-long view ridge. The first, tottering pole-platform is followed by a modern cabin-topped tower. There is plentiful water just before the second tower, about 500 feet down off the ridge. A little farther along, the Coal Ridge cabin is another potential hiker shelter. June snow water is handy everywhere at this elevation. Coal Ridge Trail No. 14 continues over Knobs 7285', 7202', 7175', 6945', and 7125' with spectacular ridgetop views in all directions.

The Whitefish Divide is a major ridge system, which threads its way from near Whitefish, Montana, northwest about 60 miles to the Canadian border. Our PNWT route includes about half that distance from our junction with Trail No. 26.

Government mapmakers incorrectly drew the junction of the Coal Ridge and Whitefish Divide trails on the topographic map. So instead of following the top of the Coal Ridge formation to where it abuts the Divide, we drop down to the beautiful cirque at the head of Coal Creek and follow the easily spotted trail that climbs the far edge of the basin. Up there we join Trail No. 26 at a many-blazed, wind-stunted tree. (This guidebook's map shows the correct route.) A pond in this cirque is a good late-season water source.

The Divide trail proceeds northwest along the height of land. One-half mile along, beware of making a false left turn down onto a little spur ridge. Instead, you should follow the cairns up the ridge a total of about 1 mile to where the trail recrosses the Divide and drops off it in a very long descent across open slopes to a burned-over area at the head of Hay Creek. (By following the Coal Ridge trail and now the Divide trail, we have made a big loop around the headwaters of Hay Creek.)

At a saddle beyond the burnt snags, we hit a new extension of the Hay Creek Road. There is a good (though possibly seasonal) stream at this saddle, which will be a refreshing find to those early-season pilgrims weary of drinking only boiled snow. These woods also make an adequate, protected campsite. The Hay Creek Road does not continue across this saddle, and we follow No. 26 down a brushy descent to Road 589 along Swift Creek. Turn right onto this gravel road by some small bluffs, and follow it northwest to a junction with the Link Lake Trail. Along the way Road 115 provides access to the nearby Red Meadow Campground. This has been the only area where our road/trail route does not actually follow the Divide itself.

But if you like ridgewalking, the next scenic miles will be pure delight as the trail hugs the northwest course of the Divide. You will have Fitsimmons Creek, the Stillwater River, and Blue Sky Creek to the west and the Whale Creek drainage to the east. Numerous trails connect Trail No. 26 with each of these valleys. For the thorough hiker the most important trails are No. 374, which leads about 1 mile north to Huntsberger Lake, and No. 11, which goes ½ mile north to Whale Lake. Note that the first road we reach on the Divide after Road 589 is at the headwaters of Shorty Creek and is marked merely as a trail on all the maps. Turn right where Trail No. 26 hits this road, and follow it along the east side of the Divide to a hunting camp and beyond. But after a long descent, be careful to return to the faint trail on the spine of the Divide where the road crosses over to the west side, soon to dead-end in the brushy forest.

Locke Lookout (destroyed) and Mount Locke cabin are both excellent observation sites. The latter is 2 miles north of the former, though both are at exactly 7205′ elevation. The "new" trail bypasses Mount Locke's summit; if you cannot find the old lookout trail (as shown on the topo maps), siwash straight up to the summit. Snow is the water source here. If you stay in the historic cabin, now sadly lacking windows and chinking, please help us to make it more weatherproof. From here you will have a good view across the mountains of the Ten Lakes Scenic Area to the Kootenai River Valley; this is Montana's long-distance hiking at its best.

The old summit trail is still in excellent condition from where it drops down the ridge from the lookout cabin to join the bypass trail. Shortly after Mount Locke, a side trail leads about ½ mile downhill to the water of Blue Sky Creek. And several strenuous miles ahead, Trail No. 28, our Ideal (though totally overgrown) Route, offers a side trip to the waters of Yakinikak Creek. Beyond that junction (which you are unlikely to see unless you have eyes like radar), Trail No. 26 winds its way about 4 miles northward. Do not go astray and find yourself much to the west atop Mount Lewis (7322), which is recognizable by the burnt remains of an old lookout there.

Trail No. 26 does not follow the Divide's last mile north to Timothy Meadow but instead shortcuts west to the Lewis Creek Road at 4519′ elevation. A real difficulty on the up-and-down 30 miles of Trails 14 and 26 is that they are so overgrown from lack of maintenance that your progress will be painfully slow. Often, instead of travelling a blazed pathway, you will find yourself bushwhacking. And in late June would-be end-to-enders will do a great deal of snow walking. However, if you have the time and the patience, you will be well rewarded for your efforts.

If you are in a hurry, the quickest way westward from Polebridge is our stock route. To follow this route, from the Polebridge Mercantile go .3 mile west to the North Fork Road 210 and north 15.2 miles on it to a left onto Trail Creek Road 114. Consecutive points along the North Fork Road's dusty logging-truck raceway include: Red Meadow Creek Road 115, 5.7 miles; Whale Creek Road 318, 4.5 miles; Ford Work Center at Teepee Creek, .3 mile; and Trail Creek Road 114, 4.7 miles, a relatively narrow, undeveloped dirt track. It was only punched over the Divide in 1960 by Herb Wilke on his "Cat." (Herb's father, the late Bert Wilke, is a storyteller in *River Pigs and Cayuses: Oral Histories from the Pacific Northwest.*)

Our stock route goes 6.7 miles up the Trail Creek Road to the Tuchuck Campground (look for the old Indian Caves at the Thoma Creek junction), then 2.5 miles farther to an overlook (4953) across a wide, beaver-dammed section of the valley opposite Kootah Creek. It continues 2.9 miles to a spring so delicious that Bert Wilke's mule string always preferred its water to any other hereabouts. It is then .5 mile to Nokio Creek (an excellent place to see anything from deer to grizzly to elk), 1.1 miles to the Whitefish Divide, 1 mile down to the Trail No. 26 junction (4968), and 1.7 more down the Lewis Creek Road to its junction with Grave Creek Road 319 (from which it is 14 miles south to U.S. Highway 93 and 14 miles northwest to Big Therriault Lake). The total road distance between Polebridge and the Grave Creek Road 319 is about 35 miles.

The Ideal Route heads west from the future bridge at Abbott's Flats and up the Trail Creek Road. From the beginning of Cleft Creek Trail No. 13, it is 6 miles to Cleft Rock Mountain, 15 miles to Seemo Pass, and 4 miles to Divide Trail No. 26. The Cleft Creek Trail is reported to be in poor condition to Mount Thompson-Seton. However, except for seasonal snowbanks, this route is always very dry. If you carry water, Seemo Pass is a good place to camp. (Trail No. 22 has been recently brushed out to provide access to Seemo Pass from the Tuchuck Campground; Trail Creek must be forded, however, at the campground.) And, as mentioned earlier, once you finally reach Trail No. 26, traces of the old path become very faint indeed. But take heart; this is beautiful country.

Next on the PNWT before we reach Eureka, Montana, is the sharply glaciated Ten Lakes Scenic Area. The Ten Lakes country, like the Whitefish Divide, features 6000' ridges, long views of heavily logged forests, and tantalizing hints of distant ranges. A number of creeks spin out of the core Galton Range and its southern outlier Gibralter Ridge. The PNWT approaches this wildlife-rich core area on a long ridge directly from the Lewis Creek/Grave Creek road junction. Throughout this part of the PNWT we are treated to many views of the lakes and ponds that give the area its name.

For the most part we follow Highline Trail No. 339 westward. However, its original builders began it at the Mount Wam Lookout, leaving 3.7 miles of the ridge trailless east of there. This future Ideal Route is not too hard to bushwhack, and it is definitely the shortest way to reach your goal. From the Lewis Creek/Grave Creek junction, climb the wooded slopes westward, contouring around toward the south side to get as much southern-exposure openness as possible. The predominant tree here is subalpine fir, but whitebark pine grows well, too, on the windiest aeries. Especially on the southern exposures, the forest is semi-open, rather grassy, good walking. So climb steadily from the thickly forested road junction (4519), and gain the first knob on this ridge at 6785'. A much larger, forested summit will appear slightly east of north, above clearcut Foundation Creek. The open, cabin-topped summit of Mount Wam will be northwest of you. Continue cross-country up this ridge until you reach the Highline Trail above the unnamed lake.

An alternative approach to Mount Wam is to walk 4 miles north, then west up the Grave Creek and Foundation Creek roads to the end of the clearcut road at elevation 5797'. From there walk a trail 1.3 miles to the unnamed lake, a possible camping spot. Next siwash 700 feet up northwest to the Highline Trail. Or, to avoid this 700-foot, off-trail climb, you could go south from the Lewis Creek/Grave Creek junction to Clarence Creek Road 7021 and up it to the trailhead of the Clarence Creek/Rich Creek Trail No. 78, a total of 7 miles. Then climb the trail through thick huckleberries to the Highline Trail, 1.5 miles. This last approach to Mount Wam is not only longer than the previous two but also involves much initial elevation loss and considerable road walking. And this roundabout way does not come out at Mount Wam, but 2 miles southwest of it. However, it is definitely the best route for pack or riding stock.

Mount Wam (like Stahl Peak, 3 crow's-flight miles to the southwest across Clarence Creek Valley) is an ideal spot to get an overview of the Ten Lakes country. At first your gaze is likely to wander eastward toward the Whitefish Divide, Mount Thompson-Seton, and even the tallest peaks in the International Peace Park. Looking southwest, you'll observe the heavily wooded Highline Trail ridge leading over to sharply defined Therriault Pass between the rugged walls of St. Clair Peak and the long cliff that ends in the massive bulk of Stahl Peak. From here Stahl's lookout cabin shines white in the sun, a tiny house precariously perched above sheer cliffs.

Arrow-like subalpine firs ring the grassy knoll where the Mount Wam Lookout was built in 1927. By the way, this unusual name was given the peak by an Englishman on a turn-of-the-century border-survey expedition. He named a Mount Wig on the Canadian side and a Mount Wam at this point. Wig/Wam. Some imagination! Mount Wam's fire lookout is a good example of a functional, windows-all-around wooden cabin with a commanding view of a vast mountainous area. Such lookouts were connected in pre-radio days by a battery-operated network of field telephones; occasionally you can see the bare, thick wire that was used between lookouts still snaking its way across the Northwest's mountains.

Mount Wam's cabin, like many of the other lookout cabins, is deteriorating rapidly. A major goal of the Pacific Northwest Trail Association is the restoration of these priceless historic structures for the use and safety of future generations of PNWT travellers.

Therriault Lake

From Mount Wam walk south and west 2 miles to the Highline Trail's junction with the Rich Creek Trail at the north end of the pass between Rich Creek and Clarence Creek. This spot is a protected, though rather dismal, campsite with a reliable spring 100 yards from the trail junction at the end of a way trail. Continue west, then south on the Highline Trail across the forested ridge 3 miles to the Stahl Peak Trail. Along the way the rough-cut bulk of Stahl Peak (7435) becomes more and more impressive.

Stahl Peak is definitely worth a visit, though its hand-built, ¾-mile trail is very steep and is not for people afraid of heights. If you wish to camp overnight in the quaint two-story cabin, be sure to carry up an adequate supply of water. You will be rewarded with memorable dawn views of the promontories, drops, plains, and peaks of the sedimentary Ten Lakes formations. Where Therriault Pass reveals a more distant western horizon, you can see part of Libby Dam's long reservoir.

Stahl Peak is also a good place from which to chart your next course along the PNWT. We loop south around Big and Little Therriault Lakes and skirt the top of the great rock cleft known as Therriault Pass—the headwaters of Therriault Creek. Before you reach the sandy junction with the southerly Therriault Pass trail, you will encounter two successive steep trails leading down north to Big Therriault Lake. The first of these lake trails is a cut-off joining the second (Trail No. 80) about ¾ mile downhill; a good spring is a bit farther downhill, left of the trail, where the little valley widens out.

The trail junction at Therriault Pass can be confusing. If you find yourself going down the mammoth rock cut that you have been seeing for the last many hours, back up and take the turn to the northwest that you missed. This part of the Highline Trail will take you beneath the cliffs of Mt. Barnaby and St. Clair Peak. If you watch carefully for moving white specks above, you may discover some of the Ten Lakes' mountain goats. Since they, like all the big game animals west of Glacier National Park (including grizzlies), are hunted by sportsmen, they tend to be secretive and easily spooked.

This is dry country, and beyond the Trail No. 80 spring, the only late-season water source is the mud hole (water must be boiled) 1.2 miles beyond Therriault Pass. Although later you will encounter two steep way trails down to Little Therriault Lake, this bug-filled stuff is much easier to fetch.

Highline Trail No. 339 crosses a long section of scree slope above Little Therriault Lake and clearcut Bluebird Creek and then climbs to a wooded pass. There, instead of continuing northwest to the Bluebird Basin, we drop off on Trail No. 88 down the St. Clair Creek Valley. Very shortly after the wooded pass, there is an open area where two trails, branches of No. 88, take off separately at either end of the clearing. Follow the rightmost trail down. Trail No. 88 is a well-used horse trail, and what it lacks in views it makes up for in good maintenance. And through the trees you can begin to appreciate the Tobacco Plains ahead. (The Tobacco Plains, where the Indians used to grow tobacco, are now sown with wheat.) A water source is ¾ mile below the initial clearing.

Trail No. 88 comes out at a relatively new dirt road and a unique, stone, trailhead marker. Cross this road and descend the embankment beyond to a PNWT white blaze that marks the continuation of the original trail, which itself comes out at a lower road (and more PNWT blazes) for a total of 5 miles on No. 88. Follow the lower dirt road out 1.3 miles to the paved St. Clair Creek Road 7125, where you will turn right and follow 7125 for 6 miles through woods and rolling farm country to Eureka. (About 2½ miles down this road, Mary Ellen Campbell sells convenient camping, lodging, and showers to PNWT travellers at her ranch, R.R.1, Box 64, Eureka, MT. (406/889-3344.) Eureka has a full range of PNWT facilities.

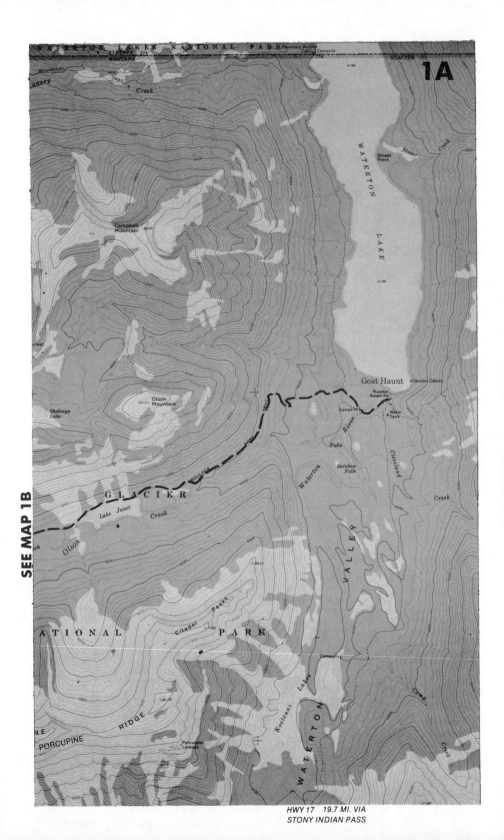

SEE MAP 1B

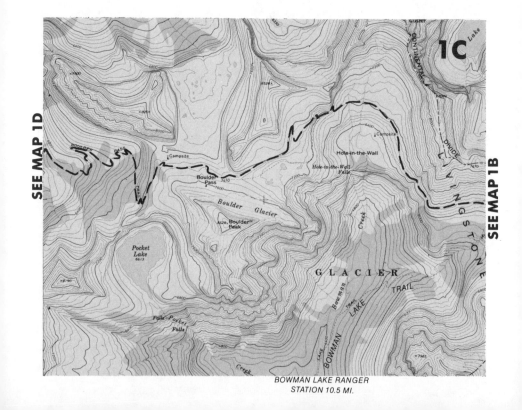

SEE MAP 1C

1B

SEE MAP 1A

Chapman Peak

Waheecja Lake

Shaheeya Peak

CONTINENTAL DIVIDE

FLATHEAD CO.
GLACIER CO.

Brown Pass

BOULDER

Creek

PASS

Thunderbird Pond

Thunderbird

The Hawksbill

Thunderbird Falls

Campsite

Lake Frances
5255

Lake Frances
5255

BOULDER

PASS

TRAIL

Olson

Obr

Creek

N

Thunderbird Glacier

Dixon Glacier

The Sentinel

Falls

1C

Lake

CONTINENTAL

Campsite

Hole-in-the-Wall

SEE MAP 1D

BOULDER

Campsite

Boulder Pass
7470

Hole-in-the-Wall Falls

Boulder Glacier

DIVIDE

NGSTONE

SEE MAP 1B

Mt. Boulder Peak

Creek

Pocket Lake
6613

G L A C I E R

Bowman

TRAIL

LAKE

Falls Pocket Falls

Trail

BOWMAN

Creek

BOWMAN LAKE RANGER
STATION 10.5 MI.

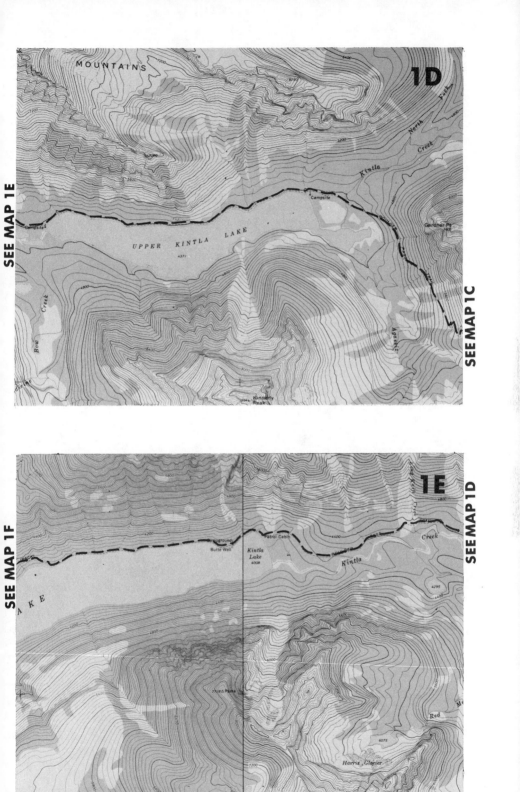

SEE MAP 1E

SEE MAP 1C

SEE MAP 1D

SEE MAP 1F

1D

MOUNTAINS

North Fork

Kintla Creek

Campsite

Gardner Pt

UPPER KINTLA LAKE

4371

Bow Creek

Agassiz

Kinnerly Peak

1E

Long Knife Creek

Campground
Butte Well

Patrol Cabin

Kintla Lake
4008

Kintla

Creek

4295

LAKE

Parke

Red

6075

Harris Glacier

Kintla Parke Peak

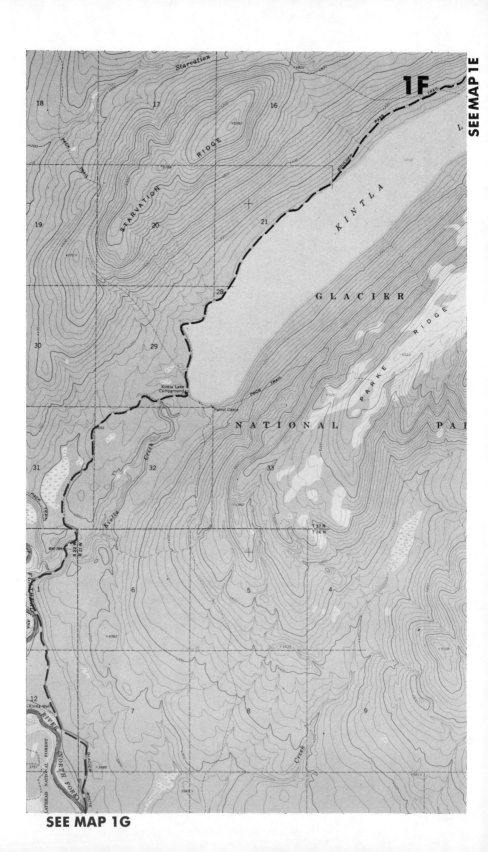

KINTLA

GLACIER

PARKE RIDGE

STARVATION RIDGE

Starvation

NATIONAL PA

18 17 16

19 20 21

30 29 28

31 32 33

1 6 5 4

12 7 8 9

Kintla Lake
Campground

Patrol Cabin

Kintla Creek

NORTH FORK

RIVER

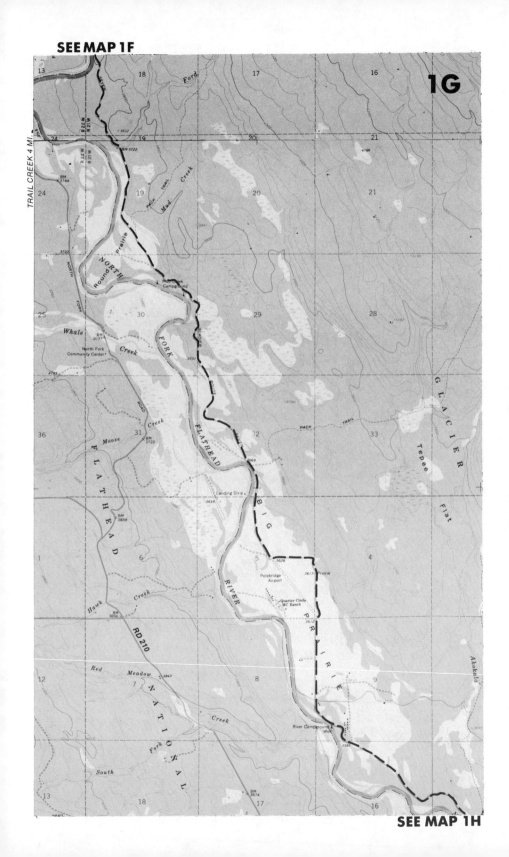

1H

SEE MAP 1I

SEE MAP 1I

TR 4

RD 210

RD 376

RD 909

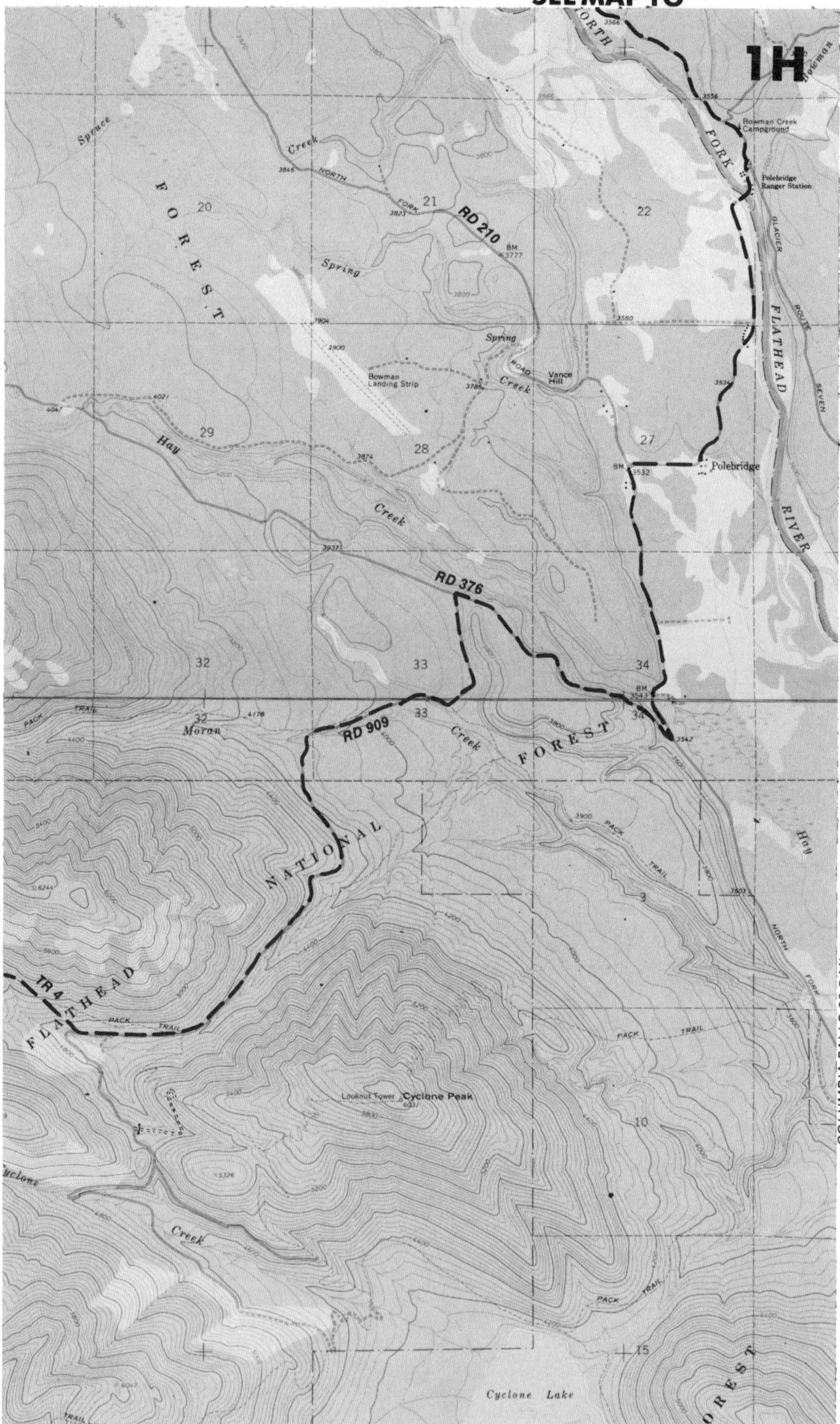

BOWMAN LAKE RANGER
STATION 4.7 MI.

COLUMBIA FALLS 30.5 MI.

Bowman Creek
Campground

Polebridge
Ranger Station

Polebridge

Vance
Hill

Bowman
Landing Strip

Moran

Lookout Tower Cyclone Peak

Cyclone Lake

FOREST

NATIONAL

FLATHEAD

NORTH FORK FLATHEAD RIVER

Spruce

Creek

Spring

Creek

Hay

Creek

Creek

Spring

Road

Hay

Creek

Cyclone

Creek

Creek

North

Creek

20

21

22

27

28

29

32

33

34

32

33

34

10

15

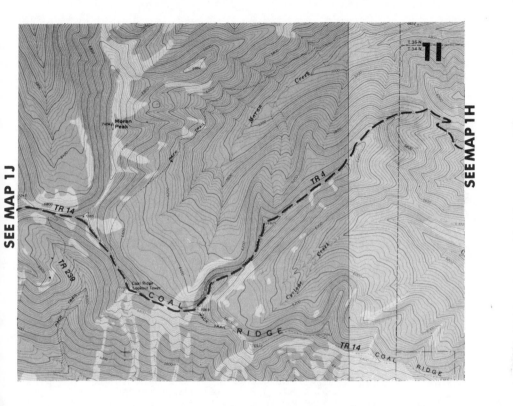

SEE MAP 1J
SEE MAP 1H

1I

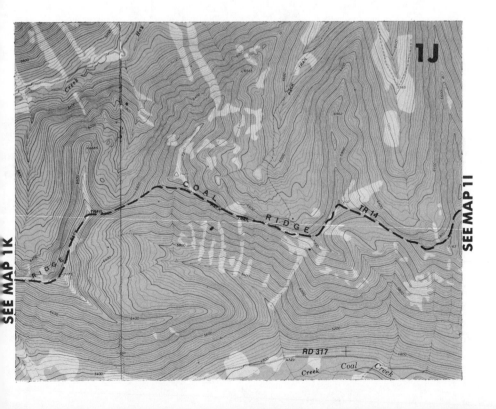

SEE MAP 1K
SEE MAP 1I

1J

1K

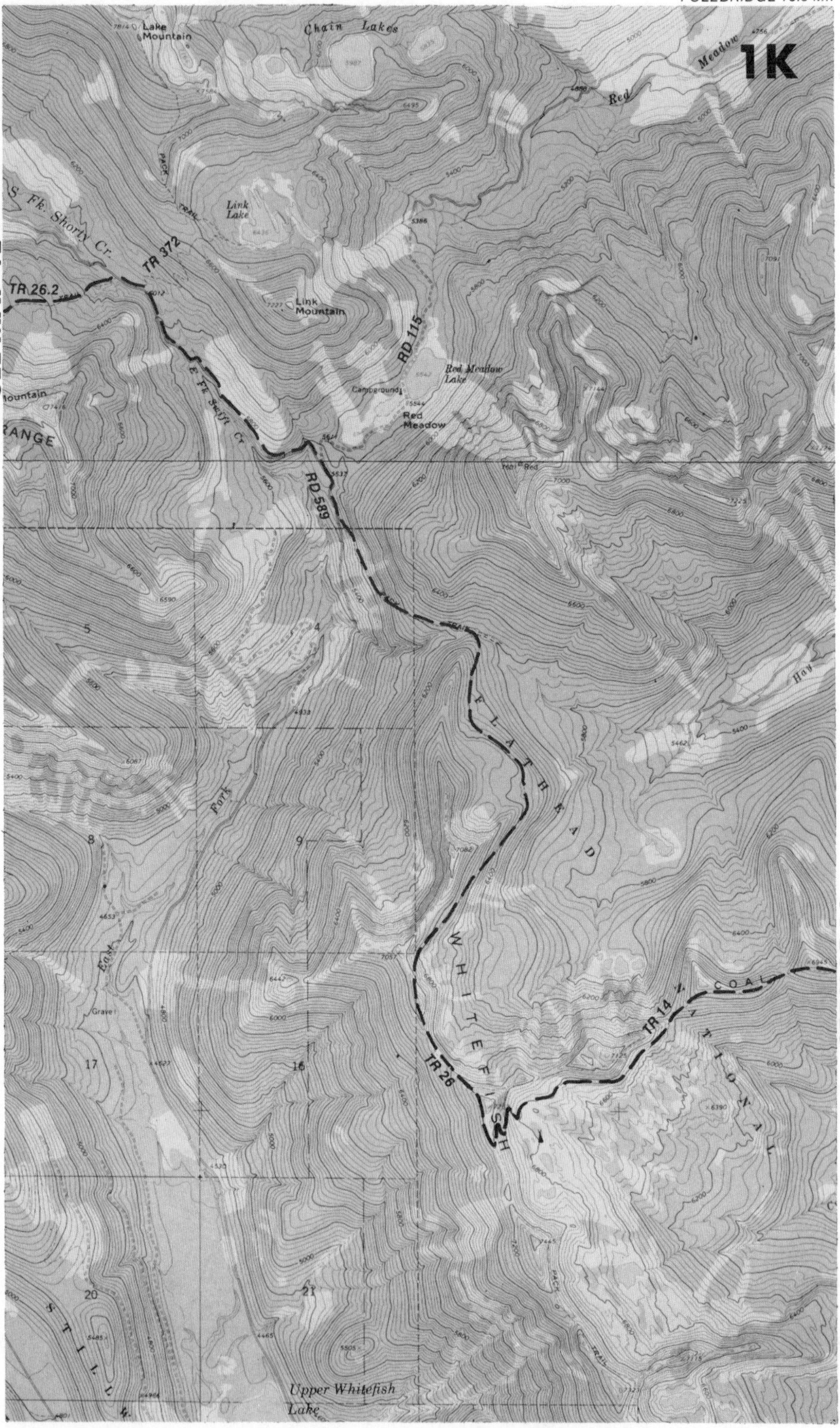

SEE MAP 1L

SEE MAP 1J

TR 372

TR 26.2

S. Fk. Shorty Cr.

E. Fk. Shorty Cr.

RANGE

Mountain

Lake
Mountain

Chain Lakes

Red Meadow

Red

Link
Lake

Link
Mountain

RD. 115

Red Meadow
Lake

Red
Meadow

Campground

RD. 589

Fork

Hay

FLATHEAD

WHITEFISH

COAL

TR 14

TR 26

NATIONAL

East
Fork

Grave

STILL

Upper Whitefish
Lake

5

4

8

9

17

16

20

21

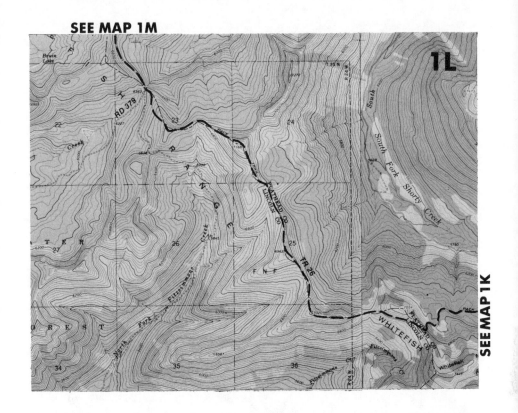

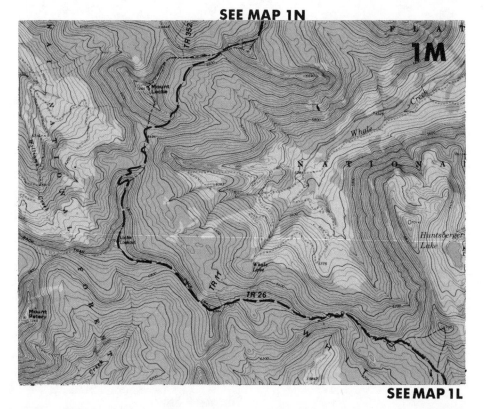

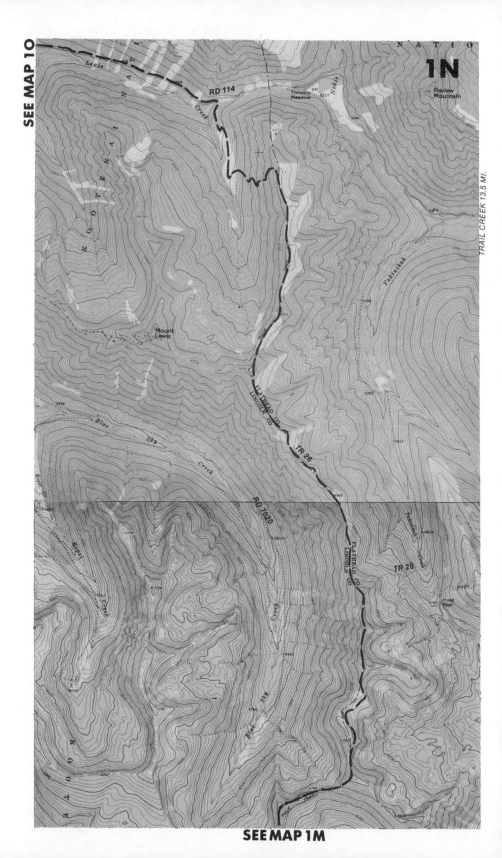

TRAIL CREEK 13.5 MI.

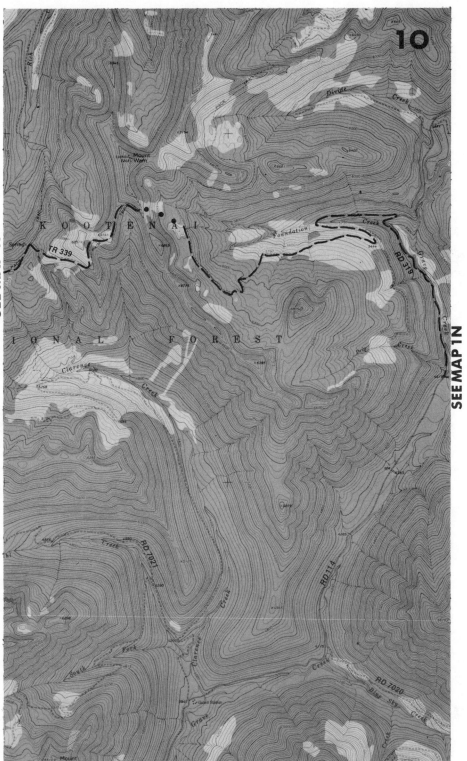

SEE MAP 1P

SEE MAP 1N

K O O T E N A I

TR 339

I O N A L   F O R E S T

Foundation

RD 319

Grave

Mount
Wam

Spring

Clarence

Creek

Creek

Creek

Divide

Creek

Dry

Creek

Gary

RD 7021

RD 114

Clarence

Creek

South

Fork

Grave

Mount
Scotty

Guard Station

RD 7020

Blue Sky

Creek

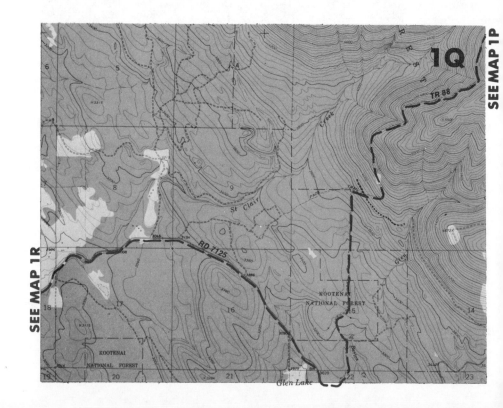

1P

1Q

TO BLUEBIRD BASIN

Bluebird

RD 319

TR 339

Little
Therriault Lake

Big
Therriault Lake

Big Therriault
Lake

Campground

St Clair
Peak

TR 88

Spring

Therriault
Pass

Finbow
Lake

N A T

Cornbud
No. Peak

Mt Barnaby

TR 339

TR 88

Creek

St Clair

RD 7125

KOOTENAI
NATIONAL FOREST

KOOTENAI
NATIONAL FOREST

Glen Lake

6   5

8   9

18   17   16   14

19   20   21   22   23

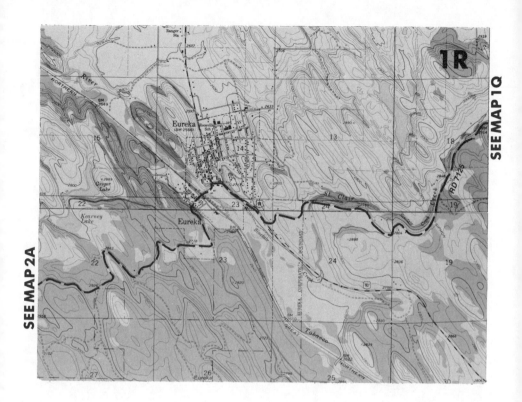

SEE MAP 1Q

SEE MAP 2A

THE PURCELL MOUNTAINS

(Eureka, Montana, to Copeland, Idaho)

Lake Koocanusa Bridge

INTRODUCTION

The Kootenai River marks the beginning of this section of the Pacific Northwest Trail, though for convenience' sake I have added nearby Eureka, Montana, which is not actually on the river. (The Kootenai, one of the greatest tributaries of the Columbia River, originates in Canada but leaves British Columbia for a deep loop into Montana and Idaho before returning to join the Columbia on its long journey to the Pacific Ocean.)

Kootenai country is a fabled land of glaciers, giant sturgeon, gold stampedes, canal-building schemes, hot springs, pioneer fortitude, and hydroelectric development. Northwestern Montana's few major towns (Eureka, Libby, and Troy) and Idaho's (Moyie Springs and Bonners Ferry) are all on or near the Kootenai River.

In this vast area of large mountains, along the PNWT the most prominent peaks are Mount Henry (7243), Northwest Peak (7705), and Bussard Mountain (5968). The Kootenai River (a.k.a. Lake Koocanusa), the Yaak River, and the Moyie River cut across our route, as do numerous major creeks.

As would be expected of such remote country, the Purcell Mountains, around which the Kootenai loops, are rich in wildlife, including everything from the big bruins to the endangered woodland caribou. Fish, too. That's no "fish story" when you land one of the Kootenai River's 9-foot sturgeon; they really do exist.

PROBLEMS

Navigation will be your chief worry in the Purcells. This section will be a test of your map and compass knowledge and of your ability to deal with the uncertainties of primitive backcountry travel. Some of the trails between Webb Mountain and Mount Henry have been neglected for so long that you will have to be very careful not to lose your way. However, the fun you have in bucking the brush will transform you from a green cheechako into a seasoned veteran.

Water is not readily available on some of this section's ridges. Plan your supply in advance and carry enough for all your needs on Webb Mountain, Thirsty Mountain, Bunker Hill, Davis Mountain, and Ruby Ridge.

Bears are not likely to be a problem here if you follow the standard procedures listed elsewhere in this book. Both black and grizzly bears inhabit this section.

Hunters take over these mountains every autumn—mainly the roads. If you choose to be out then, wear bright colors and make lots of noise. If fired upon, don't return the fire until you can see the whites of their eyes.

SUPPLIES

Two excellent supply points—Eureka, MT 59917, and Bonners Ferry, ID 83805—are at either end of this section. All services, including laundry and showers, are available at each. Near, but not on the route, are Rexford, MT 59930, Eastport, ID 83826, and Porthill, ID 83853; all have post offices. Eastport has a general store, as does Yaak, MT. The Yaak Mercantile and the Yaak River Ranch will hold PNWT cache boxes for you. Porthill has no store, but two bars; no bridge or ferry, either. The Mission Creek Store is about 2 miles from Copeland. Kootenai River bridges are located at Bonners Ferry, Copeland, and 3 miles north of Creston, B.C. Creston has a full range of supplies and services.

DECLINATION   21° E

USGS TOPOGRAPHIC MAPS

Eureka North	Bonnet Top
Eureka South	Garver Mountain
Beartrap Mountain	Northwest Peak
Webb Mountain	Canuck Peak, Idaho—Montana
Boulder Lakes	Eastport, Idaho
Lost Horse Mountain	Hall Mountain
Mount Henry	

MILEAGES (total 120.6)

		Total
Eureka City Park on St. Clair Creek (2600)	0.0	0.0
Pinkham Wye (3107) via Road 854	5.6	5.6
Beginning of Camp 32 Road 7182 (3138) via Road 856	1.8	7.4
Camp 32 (2750)	2.1	9.5
State Highway 37 via Pinkham Creek, Road 7182	2.0	11.5
Koocanusa Bridge via State Highway 37	1.6	13.1
Webb Mountain Trail No. 435 (2400)	1.3	14.4
Webb Mountain (5988)	5.0	19.4
Boulder Mountain (7058) via Thirsty Mountain (6264)	6.0	25.4
H junction above Boulder Lakes with Trail No. 91 (6600)	1.0	26.4
Larry Reed Camp via Trail No. 91 (5640)	1.7	28.1
Ridge 6903′	1.2	29.3
Lost Horse Mountain Lookout Trail junction (5960)	1.3	30.6
Janet and Rex Spring, and Basin Creek Trail No. 233 junction (6450)	.9	31.5
Mount Henry (7243)	4.9	36.4
Turner Creek Falls (3560) via Vinal Creek Trail No. 9	5.0	41.4
Road 1746 (3220) via Bunker Hill Trail No. 51	8.5	49.9
Road 92 (3074) via Yaak River Ranch Road	3.5	53.4
Garver Mountain (5874) via Road 276 and 5857	11.0	64.4
Pete Creek Meadows (4301)	4.5	68.9
Jungle Creek Road 5900 (4520)	2.0	70.9
Northwest Peak trailhead	8.1	79.0
Northwest Peak (7705)	2.5	81.5
Canuck Peak (6934)	5.0	86.5
Spread Creek Road (6160) via the Alpine Ridge Trail	1.0	87.5
Canuck Pass (5810) via the Alpine Ridge Trail and Knob 6491′	3.1	90.6
Copper Ridge Road 403 (5840) via the abandoned upper end of the Ruby Ridge Trail	1.0	91.6
Moyie River Road (2500) via Ruby Ridge Trail No. 35	7.0	98.6
Bussard Mountain Trail No. 32 (2540) via the Moyie River Road	2.1	100.7
Bussard Mountain (5968)	3.2	103.9
Camp Nine Road	5.0	108.9
Hall School junction (2194) of U.S. Highway 95 via Ace Creek and the Camp Nine Road and U.S. 95	9.0	117.9

Wallen Road (214) via State Highway 1	1.0	118.9
Copeland Bridge (Kootenai River, 1763) via the Wallen Road	1.7	120.6

ROUTE DESCRIPTION

Eureka, Montana, is sometimes called the Christmas tree capital of the world. The town (population 1200) stretches north quite a distance. However, everything needed by hikers is near the Town Pump gas station, where Highway 93 becomes the main street at the foot of the hill. From this central point a laundromat, drug store, and Prairie Market are within sight. Farther north is a larger grocery store. If you are a long-distance traveller, stop in to say hello at the Tobacco Valley News, across from the picnic park near the market.

The police station is in the small town hall near the laundromat; inquire there for permission ($5 key deposit) to use the free cold showers at the back of the fire station next to the St. Clair Creek city park. It would be convenient to camp at this centrally located park ($5) near the Town Pump. The park is across the creek from the interesting collection of salvaged old-time buildings called the Historic Village. The old Rexford, Montana, general store of Bill Fewkes serves as the Historic Village's museum. Rexford was inundated in the late 1960s when the new Libby Dam flooded the Kootenai River Valley to create Lake Koocanusa.

From the city park, the PNWT crosses the white-blazed St. Clair Creek bridge and goes southwest, crossing the Tobacco River and the tracks of the Burlington Northern Railroad. Near a church the road curves and climbs southeast out of town. Continue westward to scenic Baker Lake (2899) and Othorp Lake (3018) via Road 854, a pleasant, very easy grade. Neither of these largely private lakes has camping facilities. Continue southwest—more level walking—at the foot of Black Butte (4064) to the road junction called the Pinkham Wye (3107). It's 5.6 miles from Eureka to the Wye.

Take the right fork (heading southwest, then northwest) via Road 856 toward Mud Lake. But at a junction ½ mile before the lake, turn left (southwest) on Road 7182 and go 2.1 miles to Camp 32 (2750). Camp 32 is on a less-travelled side loop down from the main Road 7182.

Camp 32 is an old logging-camp site. You can still see the old springboard cuts in nearby stumps. (Springboards were wooden pole steps on which loggers stood high enough up the butt end of a tree trunk to leave a high stump, since the wide, lowest part of the trunk was considered undesirable by sawmills.) This camp is suitably rustic and unimproved for hikers, though car campers use it, too. If you walk upstream through scenic, rocky Pinkham Creek canyon, you will reach an attractive waterfall. During the summer be prepared for bugs here.

Continue west 2 miles along Pinkham Creek, eventually rejoining Road 7182, which comes out onto State Highway 37. Turn south toward the Koocanusa Bridge, passing the rocky gorge of Pinkham Creek and enjoying numerous views of this impressive reservoir. (The Rexford post office, by the way, is 6.3 miles north on Highway 37.) The name Koocanusa was lobbied into official acceptance by Rexford residents (including the PNWTA's Bill and Clara Fewkes). The first syllable stands for Kootenai, the second for Canada, and the third for U.S.A.

The ½-mile-long Koocanusa Bridge is not only the mightiest on the PNWT but also the longest and highest in Montana. Its steel girders span a reservoir that backs up 90 miles—well into Canada—from the Libby Dam (420' high) near Libby, Montana. A museum and summertime guided tours of the otherworldly interior are available at the well-designed Libby Dam visitors center. Write to the U.S. Army Corps of Engineers for information about local history seminars.

From the west end of the bridge, walk 1.3 miles south along the highway blasted into the mountainside. Boulder Creek's noisy torrent at Road Mile Post 44 is immediately before the Webb Mountain trailhead. Hikers must supply themselves with water here for the upcoming dry ascent of Webb Mountain. Water can usually be found about ⅓ mile short of the summit, at the end of a 900-foot side trail marked by a red sign.

Wooded Webb Mountain Trail No. 435 switchbacks relentlessly up about 3600 feet in only 3 crow's-flight miles. The trail is usually in reasonable condition. Do not miss the first right turn about 200 feet from the roadhead. The dry, steady grind of this trail is a killer on hot days. But from the concrete block lookout tower at the summit, you will be rewarded with a comprehensive view of the Ten Lakes Scenic Area, the Tobacco Plains, Hold-Up Gulch, the Koocanusa Bridge, and the long, curving ribbon of the reservoir. (This lookout is locked and has no water, but water is available 1.9 miles down the lookout access road toward Boulder Creek.)

Look west from the lookout at the three mountain knobs stretching to the horizon. Due west is wooded Thirsty Mountain, with clearcut Boulder Creek Valley to your right. The next higher point is Boulder Mountain. Beyond and to the right is cone-shaped Mount Henry. Keep this picture in mind as you cross the poorly maintained trails ahead.

Because of the newish lookout access road and the numerous logging roads and clearcuts farther west, Trail No. 248 is no longer used except by animals, hunters, renegades, and PNWT hikers. To most easily find its mossy, abandoned track, go down the road about 100 yards and look for a red-blazed tree on the left. Enter the lodgepole pine woods and find the old trail along the ridge.

After the monotonous grind up from Lake Koocanusa, this is a very pleasant stroll. Thirsty Mountain (which is as dry as its name implies) is two miles west.

Our Trail Association must create a new link between Thirsty Mountain and Boulder Mountain Trail No. 248 to replace the old abandoned and cutover route. For now, a good way to go is to contour north short of Thirsty Mountain into an old clearcut and then follow the edge of the trees west to the Boulder Creek road (5400). Do not try to cross Thirsty's lodgepole blowdowns.

From the road our next destination is the 7058' summit of Boulder Mountain 3 miles west. The road contours south through a pass and curves west. Look for a right turn up into a clearcut. (If you reach a branch of the Little North Fork, you have gone too far.) Follow that logging track out across the stumps to where it becomes the Boulder Mountain Trail.

Boulder Mountain once had a fine, wooden lookout tower, but it has been burned down. The sagging walls of an old cabin still stand, a potential shelter-restoration job for PNWTA volunteers. Boulder Mountain will help to orient you to Webb and Thirsty Mountains. It is especially important as a rare, relatively close-up view of Mount Henry, our next destination and the highest peak in this area.

An alternate approach to Boulder Mountain from the Boulder Creek Road is to follow the old logging road signed "Boulder Lakes Trail." Then turn left at the Y onto a smaller road crowded with alders. The trail leaves the brushy track at a good creek (with a deteriorating stock-loading ramp) and climbs above the northernmost of the two Boulder Lakes. (A short side trail provides easy access to lakeside camping.) At the junction where the trail finally tops out above the lake, we connect with the main PNWT route from the summit of Boulder Mountain. This also makes a good circuit hike to the road.

Where the Boulder Lakes Trail and the Boulder Mountain Trail meet at the lip above the lake (6600), turn northwest at a red blaze. The USGS 7½' Boulder Lakes map incorrectly portrays this junction, which is actually an H and not a cross. This heavily wooded area is called the Purcell Summit. Imagine the Boulder Lakes Trail curving up around from the lakes onto the high ground and continuing toward Boulder Mountain. Imagine a pack trail coming from the north, nearly touching the former trail, and swinging westward. These two separate trails are linked by a 50-foot way trail to form a kind of H. Cross over to the new trail; there a right (north) turn would bring you to the Dodge Summit in 1.5 miles. However, we turn left (west) on Trail No. 91.

As you may have noticed by now, the old, disused pack trails in this area have been red-blazed by the Forest Service as fire trails. So red paint is one trail identification clue—sometimes. Look for old tread, axe blazes, and chopped logs. And promise to sign up for a PNWTA volunteer work party.

Trail No. 91 is brushy and hard to follow at this writing, but improvement has been promised by the Forest Service. In rainy weather expect miles of wet menziesia brush, which will soak you badly unless you have rain pants or gaiters. The trail descends in ½ mile to a wet area where a red blaze on a 5-foot-high, broken-off tree tells you to turn sharply right uphill. (If you miss this turn, you immediately have to crawl over an enormous fallen tree.) Continue uphill away from the wet area through heavy brush and over many deadfalls. This enclosed, uphill course is broken in 1.2 miles by the welcome openness of a partially grassed-in pond at the head of a drainage. A very small site, Larry Reed Camp, is available at the outlet of this pond.

Trail No. 91 climbs west 1.2 more miles to a ridge, of which the highest nearby point is 6903'. At the top of this uphill section look for a double-red-blazed tree. To your left is a clearly red-blazed trail going south to Bunker Hill. Don't take that fine-looking path. Instead, grope to your right for a not-red-blazed trail, which is very faint indeed. Trail No. 91 has changed direction and now you will follow it north to Mount Henry.

After 1.3 miles, initially uphill, then downhill, we reach the Lost Horse Mountain Lookout Trail junction and a sign which says, "Purcell Summit Trail No. 7." The distance ahead to Mount Henry is recorded as 4.8 miles. It is .9 mile to Trail No. 233, which connects with Basin Creek (east) and Vinal Creek and Turner Creek (west). The latter makes a good Mount Henry circuit hike from the Fish Lakes. Just 100 yards before this junction on the right side of the trail is a wooden sign pointing downhill to the Janet and Rex Spring ¼ mile away. Immediately after this water-source side trail, we reach an excellent, small trailside site. Mount Henry is 4 miles beyond.

Where the trail starts down to a large, flat, wooded col, we get a good view of Mount Henry, its lookout tower clearly visible. If you have brought adequate water with you, this high forest plain is a good stop, especially if you anticipate a storm atop Mount Henry. (You will probably find early-season water along here.)

The wilderness cone of this grand mountain is quite rocky. Where we hike up out of the woods onto open scree, a sign proclaims the junction of Purcell Summit Trail No. 7. Go to the right and you soon reach Mt. Henry Lakes. But west on the PNWT takes you to Vinal Creek Trail No. 9, the summit trail. However, to reach the summit from this side, take the clearly marked lookout spring trail. Mount Henry (7243) is definitely a jewel of the American Purcells. Most of northwest Montana's entire PNWT is visible here.

Vinal Creek Trail No. 9 descends 5 miles to a narrow, picturesque valley near the junction of Turner Creek and Vinal Creek. From the summit junction go about 1 very steep mile down to the first flat area. There is a side trail to the Kettle Spring, which is 100 yards off the trail. Half a mile farther through open lodgepole woods you will come to the edge of a clearcut (from here the Solo Joe Creek Road is ¼ mile north).

Finally, we push our aching knees to a sharp-cut little valley at 3560' and a major trail junction. Here we can choose to continue 3 beautiful miles west via Vinal Creek to Vinal Lake Road 1746 (with access to the hamlet of Yaak, Montana). Vinal Creek has an outstanding rocky canyon with firs above and red cedar and giant larches along the water. Actually, our mainline PNWT does not go that way, but be sure to make a side trip 175 yards downstream, past the beaver dam, to the dramatic pools and chutes of Turner Creek Falls, a welcome relief in hot weather and always a good campsite.

From the junction you could also go ½ mile through dense cedars to the narrow, talus-walled Fish Lakes and 5 miles farther north to Okaga Lake (private) via Windy Creek Trail No. 397. This is another way to reach the Vinal Lake Road.

Fill your canteen at Turner Creek Falls. The PNWT goes north .2 mile at the little valley junction, then follows Bunker Hill Trail No. 51 for 8 miles, northwest across Bunker Hill (5368) and into the Yaak River Valley (2992). This trail is usually in fair condition up and over Bunker Hill and down to the first clearcut on the other side. From there Trail No. 51 becomes progressively more difficult to follow because the Forest Service has replaced it with Road 6047. However, this old trail *can* be followed down to the paved Vinal Road. At the first clearcut, go left downhill along the margin of the trees until you reach this road in a loop through the woods down to a position directly below your starting point, thus skipping a small section of the old trail. Regain the trail at a red and white surveyor's tape along the road. From here on, follow the old trail despite terrible blowdowns and many tempting road crossings. There is a good campsite where the trail intersects Bunker Hill Creek; at that point do not cross the creek but turn left onto the trail going downstream. (The only other reliable water on this trail is one-third of the way up from the Fish Lakes junction.)

At the paved Vinal Lake Road 1746, walk north .6 mile to a left onto the Vinal Access Road; descend the latter west to the Upper Ford Guard Station Road. Turn right on this dirt road and go 1.9 miles to the Yaak River Ranch Road. Turn left, pass the Yaak River Ranch, and reach paved Road 92 in 1.3 miles at elevation 3074'. (The Yaak River Ranch—Rt. 1, Yaak, Troy, MT 59935—offers lodging, camping, PNWT cache box service, and showers.)

The hamlet of Yaak is 7 miles south of the decommissioned Upper Ford Guard Station on Road 92. The Yaak Mercantile (Rt. 1, Yaak, Troy, MT 59935) is a new general store selling groceries, gasoline, and some camping supplies; they will also hold PNWT cache boxes. The Yaak Mercantile and the Dirty Shame Saloon are Yaak's only attractions.

Instead of walking entirely via Road 92 to Yaak for supplies, you could take a shortcut along Hoskins Lake Trail No. 162 or the Vinal Lake Road 1746. The old pack trail reaches a private Yaak River crossing at elevation 2966'. That crossing also ties in with the Vinal Creek Trail No. 9 and makes a good circuit hike or ride.

The next two major destinations on the PNWT are Garver Mountain (5874) and the Northwest Peak Scenic Area. The Ideal Route ascends Waper Creek to Waper Ridge (5048) and follows Garver Mountain trail northwest.

However, because of the intensive logging on Waper Ridge, we must temporarily take a Practical Route detour from Road 92 to Garver Mountain instead of ascending Waper Ridge and the Garver Mountain Trail. Our 11-mile PNWT road route to Garver Mountain begins as Road 276, the West Fork Yaak River Road, and ends as Road 5857, the French Creek Road. The road zigzags up an elevation gain of 2800' through forest and clearcuts. The lookout tower is a good place to camp—if you have carried water up from French Creek. To reach it, make a .5-mile side trip by turning left at the far end of the uppermost clearcut and walking a short skid road to the lookout trail.

From 5874' Garver Mountain we have a very good view of the Northwest Peak Scenic Area 8 miles to the northwest. In the foreground beyond Pete Creek is the 5500' ridge of Mushroom Mountain. Beyond is the West Fork Yaak River Valley and then the roadless, jagged 7000' + ridge that includes Northwest Peak (7705), Davis Mountain (7583), and Ewing Peak (7540).

To reach Northwest Peak, descend the waterless, moderately scenic, good-condition Garver Mountain Trail 4.5 miles northwest to the Pete Creek Meadow Creek Meadows (4301). Follow Pete Creek Road 338 north 2 miles past the meadows (which are the source of Pete Creek) and around west to a junction with obscure Jungle Creek Road 5900. Continue southwest along the West Fork Road to Winkum Creek Road 338, which connects to the 2.5 mile, good-condition Northwest Peak Trail. The distance from the Garver Mountain Lookout to the Northwest Peak Lookout totals 17.1 miles.

Our Ideal Route branches off at the Jungle Creek Road and goes 3.5 miles up Jungle Creek to elevation 5294', making a wide swing away from the creek higher up. If you go to the end of the road, obtain water there. Or, at a sharp left turn after 2.5 miles, look for the old trail, now a potential shortcut closer to the creek than the road. From the road end continue 2 miles via the Jungle Creek Trail's many switchbacks up to the 6440' ridge between Cooney Peak and Marmot Mountain. Next we have a 2-mile bushwhack traverse. Turn south and siwash along this wooded, easy ridge to the 6921' summit of Marmot Mountain; turn southwest down along the height of the ridge to the Winkum Creek Road in a little pass at elevation 6378'.

Go downhill .2 mile on the road to the Northwest Peak trailhead in an old clearcut. This is a good place to fill your canteens because, except for a nearby, hard-to-find lookout spring, there are no water sources (other than seasonal snow banks) until beyond Ewing Peak.

The Northwest Peak Lookout is a small, square, frame hut atop a mammoth summit of granite scree. The unlocked wooden cabin looks lost in the vast landscape. On a very clear day you can see all the way from the Rockies to the Selkirks; the horizon is so wide that the eye is almost overwhelmed. We gravitate nearby to the long ridge that connects south to the great, bare hump of Davis Mountain. We visually estimate the difficulties along that airy corridor, then follow the ridge with binoculars as it spins away westward around Lake Florence to Canuck Peak.

This is one of the roughest ridges on the entire PNWT. In bad weather take our alternate Spread Creek Road stock route instead. What makes the Northwest Peak traverse difficult is not only its elevation but also its exposure. Glacial basins drop away sharply on either side. There is no trail, only a long, fascinating scramble.

About halfway out, the bald bulk of Davis Mountain rises from the rest of the wall to obstruct our passage. But the climb over it is not difficult. Beyond Davis is a traverse around Ewing Peak. We clamber down and across the West Fork Yaak River's high, rocky headwater basin to a saddle between Ewing Peak and Rock Candy Mountain. Search there for the good-condition trail that contours west to Canuck Peak (6934). The West Fork Yaak basin has seasonal water and potential campsites.

If you are careful, you will have no trouble slowly traversing the 5 glorious miles between Northwest Peak and Canuck Peak. If you are carrying water and a windproof tent, you may wish to camp at one of several outstanding spots along this world bridge.

From Canuck Peak, Montana is almost all behind us and the cliffs of the long ridge that we have just walked stand out bold and rugged against the horizon. The west's new ridges and mountains welcome us to the Idaho Panhandle.

From Canuck Peak the Alpine Ridge Trail drops down 1 mile of huckleberry switchbacks to the Spread Creek Road (6160), our all-road, pack-stock alternate route from the Yaak River Road. The Alpine Ridge Trail crosses the Spread Creek Road at the col we have named Kounkel Pass (in honor of longtime PNWT activist Chris Kounkel of Spokane). Expect no reliable water at this pass. Trail No. 51 originally provided Forest Service access to wildlife-rich Buckhorn Mountain (6177), the Scout (6300), and Keno Mountain (6542).

From Kounkel Pass, Alpine Ridge Trail No. 51 climbs and contours around an arm of Knob 6567' and slides southwest over Knobs 6614' and 6491'. Here we are following the divide between the Moyie and Yaak Rivers. Much of the country from here south burned up in 1931, and the evidence is visible everywhere in the young forest growth. Toward the end of these 2 miles of fine tread but heavy menziesia brush, we pass plenty of streams on our way to a fine meadow and the ruins of an old cabin. We find an abandoned way trail to connect us to Canuck Pass the second time we hit an old dozer road, about 200 feet up the road to a rock cairn. Follow this passable, but unmaintained, spur ridge trail northwest 1.5 miles to Canuck Pass, crossing the Idaho state line halfway there. This is a fine, wild place to enter the Gem State; we will leave Idaho in even wilder country.

At Canuck Pass (5810) a cairn of rocks marks the beginning of an abandoned segment of the Ruby Ridge Trail No. 35. Canuck Pass is an attractive viewpoint for the Canuck Creek Valley. Its paved Deer Creek Road connects 20 miles south with U.S. 2; north is a connection to Eastport, Idaho. There is no water available at Canuck Pass, nor is there any until near the bottom of the coming 8-mile descent of Ruby Ridge.

From the PNWT cairn (5810) contour easily west along the wooded old trail to the end of the unmaintained first mile. Although the trail is often overgrown, the only difficult part is a sharp left turn in a little defile high on this forested route. A sign at Copper Ridge Road 403 marks the beginning of the official Ruby Ridge Trail No. 35.

Ruby Ridge is a pleasant, easy-to-follow trail with many fine views in its upper section. Note especially the Deer Ridge Lookout due south. West are the sharply eroded cliffs of Bussard Mountain, which we will not reach until after a strenuous crossing of the Moyie River Valley. From the trail's upper meadowed slopes we finally drop into dense forest for our final run near Orser Creek—our first water—to the river. At the bottom of this long knee-tester, the PNWT angles right in a poplar forest along the flat margin of valley and mountain, then shoots straight out to the train tracks and dirt highway on what looks like a ranch pathway.

From 7705' at Northwest Peak we have dropped rather fast to only 2494' at the Snyder Guard Station, one of the PNWT's many dramatic elevation changes. Although the climb on the west side of this valley does not go quite as high (only to 5968'), the sensation is greater because the distance is more compressed.

From where the Ruby Ridge Trail joins the Moyie River Valley Road, you will be able to see the signless entrance for the inoperative Snyder Guard Station to your left. Our Ideal Route will, we hope, someday use a cable car (and the old horse ford) there to reach Sidehill Trail No. 415 and our Bussard Mountain route to the Kootenai River Valley.

For now, however, our Practical Route follows the Moyie River Valley Road north (upstream) 1.5 miles to a wooden bridge. Cross it and follow the dirt track north to the Bussard Mountain Trail. The trailhead was moved north a few years ago and is no longer where it appears on the USGS map. Look for a sign pointing up a narrow corridor between two barbed-wire-fenced pastures. The trail switchbacks up through thick forest to a junction with the Sidehill Trail. Continue zigzagging uphill to Bussard Mountain (5968).

If you have come directly from Snyder Guard Station via the Sidehill Trail, obtain water at Bussard Creek. Or obtain water at the first and only stream you cross not far above the pastures. (According to Bill Tilley, there is also water 500 feet before you reach his jeep trail off to the left.)

After you have begun to fear that you will never break out of the trees, the long climb finally peaks out at a rock outcrop. From this great picnic site you get a fascinating new perspective on Bussard Lake, the Moyie River, the long eastern ridge, and even Keno Mountain.

Not far above this lookout ledge is a jeep road, which comes down from Bussard Mountain to Bill Tilley's Tilley Mine. Turn left on the Tilley Mine jeep road and follow it to a signed road junction atop heavily wooded Bussard Mountain. ("6.5 miles to Camp Nine Road.") We turn left and continue toward an unseen microwave-relay tower. Be careful to stay on the main track here. Over the years several prospectors have bulldozed roads throughout these woods; none are signed. If you reach the microwave station, you have gone too far. We turn off (left) down a relatively well-travelled-looking road, which takes us south on or near the route of the old Ace Creek Trail No. 32. Follow this rough road, recently improved lower down for new logging, to the Camp Nine Road, and take the latter northwest to the Brush Lake Road, which in turn takes us to U.S. Highway 95. Go left on 95 to Hall School (and the junction of State Highway 1). This 20-mile-long road route may be unexciting, but it will get you there. Camping is available at Brush Lake (2998), a free Forest Service facility 1.7 miles southeast of the Camp Nine/Brush Lake roads junction.

Turn right on State Highway 1 and walk 1 mile north to the Wallen

Road. Turn left toward the Copeland Bridge, which is 1.7 miles farther at the Kootenai River. You will pass several houses, the Copeland grain elevator, and a crop-duster-airplane hangar. The Copeland Bridge is famous in our Association's history as the site of the first PNWT sign—erected by Trail volunteers in 1977 (and stolen in 1983).

The Ideal Route from Bussard Mountain will someday offer a much better approach to the Kootenai River from the Purcell Mountains. First it will include Bethlehem Mountain (4857) 2.5 air miles west. Actually, a good pack trail, the Danquist Trail No. 225, once connected Bussard and Bethlehem Mountains along the north side of the 5600' ridge between them. The first part of that old homesteader trail still exists and can be found where the microwave station road makes a final sharp left uphill. If, instead, you go straight at that point on the old Danquist Trail, you will find an excellent path, which takes you out onto the ridge. But since that way soon drops north into a clearcut, we will route the Ideal PNWT on the other side of the ridge along a course pioneered long ago by the colorful old miner Tom Moran. His exact way is hard to find and it traverses a few brush-choked draws, but a good map-and-compass person should have no trouble arriving at the spring near the Tungsten Hill Mine. A jeep road connects that mine west with 4857' Bethlehem Mountain and south with the Camp Nine Road via Rock Creek. However, the Ideal Route should contour directly down the southwest slopes of the mountain to the Bethlehem Mine and Brush Lake. Brush Lake sits in a snag-filled bowl, which is revegetating from a 1943 forest fire; hence the name *Brush* Lake. However, it is easily reached via a compass course from the Camp Nine Road. Altogether, this Ideal Route would have water, directness, views, and campsites. But for now it is a brushy, challenging cross-country trek.

Due west of the Brush Lake Road is a swamp, which eventually drains into Mission Creek. By following this drainage the Ideal Route would avoid all highway walking. Yet U.S. Highway 95 would be available for supply trips into Bonners Ferry 16 miles south. Mission Creek emerges from the hills onto the dramatically different, totally flat wheat fields of the Kootenai River. The creek hugs the field/hill margin; we follow it north to the Copeland Bridge atop a farmland dike. A left on the Wallen Road returns us to the Kootenai River, here flowing north toward Canada and its meeting with the Columbia River.

We have crossed the Purcell Mountains, beginning and ending at the Kootenai River.

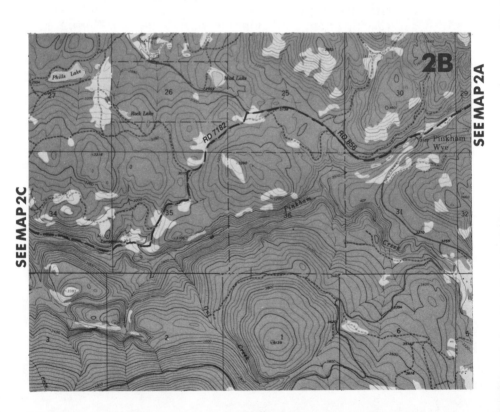

SEE MAP 1R

SEE MAP 2B

SEE MAP 2A

SEE MAP 2C

2A

2B

Eureka

RD 854

RD 7182

RD 856

Pinkham Wye

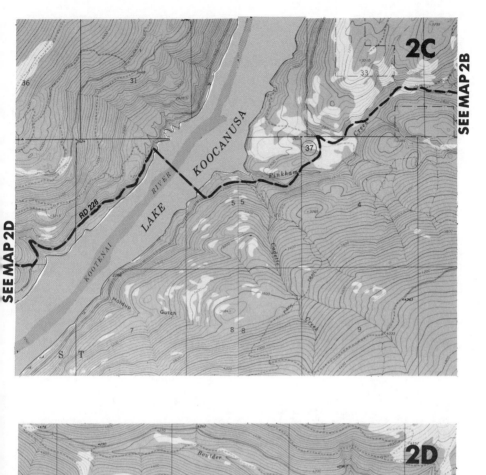

SEE MAP 2B

SEE MAP 2D

2C

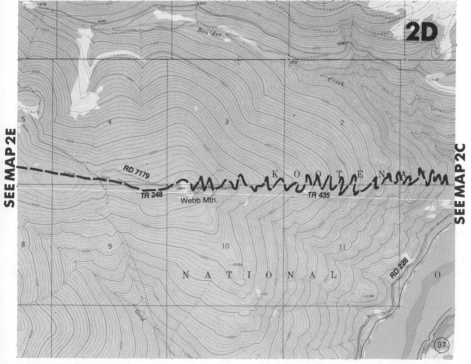

SEE MAP 2E

SEE MAP 2C

2D

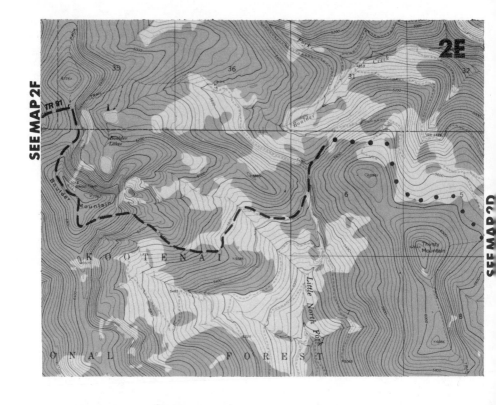

SEE MAP 2F

SEE MAP 2D

2E

TR 91

Boulder Lakes

Boulder Mountain

K O O T E N A I

Little North Fork

Thirsty Mountain

O N A L

F O R E S T

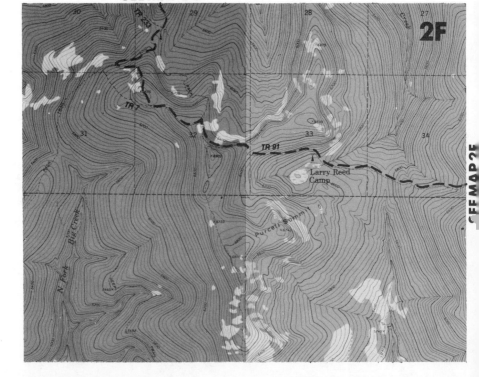

SEE MAP 2G

SEE MAP 2E

2F

TR 7

TR 91

Larry Reed Camp

Purcell Summit

N. Forks Big Creek

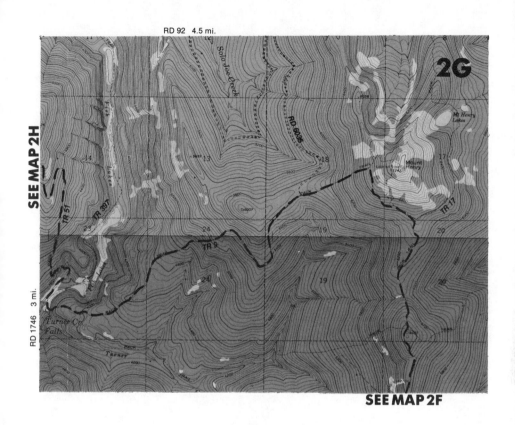

2G

SEE MAP 2H

SEE MAP 2F

RD 1746   3 mi.

Mt. Henry

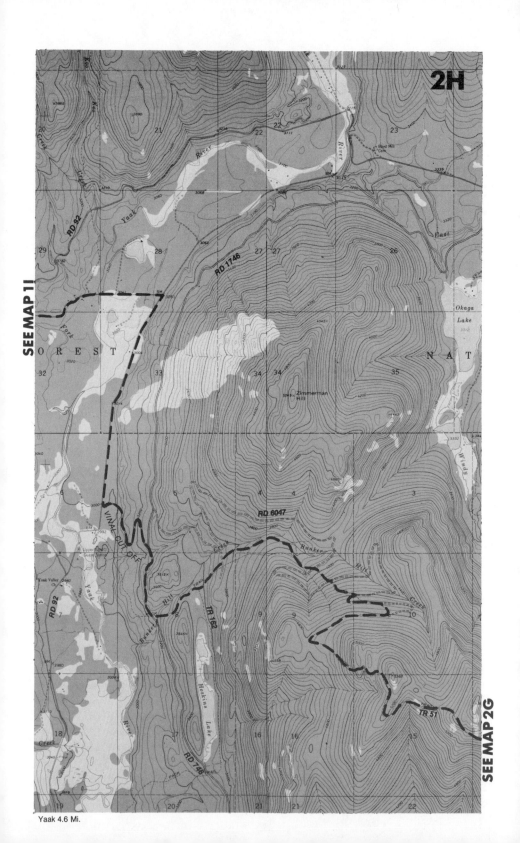

SEE MAP 1I

SEE MAP 2G

Yaak 4.6 Mi.

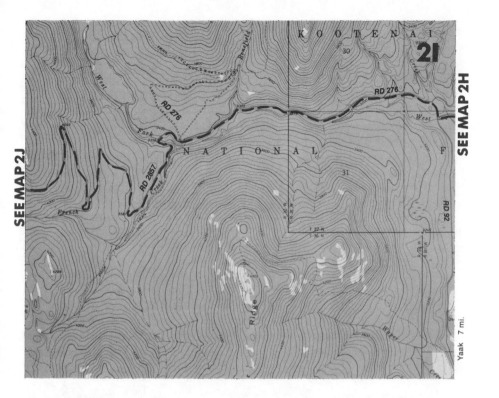

SEE MAP 2H

SEE MAP 2J

Yaak 7 mi.

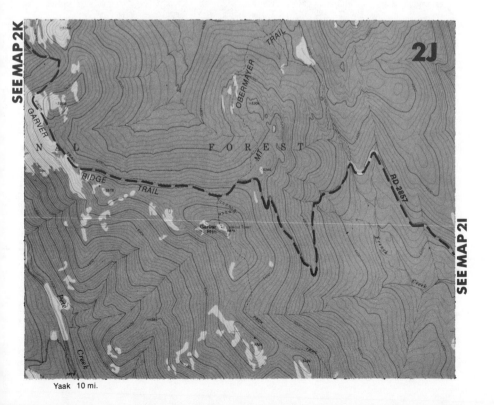

SEE MAP 2K

SEE MAP 2I

Yaak 10 mi.

SEE MAP 2L

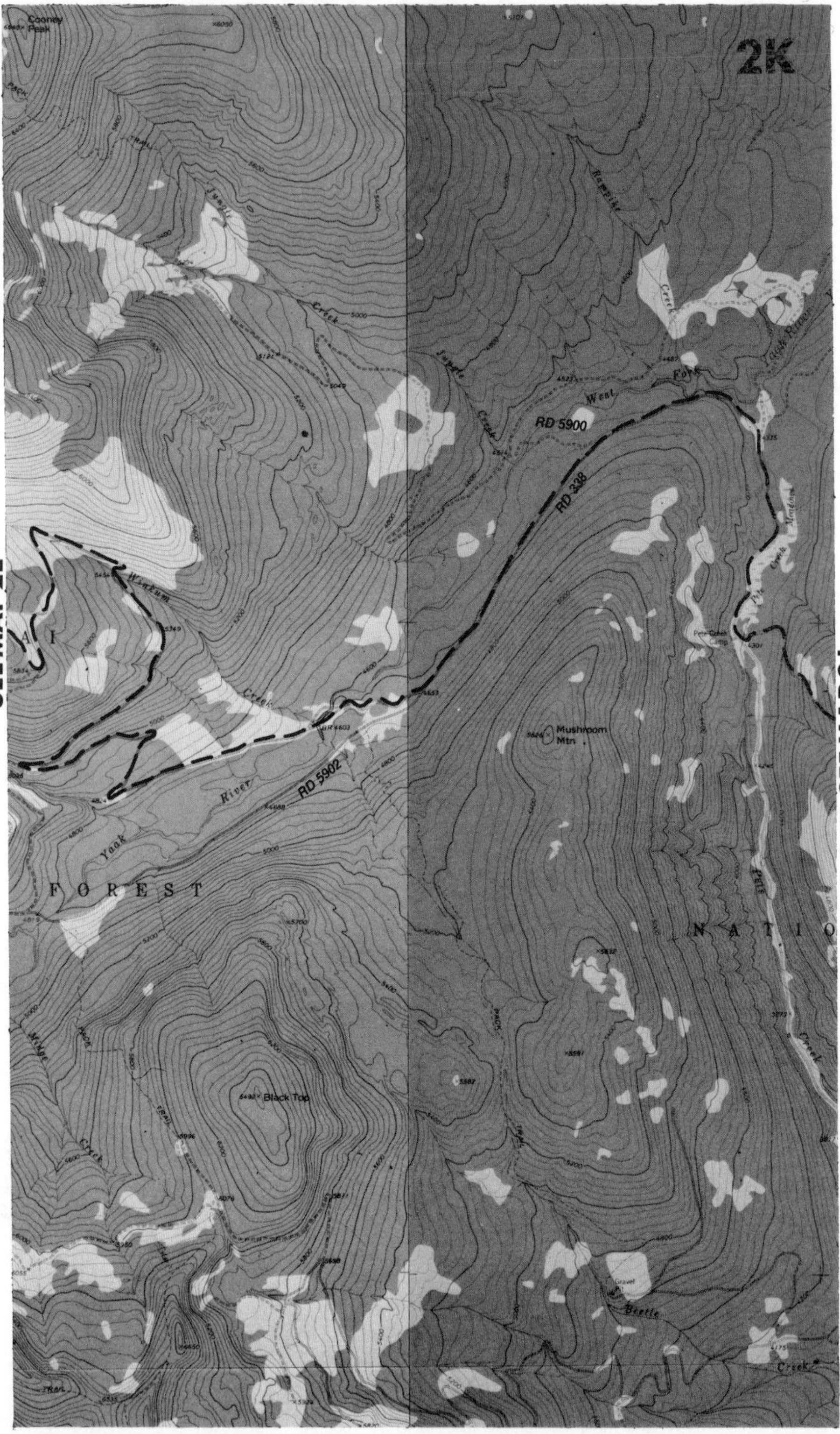

SEE MAP 2J

Cooney Peak

Jungle Creek

Rosmilk Creek

West Fork

RD 5900

RD 338

Teich River

Montana

Ferry Creek

Mushroom Mtn

Yaak River

RD 5902

FOREST

NATIO

Black Top

Beetle

Creek

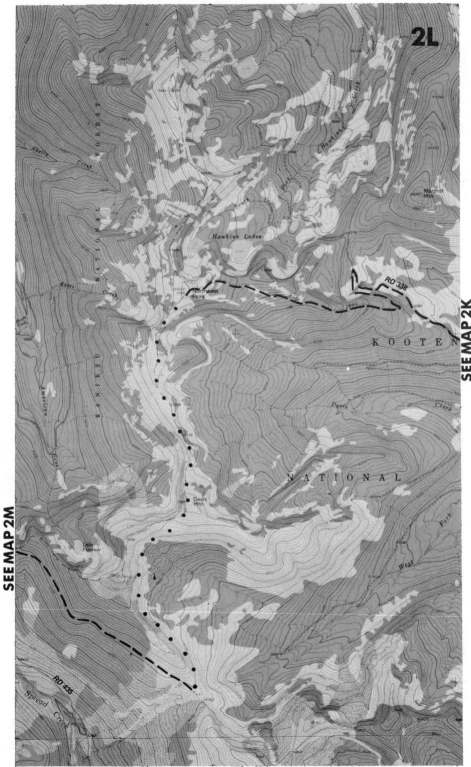

SEE MAP 2K

SEE MAP 2M

2L

Yaak River Road   7.8 mi.

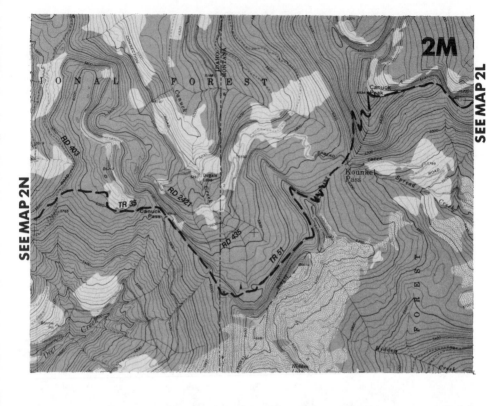

SEE MAP 2L

SEE MAP 2N

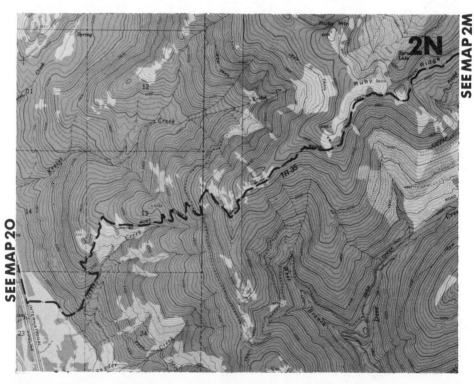

SEE MAP 2M

SEE MAP 2O

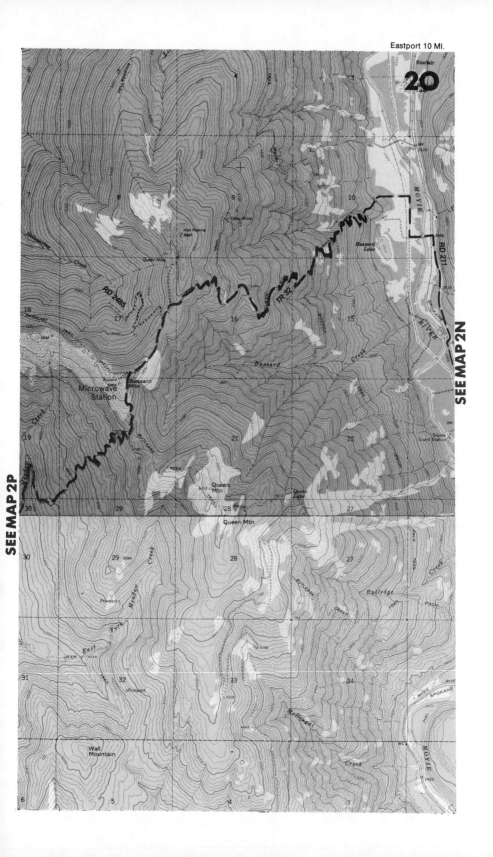

SEE MAP 2N

SEE MAP 2P

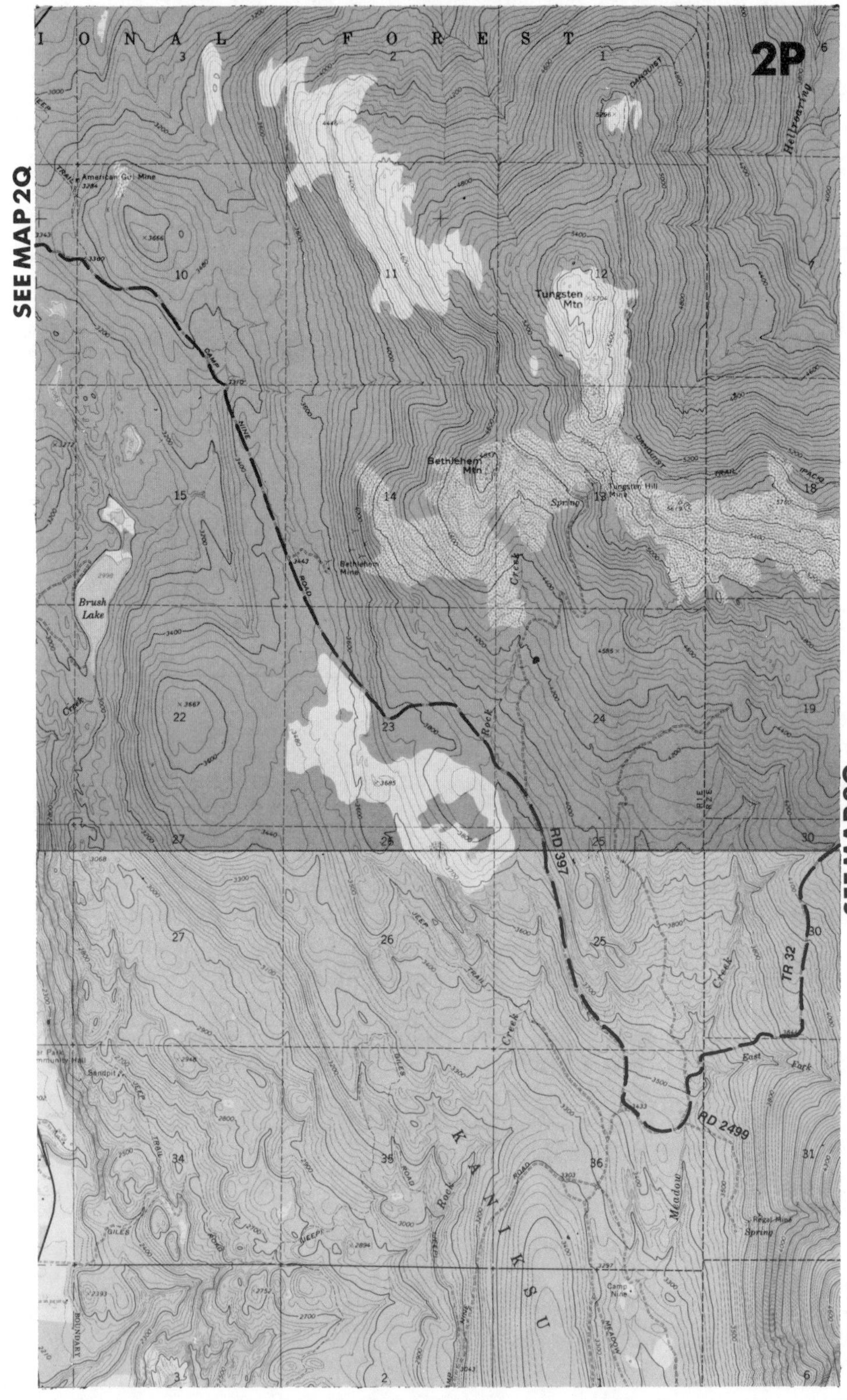
2P
SEE MAP 2Q
SEE MAP 2O
N A T I O N A L   F O R E S T
American Girl Mine
Tungsten Mtn
Bethlehem Mtn
Bethlehem Mine
Tungsten Hill Mine
Spring
Brush Lake
Creek
Rock Creek
CAMP MINE ROAD
RD 397
RD 2499
TR 32
DANQUIST TRAIL
Hellroaring
East Fork Creek
Meadow
Camp Nine
Regal Mine
Spring
JEEP TRAIL
GILES ROAD
K A N I K S U
BOUNDARY

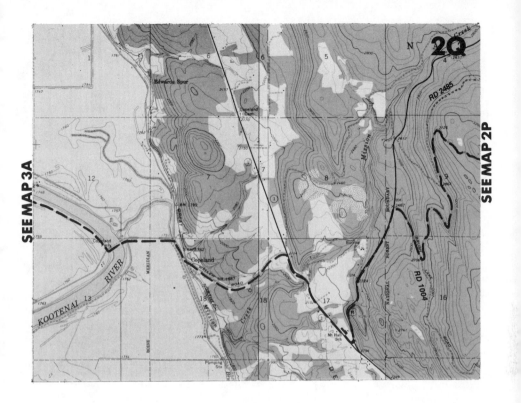

THE INLAND EMPIRE

(Kootenai River, Idaho, to Northport, Washington)

Kootenai River and Copeland Bridge

INTRODUCTION

The Inland Empire is that area of northern Idaho and northeast Washington that looks to Spokane as its shire city—despite the existence of two official capitals hundreds of miles away.

Don't expect much social or cultural continuity from one valley to the next. The Kootenai River, Upper Priest River, Pend Oreille River, North Fork Deep Creek, and Columbia River valleys are all north-south corridors with little east-west connection. In fact, the PNWT is usually the most direct way to move from one of these drainages to the next. From the settled precincts of one valley you will climb into wild backcountry, descend to another isolated settlement, and repeat the process again and again.

This remote Inland Empire section of the PNWT is anchored at both ends by major river corridors. We begin with the Columbia-bound Kootenai River and end at the Columbia itself. We thread our way along the Selkirk Crest, where a special management area includes 14,640 acres of Idaho State land and 21,140 acres of U.S. Forest Service land. The PNWT follows the Crest south from Long Canyon in very fine, lake-studded country. Priest Lake is a resort area where the possibility of a lengthy boat trip could put you in touch with the old voyageur and trapper days. Upper Priest Lake's primitive shoreline will give you a sensation of ancient wilderness; listen for loons at dawn and wolves at dusk. The Upper Priest River Trail is another such place—the entrance to the proposed Salmo-Priest Wilderness. Giant cedars and hemlocks moistened by Fraser River–borne rains evoke damp, mossy Puget Sound far to the west. Beyond the abrupt elevation changes of the Salmo-Priest, Washington State begins to ply you with treats—Gypsy Peak, Crowell Ridge, the Z-Canyon, Hooknose, and Abercrombie and Sherlock, the misty meadows of the Lind Ranch, and the long views down the great Columbia toward salt water. One third of all Lower U.S. waterpower flows seaward out this river. Its mighty tributary rivers read like the roll call of subject kingdoms of some ancient empire: the Kootenai; the Pend Oreille, the Kettle; the Okanogan; the Similkameen; the Pasayten; and the Sanpoil.

Like "separate kingdoms," too, are the wildlife populations along the Trail. The famous naturalist Henry Beston described them that way sixty years ago. If a PNWT trek is truly an education and not just a lark, its ecological aspects are some of our most lasting benefits.

Between Squawman Lookout and Salmo Mountain you will pass through critical habitat for northern Rocky Mountain wolf, grizzly bear, and mountain caribou. (This caribou is the rarest wild mammal in the United States.) Federal and state laws protect these animals and mandate the identification of critical habitat for national recovery efforts. *Every* effort should be made by you as a hiker to minimize the impact of your passage through this area.

PROBLEMS

Water will not be a problem in this section except on certain high ridges (e.g., above Kent Lake). Normally you will have more than enough water; it rains a lot here, and there are plenty of lakes and creeks. On the Selkirk Crest alone there are 24 glacial cirque lakes full of Eastern brook, cutthroat, California Golden, and rainbow trout. The PNWT visits some of these lakes, not to mention the major waters of Priest Lake and Upper Priest Lake. Amidst all this wet fun, your raingear may receive a severe test.

Our local volunteers are actively involved in wildlife preservation and in the campaign to create a Selkirk Crest National Park. Remember that you are an intruder into some of America's last remaining wilderness; practice extra-low-impact hiking.

This section utilizes the usual overgrown Forest Service Sherlock Holmes trails—although conditions here are better than, for instance, at Mount Henry. However, we also follow some high trailless ridges and do enough "bucking the brush" to really separate the compass-ready from the ready-to-get-lost. Don't attempt these cross-country wilderness sections unless you are sure that you can handle them.

SUPPLIES

In this section, distances are great between supply points, and progress is slowed by poor trails and navigational problems. Be sure to plan your supplies carefully. Freeze-dried food is your best choice here because of its low weight and because it needs little heat to prepare.

Bonners Ferry, Idaho, near the beginning of this section, is an excellent supply point. Northport, Washington, at the western end, is only slightly less good. From both, public transportation is available to Spokane if you have a major problem such as a smashed camera. If you are a would-be end-to-ender, drop in at the Bonners Ferry Herald to tell them about your trip. Bonners Ferry (83805) has both a downtown retail area and its South Hill stores. Because there are no campsites in or near town, lodging is restricted to motels.

Copeland has no post office and no facilities for travellers.

Porthill (83853), on State Highway 1 at the Canadian border, does have a post office. Creston, B.C.—famous for fresh fruit—is only 7 miles north. There is no longer a Kootenai River crossing at Porthill.

Coolin's post office (83821), at the south end of Priest Lake, is adjacent to the Leonard Paul Store. The present owners of the Leonard Paul Store, Gordon and Diana Hudson, may be able to assist PNWT hikers with hiring a boat for a ride back up the entire length of Priest Lake. Also, the owners of the Indian Creek Store, Joan and Gary Dunning, will be helpful in securing transportation by boat or auto from Indian Creek to Coolin or Mosquito Bay (The Thorofare) and in holding your cache supply box for you. Coolin is their post office address. For hikers who take the Klootch Mountain Trail, there is a mobile radio at the campgrounds at Mosquito Bay. You may be able to call Coolin and arrange transportation down. Mosquito Bay also has shower facilities; the manager there is Larry Townsend (208/443-2200).

Metaline Falls, WA 99153, has groceries, a cafe, phones, and a post office. No camping, but there are motels nearby such as the Z-Canyon Motel.

Northport (99157) has groceries, cafes, taverns, laundry machines, phones, a post office, and pay camping in the city park north of the bridge.

DECLINATION   21° E to 21½° E

USGS TOPOGRAPHIC MAPS

Copeland, Idaho	Salmo Mountain
Smith Falls	Gypsy Peak
Pyramid Peak	Boundary Dam
Smith Peak	Metaline Falls
The Wigwams	Abercrombie Mountain
Priest Lake NE	Leadpoint
Caribou Creek	Metaline
Upper Priest Lake	Boundary
Continental Mountain	Northport

MILEAGES   (total 154.7)

		Total
Kootenai River (1748), Copeland Bridge	0.0	0.0
Dike Road (1756) via river dike from bridge	2.5	2.5
Mouth of Long Canyon Creek (1747)	7.0	9.5
Long Canyon Trail No. 16 at West Side Road	1.5	11.0
Pyramid Pass Trail No. 7 (4520)	13.0	24.0
Junction, Parker Peak Trail No. 221 (6400)	3.5	27.5
Junction (6120), Big Fisher Lake Trail No. 41 (via Pyramid Pass)	1.5	29.0
Junction (5910), Trout Creek Road Trail No. 19	.5	29.5
Pyramid Lake (6050)	3.0	32.5
Ball Lakes (6708, 6605)	1.0	33.5
Myrtle Peak (7122)	3.5	37.0
Knob 7001′	3.0	40.0
Two Mouth Lakes (5831, 5842)	1.5	41.5
The Wigwams (7033)	3.5	45.0
Klootch Mountain (6048)	2.7	47.7
Priest Lake, Squaw Bay (2438)	4.3	52.0
Mosquito Bay via East Shore Road (2444)	1.5	53.5
Ruby Creek Road (2600) via Upper Priest Lake Trail No. 58	9.5	63.0
Upper Priest River Road 1013 (2634)	.5	63.5
Upper Priest River Trail No. 308 (2762)	3.5	67.0
Little Snowy Top Trail No. 349 (2960)	6.5	73.5
Shedroof Divide Trail No. 512 (6200)	5.0	78.5
Trail No. 535 (6120) via the Shedroof Divide	6.0	84.5
Salmo Mountain (6828) via Trail No. 535 and Roads 654 and 853	6.0	90.5
Crowell Ridge Trail No. 515 (6000) via Gypsy Peak cross-country	5.0	95.5
North Fork Sullivan Creek Trail No. 507 (6520)	3.0	98.5
Lime Lake (2560) via Trail No. 507	10.0	108.5
Pend Oreille River Bridge (2059), Metaline Falls	4.0	112.5
County Road 62 (2123) via State Highway 31	1.3	113.8
Flume Creek Road 585 (2566)	3.7	117.5
Abercrombie Mountain (7308) via Road 585 and Trail No. 502	11.0	128.5
North Fork Silver Creek (3708) via Baldy Trail	4.0	132.5

Leadpoint (2135)	5.0	137.5
O'Hare Creek Road (2179) via County Road 705	2.0	139.5
Lind Ranch (4300) via O'Hare Creek Road	4.5	144.0
Black Canyon Road (2984)	1.5	145.5
Deep Creek County Road 700 (1862)	3.0	148.5
Columbia River Bridge, Northport (1328)	6.2	154.7

ROUTE DESCRIPTION

After crossing the Copeland Bridge, we walk the 2.5 river miles of the PNWT that we have named the Harry Meyers Route, in honor of the late ferryman whose ferry plied the river here until the bridge was built in 1968. At the west end of the bridge, walk down to the dike at a swimming hole much used in summer by local teenagers. If you camp here, be prepared to hear loud music from car stereos until the revelers decide to drive home. (The only water source here is the river itself.)

The Kootenai River makes a great westward bend around acres and acres of wheat and loops close by the base of 6570' Eneas Peak. This bucolic scene of morning mists, grazing cows, red-winged blackbirds, and stately cottonwoods will bring you in 2.5 miles to the West Side Road. Note how the river banks have been eroding because of the sudden fluctuations in water level caused by Libby Dam.

Just before you reach the paved West Side Road, you will encounter a dirt road, which follows the river north to a pump at Mile 110½ where Long Canyon Creek slips into the Kootenai. If the river water were transparent instead of opaque, you could see some of the enormous sturgeon snuffling about in the depths.

Although the northwesterly West Side Road is a mile shorter to Long Canyon Creek, we recommend your following the dike road because of its greater intimacy with the riverside environment. After 3 miles you will reach the mouth of Parker Creek. Turn left on the road just before the creek crossing and follow it southwest .7 mile to its junction with the West Side Road.

Walk the road northwest toward the steep defile of Long Canyon Creek. Watch carefully for the Long Canyon trailhead (1800) .3 mile beyond the creek crossing. Camping is available on the West Side Road, at an informal site west of the road by the south bank of Long Canyon Creek. It is on private land, so be extra careful to leave it better than you found it.

Horsemen and non-bushwhackers should take the Smith Creek Road west to the Upper Priest River Trail rather than attempt the Selkirk Crest on the main-line PNWT.

Long Canyon Trail No. 16 runs 18 miles south and west to Long Canyon Pass. We leave Long Canyon, however, at the 13-mile point via the Pyramid Pass Trail No. 7 and continue south to fabulous lakes and ridges. From Two Mouth Lakes we head west across The Wigwams and Klootch Mountain until we finally reach Priest Lake—41 miles of uninterrupted wilderness of the finest kind!

I think that after you have walked this impossibly scenic route, you will agree with us that this area is national-park-caliber country. Its mountains, lakes, wildlife, and solitude are a priceless natural resource. And strangely enough, Idaho has no national parks. Won't you please join us in our effort to create a Selkirk Crest National Park? (1) Join our PNWT Association, and (2) write your congressman and senators in favor of the proposal.

The volunteer-maintained Long Canyon Trail rises steeply up the Kootenai Valley face. Its steep entrance is why no logging has ever penetrated this last undisturbed northern valley. After 1 mile on the trail, you can reach a good viewpoint out over the valley via an old road. Nearby, behind Knob 2641', is a potential, though marginal, campsite with a little stream. Next on the main trail we traverse open slopes high above Long Canyon Creek. The first good campsites are 3 miles in and are next to the creek. There is a ford 5 miles up which, depending on the water level, can sometimes be tricky. Another ford, at the 4000' level, is much easier. Then, beyond Cutoff Peak Creek, you will find more campsites. Next in the broad, upper valley there are relatively open, park-like stretches where camping and views are more common than during the trek up from the Kootenai Valley. Be sure to note the enormous white pines, much prized by lumbermen and now a rarity in the Northwest.

The PNWT leaves Long Canyon at the 13-mile mark. Pyramid Pass Trail No. 7 is a relentlessly steep, 3.5-mile grind. (Not much water is available, but you will find some up above.) Near the top you will be rewarded with a good view of Long Canyon and Smith Peak.

At a rocky, signed junction for the Parker Peak Trail No. 221 (6400), you could make a very scenic loop trip back north to the Kootenai River Valley over Long Mountain (7265) and Parker Peak (7670). This trail is waterless (except for seasonal snowbanks) and at its northern end, steep and unmaintained.

The PNWT turns south 1.5 miles on Pyramid Pass Trail No. 13, crosses wooded Pyramid Pass below 7355' Pyramid Peak, and descends in the Trout Creek drainage to a junction with the Trout Lake-Big Fisher Lake Trail No. 41. This junction has a reliable brook. Trout Lake (3 miles) and Big Fisher Lake (6 miles) both have good fishing and camping. Fisher Peak (7710) is the highest point in Boundary County.

Turn right at this junction and continue south .5 mile to an easily missed junction at the Trout Creek Road trail. If you arrive in a clearcut at the roadhead, go back uphill .6 mile until you find the Pyramid Lake Trail. (The Trout Creek Road would take you back to the West Side Road near the Copeland Bridge.)

Continue south 3 miles on Trail No. 43 to Pyramid Lake, a popular camping spot. It is one of the few lakes on the Selkirk Crest that have an excellent view of sunrise, especially from the rocks just above the west side of the lake.

The PNWT continues past the fir-screened campsites at Pyramid Lake

(6050) and up rock-face switchbacks above the lake to a higher bench. A short mile's hike brings us to Upper and Lower Ball Lakes (6708, 6605). The Upper Lake has few campsites; there's one nice one at the Lower Lake. Late-summer campers, fill all your canteens here because, except for seasonal snowbanks and the hard-to-find Russin Spring, the next 8-mile haul to Two Mouth Lakes has no water. This can be a slow 8 miles, too, because it is mostly ridgerunning, bushwhacking, and rubbernecking.

From Lower Ball Lake, gain the ridge southwest of the lake by climbing the scree and contouring around Knob 7265'. Don't bother climbing to the top of this rocky, mostly treeless prominence. Just go high enough to slip around its southeast side to the southward-running ridge beyond.

This ridge extends 3.5 miles to Myrtle Peak (7211). Our progress is between and over a series of bumps and knobs, dodging the wind-dwarfed firs, and sometimes hopping from rock to rock. Where you cross the glacier-polished planes of granite, you will be thankful for your Vibram boot soles. This is not a place for missteps, but it is not really difficult, either.

Keep rethinking your new positions in relation to prominent landmarks. This ridge is a series of gradually descending knobs—6923', 6862', 6799', 6865', 6541'—which are fun and easy to scramble over. From the top of each the familiar face of Lion's Head shows a new profile.

Our next goal, Myrtle Peak (3.5 miles from Ball Lakes), becomes more and more impressive as we drop down to a pass a thousand feet below it. Its bulky, forested mass looks enormous and very difficult to climb. However, the going is actually easy because at the pass we join Trail No. 11, which swings up from Turk Creek and leads us straight to the summit. In most places this trail is easy to follow. Just before the summit you will find a 1-mile side trail down to Myrtle Lake (5946), another fine fishing and camping spot.

Myrtle Peak's open lower summit is a splendid place to pitch your tent and feast on the long views of the Lion's Head country, which by now has become so familiar to you.

Myrtle has a true summit where you will find the ruins of an old lookout tower. Climb up to the charred timbers and melted glass gobs for a very special view south across as fine a wilderness scene as you will find anywhere on the PNWT. Glaciers gouged and pocked this granitic landscape into a fantastic Picasso tableau of bowls, pockets, points, arrêts, and cones. Look for Roman Nose (7260), Harrison Peak (7292), and especially Chimney Rock (7124). "Chimney" is a prosaic-sounding name for this dramatic needle, which compels our eyes to return to its spiky form again and again until, miles west of here, we can no longer see it.

Trail No. 286 descends from Myrtle Peak east to the Jim Creek Road, which in turn connects with the Myrtle Creek Road and Trail No. 268 to Two Mouth Lakes.

Two Mouth Lakes is our next destination, but the PNWT approaches it not by trail but by bushwhacking the southwest divide down Myrtle Peak and climbing to Knob 6054'. We then follow that 6000' ridge southwest to sentinel-like Knob 7001' high above Kent Lake. Next comes a ridge-walk, boulder-hop descent to the bowl where the Two Mouth Lakes (5831, 5842) nestle below Harrison Peak.

From 7122' atop Myrtle Peak we speed down through the upper forest's many openings. Then, encountering thick brush, we buck our way through as best we can until we reach a wild, narrow, brushy forest pass at 6000'.

If you are lucky, your way to the pass will take you past the Russin Spring, which is east of the true divide and not quite at the bottom of your descent. (Early in the season there are dozens of springs there.) If you cannot find it and if you badly need water, you can descend from the pass to Peak Creek not far below. Also, you could reach Two Mouth Lakes via the Peak Creek Trail and the Slide Creek Trail No. 268.

The PNWT climbs to Knob 6491' from the pass. Keep to the west side of the divide as you climb to avoid some steep rock faces. An eastern shoulder of Knob 6491' above those faces offers a narrow perch for a tent—but no water; bring some up from Russin Spring. Across Knob 6491' is a flat table of smooth granite, a potential campsite. This enormous rock pancake has been marked by the Forest Service as a helicopter landing pad.

We continue our up-and-down course above the abyss of Lion Creek and Kent Lake while enjoying new views of Kent Peak (7243) west across the void. The anticipation that builds up as we hike these ridges is a main part of the fun. Just how are we going to get up on that Knob 7001'? At the 6919' promontory rock, the answer becomes apparent. We must drop below a solid rock cleft in the ridge, contour around on glacier-scoured granite, and swing up again past scraggly trees to the ridge.

A no-trace camper with water and a sturdy tent could find no better alpine aerie than Knob 7001'. From it you can look straight down 1400' to Kent Lake or straight east to The Wigwams (7033) and Priest Lake. To the south, Chimney Rock looks more dramatic than ever. Here you feel at the top of the wilderness world. (We have named the Ball Lakes-Two Mouth Lakes ridgehop the Will Venard-Jerry Pavia Route after our two Boundary County members who pioneered it.)

A potential ridge connection to The Wigwams lies due west of Knob 7001'. However, we follow the other ridge southwest down to Two Mouth Lakes. At first there is an easy walk along the krummholz edge of the cliffs above Slide Creek. But at the end you will have to pick your way from boulder to boulder very carefully.

After the rocky, windy panoramas of the ridges, the tranquil Two Mouth Lakes are a different world. Their twenty acres are a little paradise of grassy retreats, browsing moose, sun-dappled trout waters, and excellent campsites.

The PNWT next turns west to Priest Lake. We stay north of Two Mouth Creek and cross The Wigwams and Klootch Mountain. The 3.5-mile, easy-to-follow trail to The Wigwams begins at the north end of the lower (northwesternmost) lake and contours westward. After about 1½ miles we cross a good brook, where canteens should be filled; no more water will be available until beyond the Squawman Lookout. Even before the trail begins its long switchbacks, we have good views across the wide, deep valley to the rugged Standard Lakes basin area near Goblin Knob. Also, this area gives us our last glimpses of Chimney Rock. Trees on this southern exposure become sparser, and the switchback views become better. Finally we top the ridge and reach the summit ruins of the Squawman Lookout cabin. From our 7033' perch The Wigwams present a glorious look at Lion's Head, Kent Peak, Goblin Knob, Two Mouth Lakes/Harrison Peak, etc.

Squaw Creek is our route to Priest Lake once we have crossed Klootch Mountain. From the ridgetop, zigzag 2 miles down to the col between Klootch and The Wigwams. This Squawman Peak Trail No. 30 is in very good condition and until it drops into the trees offers fine views north. From the summit we earlier could see a knife-edge ridge extending west from the precarious, old lookout site. From the bottom of that sheer rock face, a seasonal tarn feeds the South Fork of Lion Creek, which the trail crosses at a lovely spot for camping, picnicking, or just refilling your canteens.

At the pass we reach Two Mouth Creek Road 32, which will take us in 10 foot-beater miles down to Priest Lake, if we wish to avoid the PNWT's much more direct bushwhack route ahead.

At the heavily wooded pass the old trail continued west to Klootch Mountain, which also had a lookout. This trail, like that lookout, is mostly memory. You can find traces of it if you follow the south side of the ridge west, staying about 300 to 500 yards below the high point and contouring up to Klootch Mountain summit (6048). Although Klootch is mostly wooded, you will enjoy a lovely south-face pasture near the summit—a perfect camping spot for a low-impact hiker with full canteens.

Continue along the ridge past the helicopter pad, and position yourself on the ridgetop above the beautiful beargrass, sidehill park. From here the trail becomes very indistinct; go downhill through the trees on a bearing of 272° toward Squaw Creek. You will reach the creek before its trail; so descend its south bank, looking carefully for tread and old blazes, about 1½ miles from the summit. This trail becomes a logging road, and we are back in civilization. Do not be confused by the many logging roads here, but keep going downhill until you reach the East Shore Road at Squaw Bay. The distance from The Wigwams to Priest Lake is 7 miles, of which about 2.5 miles are bushwhacking.

From Squaw Bay go 1.5 miles north up the East Shore Road to the state campground at Mosquito Bay. If you need to go south for supplies, at Squaw Bay you are about 4 miles from the Two Mouth Creek Road, 17 miles from the Indian Creek Store, and 26 miles from Coolin.

Our Bonner County volunteers have devised an alternate route from Two Mouth Lakes that makes use of additional exciting ridges, visits more alpine lakes, and ends farther south on Priest Lake, nearer to the area's only supply points. This alternate may be used in conjunction with our main-line PNWT route to form an outstanding loop trip. From the southeasternmost of the Two Mouth Lakes, hike the ridge 2.5 miles south via Harrison Peak to Harrison Lake (6182). You will cross steep talus slopes of glaciated granite similar to our earlier route to Two Mouth Lakes. Harrison Lake's thirty acres of trout water make it the largest lake on the Selkirk Crest. This popular destination is only 1.5 miles by Trail No. 217 from the end of the Pack River Road.

From Harrison Lake's south shore, traverse the forested slope on a heading of 182° to the Beehive Lakes, which, like Harrison Lake, feed into the Pack River. Because the deep northern Beehive Lake (6271), also called Little Harrison Lake, is almost totally surrounded by granite walls, its color is a beautiful turquoise. Next, contour cross-country to the southern Beehive Lake (6457). At its south shore fill your canteens, then climb the ridge bearing 210°, then due west to the summit of Twin Peaks (7599). The distance from Two Mouth Lakes to here totals 5.5 miles. Twin Peaks is the highest mountain in the southern Selkirks. (Parker Peak at 7670' is the highest in the northern American Selkirks.)

Our alternate route follows the ridge north above the Beehive Lakes and then west to Goblin Knob, 7 miles. Head north bearing 37° along the southeastern side of Knob 7374', and follow the ridge past Knob 7353'. Turn onto the northwesterly side ridge bearing 298°, and go 2.5 miles along the talus and cross Knobs 6726' and 6518'. Where the ridge turns due north to the two Standard Lakes (5102, 5318), you could siwash that one-mile drop and camp at those famous fishing holes; trails connect them to the Two Mouth Creek Road.

Our alternate route, instead of following the ridge north to the Standard Lakes, drops due west to a pass at 5841', where we join the Goblin Knob trail. Follow it up 3 miles to the summit at 6606'. This peak has the best view in the area of Priest Lake—all the way from Mosquito Bay in the north, Distillery Bay in the west, to Reeder Bay in the south. To reach the lake from the summit, siwash the open northwest ridge down to the jeep trail and follow that and then the Two Mouth Creek Road to Huckleberry Bay, 7 miles. The Diamond International Company maintains a sandy-beach, public campground on the north side of this attractive, fir-ringed bay. From here it is 13 miles south to the Indian Creek Store and 22 miles south to Coolin. (A more direct route from Goblin Knob to the Indian Creek Store and state campground would take you by trail from Pass 5841' to the North Fork Indian Creek Road; from its junction with the East Shore Road, Coolin is only 10 miles to the south.)

Anyway, once you get to the Mosquito Bay Campground, you must decide whether to go north on the east or west bank of Upper Priest Lake. The 2½-mile-long Priest River drains Upper Priest Lake into its larger southern neighbor. The river was such a popular artery in the old days that it got the name The Thorofare.

The advantages of the old-growth west-bank trail include two developed campgrounds (Plowboy and Navigation). There are also excellent views of Lion's Head and other Selkirk Crest favorites. Moose are fairly common. And there is a good feeling of wildness—the U.S. Forest Service maintains this side of the lake as the Upper Priest Lake Scenic Area. Its only disadvantage is that you must arrange boat transportation to reach it across The Thorofare. If you do, Plowboy Campground is 3 miles in from the newly-renovated Tule Bay Picnic Area, and Navigation Campground is 6 miles in. We begin near Beaver Creek, where there are numerous campsites. At soggy Armstrong Meadows we scoot to the right of the wet areas. Beyond a crumbling cabin we descend to the lake and the Plowboy Campground. Then the trail keeps to the lakeshore until a rise to some fine, but dry, campsites up the hill and prior to the Navigation Campground. Deadman Creek is a reliable, if spooky, water source. A side trail connects the camp with Plowboy Mountain (4877), another former lookout site; this side trail also makes a convenient loop back to the Beaver Creek Road. From Navigation Campground continue north 4 miles via Trail No. 302 to Road 1013.

The twin advantages of the mainline PNWT east-shore route are that it is not dependent upon uncertain water transportation and that its less-travelled backwoods track looks northwest toward the spectacular Salmo-Priest Wilderness, our next goal.

From the Mosquito Bay Campground, walk west a very short distance on the road that goes to The Thorofare. Near the campground you will find Trail No. 58, which is initially a jeep trail and later a pack trail near the lake. All the way until the north end of Upper Priest Lake, we will continue to be mostly in Idaho Department of Lands territory, as we have been all the way from Two Mouth Lakes. This trail constitutes 9.5 easy miles to the Ruby Creek Road as we hug the foot of the hills. Occasional seeps and brooks are available, especially Trapper Creek at a delta near the head of the lake. A good side trip is to follow the Floss Creek Trail to the East Fork Trapper Creek Trail up Caribou Hill (4592). The Caribou Creek Road also connects this old lookout site with the Mosquito Bay Campground.

Not too long ago, had you snowshoed Caribou Hill in winter, you would have had a good chance to see some of the now extremely rare animals for which it was named. However, poaching, commercial hunting, sport hunting, forest fires, automobile collisions, and dramatic habitat reduction (clearcuts and roading) have reduced the population to about a dozen individuals.

Mountain caribou are smaller than elk but much larger than deer, often measuring four feet in height at the shoulder. They have special winter-adapted, semi-circular, concave hooves for snow travel. Both the dark brown bulls and cows carry antlers; the bulls' forward arched, amber-colored autumn ones contrast beautifully with their tawny coats and throat-to-chest, white flowing manes. Historically, their range included the North Fork of the Flathead, the Purcell Mountains, and the Selkirks. Today you will be very lucky to see even one of these roamers. They are a unique heritage of the Pacific Northwest Trail.

We reach the Ruby Creek Road via the Upper Priest Lake Trail, which here on Kootenai National Forest land is called Trail No. 302. Next go left (west) ½ mile to Upper Priest River Road 1013. Walk it north up the valley through thick forest 3.5 miles to the Upper Priest River Trail No. 308.

This trail is near the river and in the finest western-red-cedar forest east of the Cascades, making the 6.5-mile walk a very special treat. Look for wildflowers, spiny, big-leafed devil's club, and yellow-striped toads. You will also enjoy the endless ferns, the hemlock seedlings growing on "nurse logs," the old wasp nests that have fallen onto the trail, the tiny cedar cones and condensation-wet pebbles underfoot, the delicate, ubiquitous spider webs, the scattered patches of canopy-filtered sunlight, the chattering pine squirrels, the unseen-but-heard birds, and the large bumblebees winging from flower to flower. You may see cedar eight to ten feet in diameter and countless tree mushrooms, which grow on rotting wood.

There is a good campsite beside a stream 6.5 miles south of the Upper Priest Falls (also called the American Falls). Beyond Rock Creek we pass numerous features that are unnamed on the USGS topographic map—Wounded Horse Crossing, Devil's Club Creek, Twin Rocks, Mud Flats, Brunner's Crossing, Ridge Creek, Orr Creek, Boomerang Bridge, and Irene Creek. A sign at a ford 4 miles south of Upper Priest Falls tells us that Little Snowy Top is 6.5 miles west via Trail No. 349.

The ford, which in spring high-water must be crossed on deadfalls, is about four thousand feet below Little Snowy Top's lookout cabin only 1½ miles west! Expect 72 switchbacks at this, one of the most extreme elevation changes on the entire PNWT. And be prepared to make your way cross-country if the trail is obscured by snow.

The Salmo-Priest country is covered with dense forests of white pine, western red cedar, and western hemlock. Spruce and subalpine fir grow at the higher elevations. Streams contain cutthroat trout, char, and Dolly Varden. Besides the remnant mountain caribou mentioned earlier, there are also elk, black bear, grizzlies, and mule deer.

Early in the season in mid-June, much of this trail and much of the Shedroof Divide Trail above are likely to be covered with snow. In that case, pick your way from blaze to blaze to the cabin. It is old, unmaintained, and its broken windows let in the howling winds. But it is a good overnight shelter if you don't mind the sounds of hungry little mice. The lookout has an excellent view, clouds permitting, of the South Salmo River, Snowy Top (7572), the Upper Priest River, and our next goal, Salmo Mountain.

Follow the extremely scenic Shedroof Divide Trail 6 miles, almost to Shedroof Mountain and the Trail No. 535 junction (6120). On the way, just after the junction with the Hughes Ridge jeep trail and just before a 5600' col, there is a reliable water source. Shortly beyond that and Knob 5963', you will cross into Washington, the Evergreen State. In another 6 miles via Trail No. 535 plus Roads 654 and 853, you will reach the lookout tower at Salmo Mountain (6828). Be sure to locate the lookout spring just before the first big bend in the road below the tower.

From Little Snowy Top a pretty loop hike would take you north to the saddle between the lookout and Snowy Top. Descend through marvelous open parklands to the white pine woods and the Salmo River and Salmo Cabin. Continue for 6½ miles downstream on Trail No. 530 to the Cutoff Trail No. 506 ford and good campsites. Ford the river and climb

Salmo River Valley from Little Snowy Top

2½ miles to the Salmo Mountain Road. Along the way, note carefully the Salmo Cabin's strong door, windows, and walls. Some time ago that impregnable-looking cabin was heavily damaged by a grizzly bear, which should be a warning to you in your microthin tent to practice careful camp and food procedures.

From Salmo Mountain, if we sight along a heading of 218°, we see the course of our next bushwhack cross-country to Crowell Ridge Trail No. 515. We have 5 slow miles to go along the northwest spur of Crowell Ridge, which connects to Salmo Mountain. West of us beyond Watch Creek is Gypsy Ridge, a thousand-foot-higher part of a Y that begins roughly where we will finally reach the trail. The first mile of our course down and up from Salmo Mountain is brushy and tiring. But then we hit open slopes west of Knob 6345' above Watch Creek. Continue southwest over Knob 6117'. (From here you could make a nice side trip west to Watch Lake.) Climb part way up Knob 6303', and contour southwest across beautiful open slopes at the 6200' level to the trail southeast of Knob 6617'.

If you wish to avoid this 5-mile bushwhack, you could take the nearby Deemer Creek and Leola Creek roads instead. But Crowell Ridge is some of the PNWT's finest country. Be prepared to see bighorn sheep, elk, bear, and grouse. Not to mention excellent scenery, which, despite the ubiquitous clearcuts, still retains plenty of wildness. This is some of our best, most open, ridge walking.

From where you reached the ridge trail, it is only 3 miles to our turnoff down the North Fork Sullivan Creek Trail No. 507. A spring is located due east of this junction.

The 10-mile downhill to Lime Lake offers a campsite with water about a third of the way down. Halfway along we meet the Halliday Trail No. 522. At this point we continue southwest to privately owned Lime Lake on No. 507, but the Ideal Route goes northwest 4 miles via No. 522 to State Highway 31.

Today's PNWT crosses the Pend Oreille River at Metaline Falls. The Ideal Route crosses it far to the north at the Boundary Dam, one mile south of the Canadian border. To reach the dam, the Ideal Route will contour along the edge of the Pend Oreille River canyon. You will not see its rugged, reservoir-flooded bottom because the water has backed up even beyond Metaline Falls to the south. This route is currently a brushy bushwhack; you could avoid it by walking 7.1 miles on State Highway 31. There is a Forest Service campground at Crescent Lake.

The Ideal Route crosses the top of the Seattle City Light dam and continues west on the Frisco Standard Road. Next we pass Crawford State Park, the location of Gardner Cave. Although this park has a few campsites, visitors must bring their own drinking water. Illuminated, handrailed Gardner Cave has a total slope length of 1050 feet and is the largest limestone cavern in Washington state. If you wish to see its Cambrian limestone stalactites and stalagmites, inquire in advance about when the cavern will be open (Washington State Parks, P.O. Box 1128, Olympia, WA 98501).

The Ideal Route leaves the Frisco Standard Road at a big curve at elevation 3197' between the South Fork and the main branch of Russian Creek. We follow a jeep road southeast 1½ miles to its terminus at about 3600' on the slopes of Russian Ridge. From there we bushwhack up the ridge to points 4215' and 4896' and loop around the headwaters of Fence Creek to Hooknose Ridge and Knob 6092'. We continue south, switchbacking up the west side of Hooknose Mountain (7210) to gain the saddle at its southeast corner. We walk southwest via Knob 7003' to Abercrombie Mountain (7308). Here we temporarily rejoin the Practical Route, which follows the Baldy Trail cairns across the summit. But instead of dropping west on the Baldy Trail, we continue south, siwashing along the open ridge over Knobs 6502', 6379', 6549', 6631', and 6285'. Near Knob 5722' we join South Fork Silver Creek Trail No. 123 and follow it west to Sherlock Peak (6365). All along this ridge we have grand views of the Windy Ridge and the Gladstone Mountain mining district, which produced much lead and zinc during World War I. At Sherlock Peak we leave the ridge on Trail No. 139, which takes us to a jeep road and a spring. From the spring, bushwhack southwest to Republican Creek and follow its north bank down to the North Fork Deep Creek Valley (2124). About halfway down you will pick up the remnants of Trail No. 124.

The Ideal Route continues west up the Sherlock Creek Trail directly across the valley. At the northeast corner of Section 16 at about 3600' elevation, we begin to bushwhack across state and BLM land to Knobs 4650' and 4689' and to the Lind Ranch. Here we rejoin the Practical Route, which has come up to this Stone Mountain country via the O'Hare Creek Road.

The Practical Route samples some of the highlights of the way just described but avoids all of its bushwhacking. Plus, it crosses the Pend

Oreille River at the town of Metaline Falls, where some supplies and services are available. From Lime Lake at the foot of Trail No. 507, we walk the Lime Lake Road, the Sullivan Lake Road, and State Highway 31 to town. On the outskirts you will see a newly renovated hydroelectric power station and the creeping white dunes of the cement plant's tailings pile. Cross the Pend Oreille River bridge (2059). On the far bank upstream, note the old mine shaft.

Next walk 1.3 miles on State Highway 31 to the Z Canyon Motel. Turn right there at the Gardner Cave sign and walk 3.7 miles north on County Road 62. This road initially climbs several hundred feet to a good viewpoint. On a clear day Sullivan Mountain (6483) and Crowell Ridge loom over the town. From here the village of Metaline Falls seems like a place only recently carved out of the surrounding wilderness.

The road passes several mines such as the Oriole and the Gold Hill, an active cement company gravel pit, and acres of roadside fireweed, and continues up the Flume Creek Valley parallel with the Boundary Dam's high voltage lines. Note the abrupt, sharp peak to the northwest— Hooknose Mountain, part of the Ideal Route.

The Flume Creek Road 585 looks like a driveway where it enters an abandoned farm past a tumbledown house. Walk past the house and its decaying outbuildings to the power lines and the road up the mountain. Three quarters of the 11 miles up to the summit, this old logging road becomes Trail No. 502. Views will open up of a microwave relay station below and of the distant lookout cabin on Sullivan Peak. A very convenient, though tiny, campsite is located at the bottom of a long scree slope. A gentian-ringed spring provides a reliable source of water. This site is especially handy if the summit is gripped by harsh winds and snow. And at an elevation of 7308', that's a real possibility, even in summer.

From this campsite the trail makes a sharp right switchback and soon reaches the ridge, where we meet the Ideal Route, which has just crossed over from Hooknose Mountain. The old Abercrombie Mountain lookout cabin is gone, but its northwest-facing outhouse survives, with one of the best views on the PNWT. This summit is a treeless rockpile totally exposed to the fierce gales that sweep in from the Canadian north.

The Baldy Trail down from Abercrombie's summit was marked by cairns in 1983. Look along the tree line southwest of the lookout site; the trail goes out the south side of the Knob 5985' ridge. And once you are on the Baldy Trail, do not be deceived into going down Hartbauer Creek, which flows northwest. The North Fork of Silver Creek, which you want, flows southwest. The Baldy Trail switchbacks 4 miles down it, past fire-scarred ponderosa pines and through a jungle of summer brush. There is a good campsite (3708) where this trail reaches the creek.

The remaining 5 miles of high-standard Forest Service road route to the hamlet of Leadpoint are not very exciting. Leadpoint, a collection of several houses in the Deep Creek Valley at 2135', is a mile lower in elevation than the summit of Abercrombie. So if your feet hurt here, you will know why.

Leadpoint was laid out in June, 1917, at the height of the World War I zinc boom, and was named for the nearby Electric Point Lead Mine. Today no services are available in Leadpoint, but you could mail out a letter by putting it in someone's mailbox and raising the box's red flag.

To reach the Columbia River town of Northport from Leadpoint, we must cross a four-thousand-foot intervening height of land. Most of this country is privately owned, though several sections belong to the state and to the U.S. Bureau of Land Management.

Deep Creek Valley is a flat bucolic expanse of grazing cows and soaring nighthawks. Across the valley from the road, one large old mine is currently being worked.

Walk two miles north to the O'Hare Creek Road, a glorified jeep road up through logging country. From the Deep Creek Valley (2179), the O'Hare Creek Road rises quickly, in 4.5 miles to 4300' at the abandoned Lind Ranch. We arrive at this log barn and collapsed house on Stone Mountain by a dirt road northwest of the meadows, spring, and buildings, though the USGS map shows only the original homestead route southeast of them. The new road has a short connecting link to the Lind Ranch and the ranch's meadows, an excellent campsite with a reliable spring.
Ranch is an excellent campsite with a reliable spring.

Ideally, we could walk cross-country from here across Stone Mountain and Grass Mountain to Deadman's Eddy, Steamboat Rock, and Smelter Rock on the Columbia River. But lacking such a route, we walk 1.5 miles steeply down a dirt track from the Lind Ranch to meet the Black Canyon Road at a cattle spread. Passing numerous abandoned buildings, walk the pavement 3 miles out to the Deep Creek School and the Northport Highway.

Another 6.2 miles north on County Road 700 brings us finally to the Columbia River, where mail, supplies, and services are available in Northport (1328). A city park just north of the bridge has public camping.

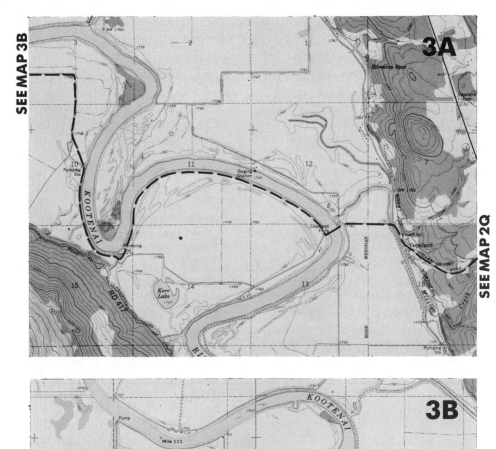

SEE MAP 3B

SEE MAP 2Q

3A

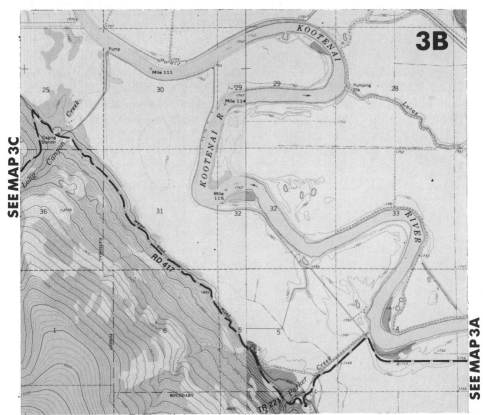

SEE MAP 3C

SEE MAP 3A

3B

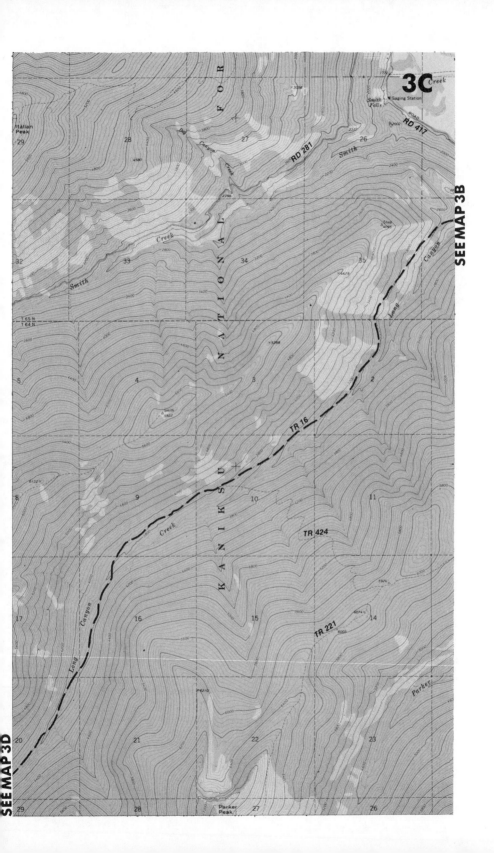

SEE MAP 3B

SEE MAP 3D

Italian
Peak

FOR

NATIONAL

KANIKSU

RD 281

RD 417

Smith Falls

Gaging Station

Smith

Creek

Smith

Long Canyon

TR 16

TR 424

TR 221

Creek

Long Canyon

Parker

Parker Peak

29   28   27   26

32   33   34   35

5   4   3   2

8   9   10   11

17   16   15   14

20   21   22   23

29   28   27   26

T 65 N
T 64 N

Ruins of Parker Peak Lookout

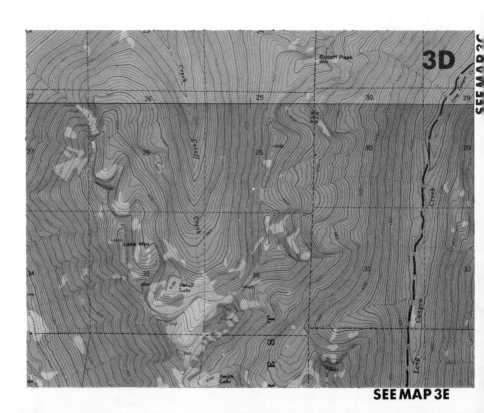

SEE MAP 3E

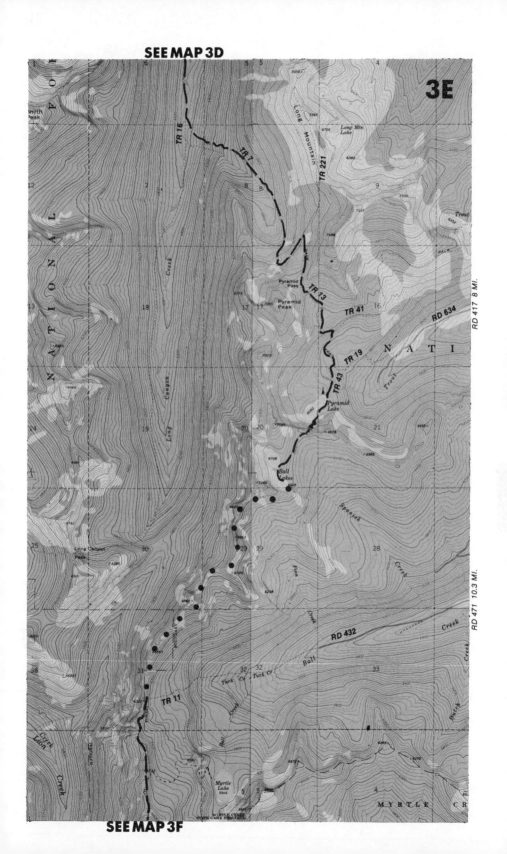

SEE MAP 3D

3E

SEE MAP 3F

RD 417 8 MI.

RD 471 10.3 MI.

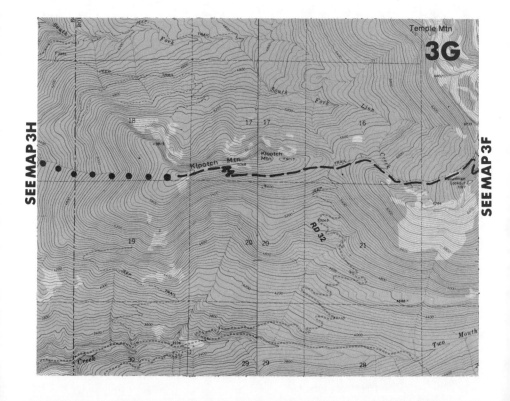

SEE MAP 3E

3F

SEE MAP 3G

RD 417 VIA
RD 633 12.5 MI.

Myrtle
Peak

TR 286

Russin Spring

Kent
Peak

Kent
Lake

The
Wigwams

TR 268

MYRTLE CREEK GAME PRESERVE

STATE FOREST

RD 633

Two Mouth
Lakes

SEE MAP 3H

3G

Temple Mtn

South Fork

South Fork Lion Creek

Klootch Mtn

Klootch
Mtn

RD 32

JEEP TRAIL

SEE MAP 3F

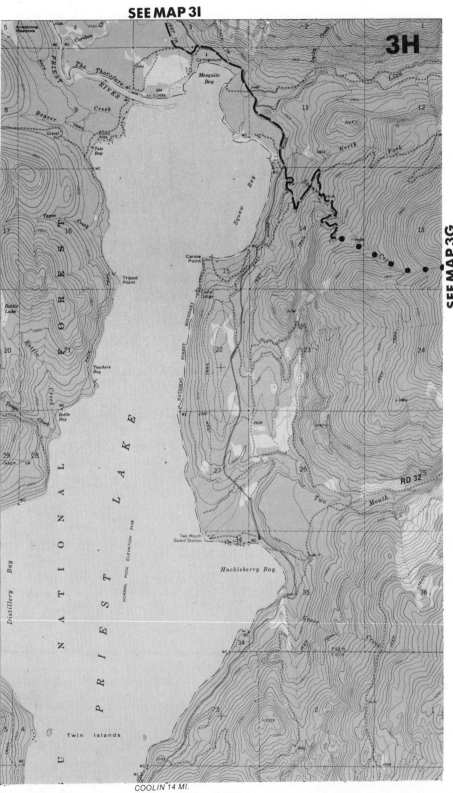

3H

COOLIN 14 MI.

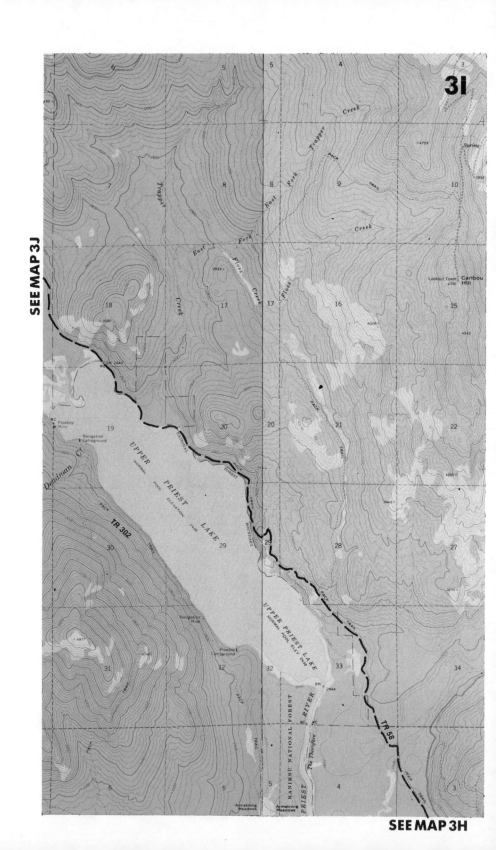

SEE MAP 3J

SEE MAP 3H

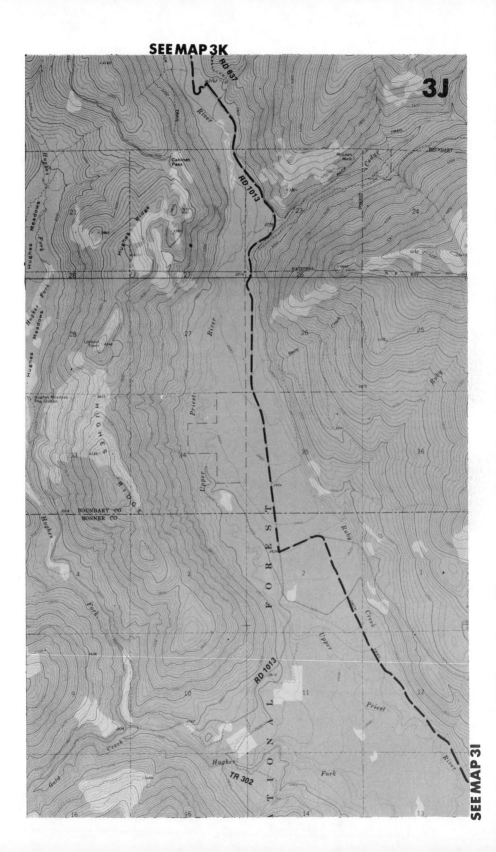

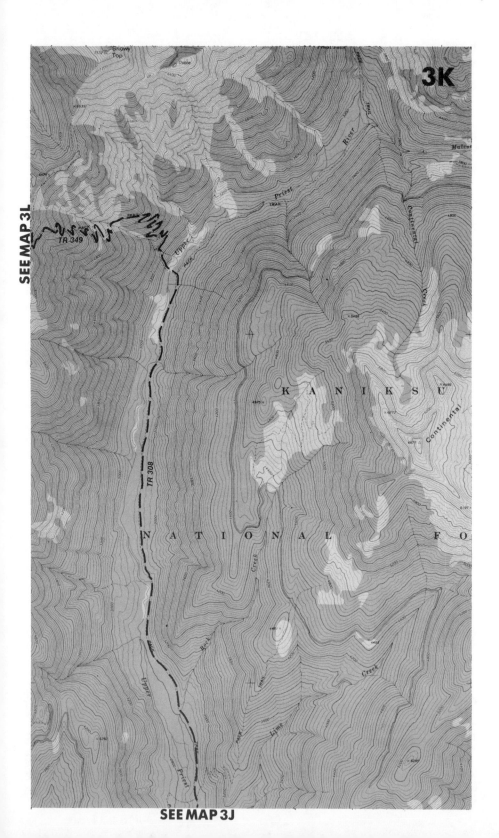

SEE MAP 3L

SEE MAP 3J

Snowy
Top

Priest   River

Mulcor

Priest   TRAIL

Continental

Upper

PACK

TR 349

TRAIL

TR 308

K A N I K S U

Continental   Creek

Creek

N A T I O N A L   F O

Creek

Creek

Upper

Rock

Priest

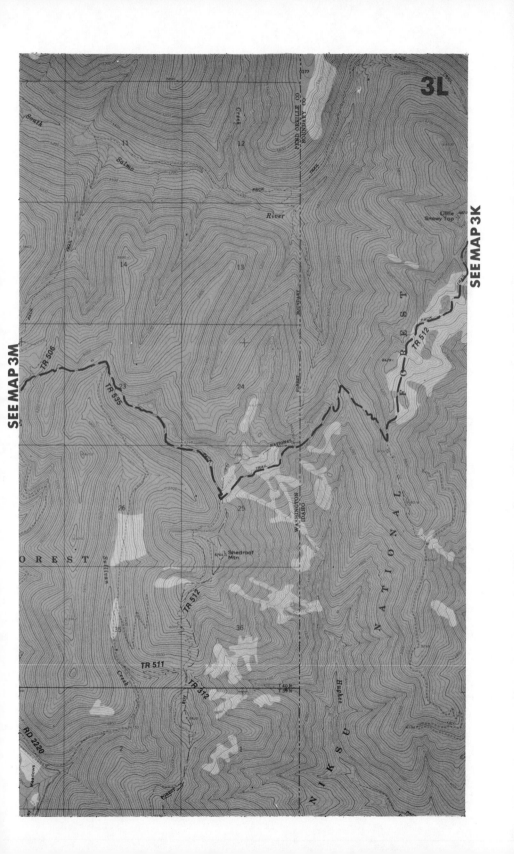

SEE MAP 3M

SEE MAP 3K

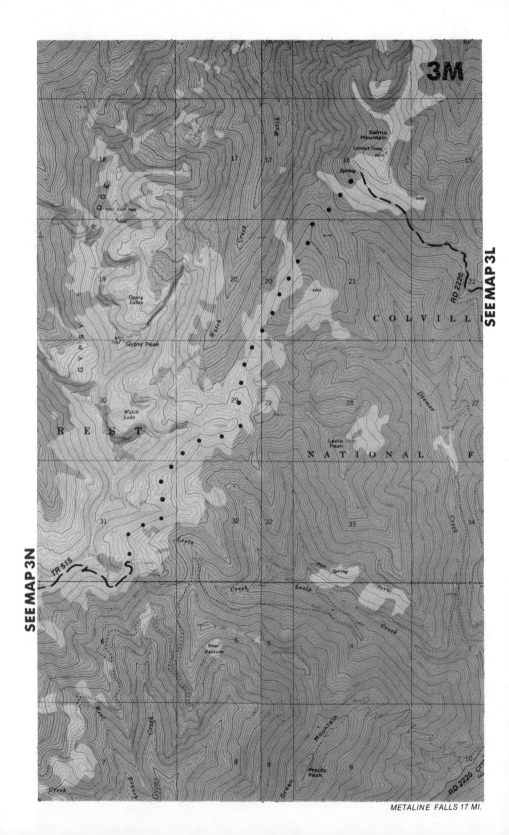

SEE MAP 3L

SEE MAP 3N

Salmo
Mountain

Lookout Tower

Spring

Watch Creek

COLVILLE

GYPSY RIDGE

Gypsy Lakes

Gypsy Peak

Watch Lake

FOREST

REST

Leola Peak

NATIONAL F

Diemer Creek

TR 515

Leola Creek

Spring

Leola Creek

TRAIL

Bear Pasture

Green Mountain

Prouty Peak

RD 2220 Creek

METALINE FALLS 17 MI.

SEE MAP 3O

SEE MAP 3M

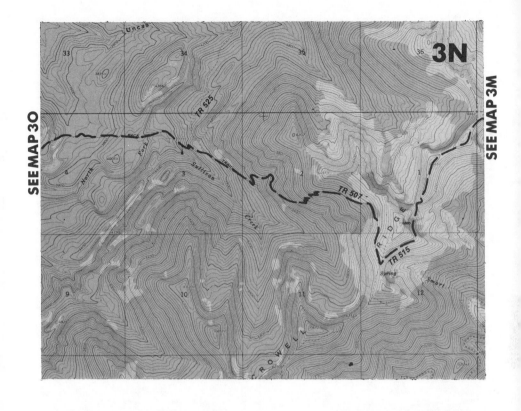

HWY 30 3.1 MI.

SEE MAP 3N

SEE MAP 3P

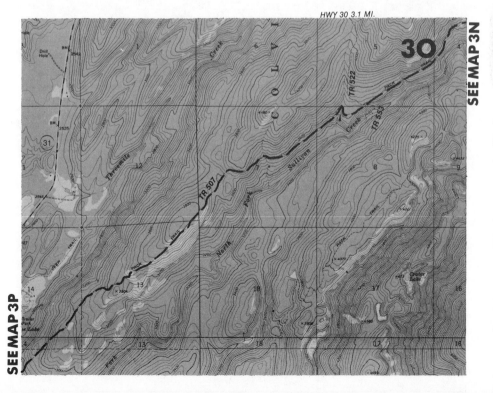

SEE MAP 3Q

SEE MAP 3O

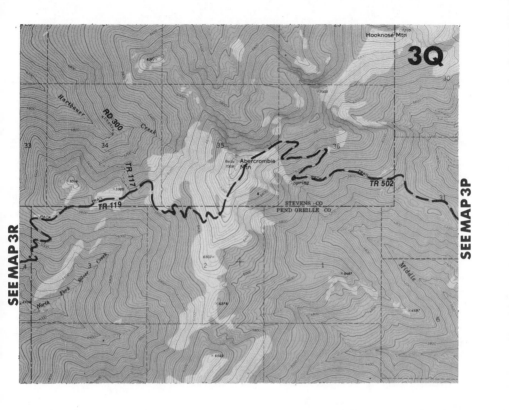

SEE MAP 3R

SEE MAP 3P

3Q

Hooknose Mtn

Hartbauer Creek

RD 300

TR 117

TR 119

Abercrombie Mtn

Spring

TR 502

STEVENS CO
PEND OREILLE CO

North Fork Silver Creek

Middle

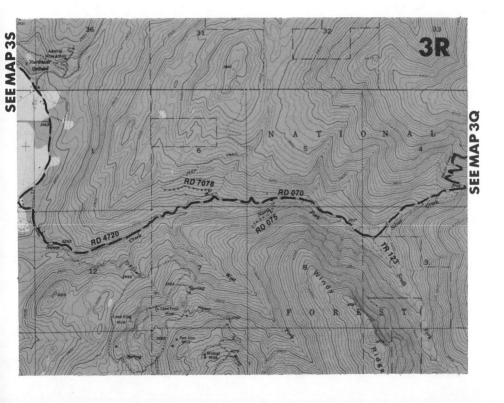

SEE MAP 3S

SEE MAP 3Q

3R

Admiral Mine & Mill
Hartbauer Orchard

N A T I O N A L

RD 7078

RD 070

RD 4720

RD 075

Silver Creek

North

TR 123

Windy

West Spring

Spring

Little Gem Mine

Last King Mine

Red-bun Mine

Wildcat Mine

F O R E S T

Ridge

TRAIL

JEEP

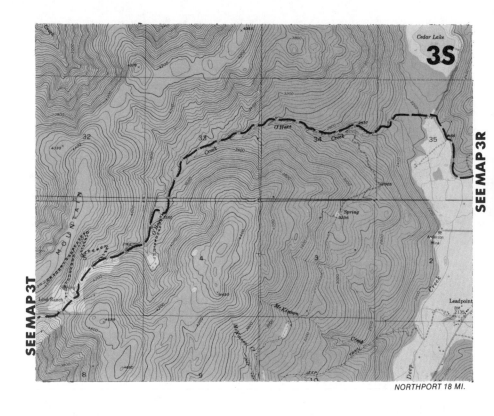

SEE MAP 3R

SEE MAP 3T

NORTHPORT 18 MI.

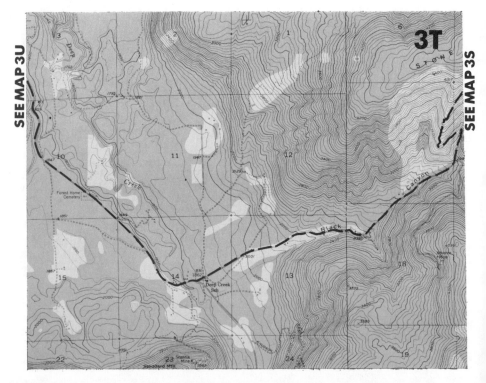

SEE MAP 3U

SEE MAP 3S

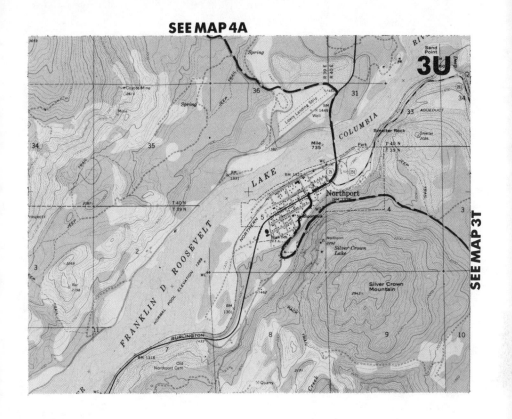

THE KETTLE RIVER RANGE

(Columbia River to Sweat Creek)

|| 4

Kettle Crest Trail

INTRODUCTION

"That trail goes through eastern Washington?" they say in a skeptical tone. "Well, isn't it awfully flat and boring?"

Even most Washingtonians—the majority of whom live in the Olympia-Seattle-Everett megalopolis on Puget Sound—know little about their own state's northeastern landscape. Flat and boring it certainly isn't. The Kettle Range area, for instance, offers visitors superb lakes, streams, forests, and wildlife. And mountains—the six-thousand-foot range west of the Kettle River is one of the highlights of the entire Pacific Northwest Trail.

There are few sharp crags and brutal fronts and ridges in the Kettle Range. Peaks such as Leona, Midnight, and Wapaloosie won't dazzle you; they are not haughty mountains. Miles-long wildflower meadows alternate with virgin stands of pine and fir. Ponderosa pine is a familiar sight in this dry country at the edge of the Okanogan. *Calypso bulbosa*, the Kettle Range's common orchid, symbolizes the beauty and grace of these little-known mountains.

Not that you won't have to work to obtain their rewards. The ups and downs here are as up and down as anywhere else. That's how Profanity Peak got its name. And the long, long miles of road walking can make even a seasoned hiker wish he had taken up sailing instead. Even so, let the Kettle Range capture your heart.

PROBLEMS

For once, route finding will not be a problem. The roads which we follow are easy, and the Kettle Crest Trail a snap. Of course, to get the most out of your Kettle Range visit, you should follow our Ideal Route south from Sherman Pass, west along Tenmile Creek, and north to Fir Mountain. Going that way will require the usual PNWT map and compass skills.

Water will not be a problem since the road sections touch many creeks and lakes and the mountain trails encounter numerous springs. If you wish to camp on some of the Kettle Range's broad, comfortable summits, you must carry up water.

SUPPLIES

Northport (99157), Orient (99160), and Republic (99166) all have post offices. Groceries may be purchased in Northport and Republic but are minimal at the Orient gas station. Kettle Falls (99141) is 29 miles east of Sherman Pass via State Highway 20.

Ollie Mae Wilson's Northport post office is open Saturday mornings.

DECLINATION   22½° E

USGS TOPOGRAPHICAL MAPS

Northport	Togo Mountain	15'
Belshazzar Mountain	Sherman Peak	15'
Churchill Mountain	Republic	15'
Laurier	Aeneas	15'
Orient		

MILEAGES   (total 105.2)

		Total
Columbia River Bridge, Northport (1328)	0.0	0.0
Big Sheep Creek County Highway 800 (1453)	.8	.8
Sheep Creek Campground, D.N.R. (1960) via Big Sheep Creek	4.2	5.0
Pierre Lake junction	4.4	9.4
Elbow Lake Campground (2875)	4.0	13.4
Roads 15, 440, and 170 junction (332)	1.7	15.1
Flat Creek Road 1520 junction	1.5	16.6
Road 15 and Fisher Creek Road 080 junction	5.0	21.6
Pierre Lake Road junction (2142)	1.4	23.0
Pierre Lake Campground (2005)	1.9	24.9

Toulou Mountain Road via Pierre Lake Road (1939)	3.8	28.7
Kettle River Bridge (1400), Orient	3.7	32.4
Slide Creek (2920)	3.3	35.7
Jungle Creek (4350)	5.6	41.3
Deer Creek Summit (4600)	5.4	46.7
Indian Creek Camp (4550)	6.7	53.4
Ryan Cabin (4850)	3.8	57.2
Neff Spring (6200)	4.9	62.1
Copper Butte (7135)	3.5	65.6
Jungle Hill (6450)	7.1	72.7
Sherman Pass (5587)	4.5	77.2
Republic (2143) via State Highway 20	19.0	96.2
Sweat Creek Campground (3499) via State Highway 20	9.0	105.2

ROUTE DESCRIPTION

The Kettle River is another of those frontier-defying streams that loop through and around the American/Canadian border ranges. In this case, the Kettle River joins the Columbia River near the town of Kettle Falls, about 25 miles downstream from Northport. There the two rivers form a 20-mile-wide V between Northport and Orient. For the PNWT traveler this is mostly a road trek because we have not yet managed to find an Ideal Route through this complex, broken-up country of dense forests and low, rolling mountains.

The situation is different west of the Kettle River in the Kettle Range, a north/south procession of major five-to-seven-thousand foot peaks. There the route is obvious—the Forest Service's excellent Kettle Crest Trail No. 13. Beyond the Kettle Range in settled Ferry County our Practical Route temporarily uses State Highway 20 from Sherman Pass through Republic to the Sweat Creek Campground at Clackamas Mountain.

The Grand Coulee Dam's Franklin D. Roosevelt Lake is the first feature of this PNWT section. After your weeks of mountain travel, this broad reach of sere brown hills will seem like a different world. Especially early in the season, the refreshing, heady scent of sweet vegetation makes it an oasis from the still-cold high country. Plan to take a slow side trip down the west bank of the river.

Our Practical Route crosses the Columbia River bridge (1328) and goes north on State Highway 25 for .8 mile to the beginning of unpaved County Highway 800, the Big Sheep Creek Road. The junction (1453) is located near the northeast corner of the Lowry Landing Strip. The road parallels unseen Big Sheep Creek north for several miles of gradually rising elevation. Near the unseen tributary fork of Little Sheep Creek, our road swings west along the south side of Big Sheep Creek. After 4.2 miles we reach the Department of Natural Resources Sheep Creek Campground (1920). This streamside spot, complete with covered picnic areas and much favored by fishermen, is a convenient place to camp on a road where campsites are located at well-spaced intervals. (The other two before the Kettle River are Elbow Lake and Pierre Lake.)

The road continues along the river, often right beside it, until a valley opens up to our left—Sleepy Hollow, a trail route for a circuit trip to the beautiful, rocky Pepoon Canyon and the 4253' Columbia River lookout on Flagstaff Mountain. About a mile farther (and 4.4 miles after the Sheep Creek Campground), we encounter a junction. The Big Sheep Creek Road turns right, but we bear left toward Pierre Lake along the American Fork. In .7 mile we pass through an immense clearcut, a clearcut so big that the road distance through it measures .7 mile. This vast opening in the heavily forested area gives us good views of Lead Pencil Mountain (3668) and other scenery to the northwest. At this point we are within about 2 miles of the Canadian border.

The road twists southwest up and away from the American Fork. We climb and turn steadily for 2.4 miles to a big fir-ringed meadow and the Rose Ranch. (Do not stray right onto a travelled-looking logging road just before the meadow.) After another mile of steady climbing, we reach Elbow Lake (2875). This agreeable, hill-surrounded campground is usually deserted; few car campers stray so far into the boonies. But the lake has wildlife, such as mink and waterfowl, which make it a refreshing contrast to the constant road walking. Usually one or more Robinson Crusoe–type homemade rafts are ready to help you explore these delightful waters, which are actually two interconnected lakes.

From Elbow Lake, Orient is 19 miles farther. Pierre Lake Campground (11.5 miles beyond Elbow Lake) is a practical intermediate destination. The road continues its climb through thick fir and cedar forest. In 1.7 miles we reach a junction near Kiel Springs, where we turn left on Road 15. (Do not turn by mistake onto the first road at this junction, the Kiel Ridge Road 440.) Flat Creek Road 1520 goes left (southeast) 1.5 miles farther south, but we continue south, then west. At a swampy height of land we cross over into the Pierre Creek drainage. Passing Mineral Mountain Road 070 (3123), we continue 5 miles down to a 4-way junction with Road 15 (which has paralleled our course up in the hills north of Pierre Creek) and the Fisher Creek Road 080.

We continue west 1.4 miles to the paved Pierre Lake Road junction, where the PNWT turns left onto the paved Pierre Lake Road and descends 1.9 miles through a beautiful, narrow, cliff-bordered ranch valley to Pierre Lake. This popular, free Forest Service Campground has a lakeside trail, picnic tables, and campsites.

Beyond this mile-long lake the valley widens and we pass more cattle ranches. After 3.8 miles we reach the turnoff west (1939) on the Toulou Mountain Road to Orient. This road rises through pleasant woods to a 2140' height of land and descends to a pre-World War I iron bridge on the Kettle River.

If you camp at Orient's quaint city park across from the gas station, you will be thankful for the village's amenities. You may use the outhouses of the tavern near the park. And junk food and groceries are for sale at the gas station/cafe. Daily bus service is available via the Republic/Colville Stage Line (509/684-4412).

The PNWT goes south 100 yards from Orient on U.S. Highway 395, the main road to Spokane. Immediately after a highway rock cut, turn right on what looks like a dirt driveway up past several houses. This road rises ¼ mile up a birch draw to a meadowed bench. At a grassy 4-way junction, turn right uphill toward the trees. This jeep road climbs across more grassy, scenic benches, which offer good views back toward the Kettle River Valley and First Thot Mountain. (Later there is water at Slide Creek). Eventually this old, unimproved woodsy track ends at a new logging road. Climb the earth barrier and turn left on this wide, heavy-duty dirt road.

Our destination is the Kettle Crest's Marble Mountain (5973). The new logging road follows the old East Deer Creek trail past Jasper Mountain to a heavily logged area at the headwaters of the South Fork Little Boulder Creek. Be careful not to follow this seductively easy road beyond the somewhat vague ridge between the East Deer Creek and South Fork Little Boulder Creek drainages. You should pass a locked gate and make a sharp right turn on Road 9576/265. Climb to a clearcut on the ridge and cross the stumps into the trees, heading due west. (If, instead, you follow the road around northwest to a creek, you have gone too far on the road.) In the forest you will quickly intersect the old East Deer Creek jeep trail, which as of this writing (1984) will soon be logged for lodgepole-pine-beetle damage salvage. Jungle Creek is a reliable water source and a convenient bivouac site.

Beyond Jungle Creek the old East Deer Creek jeep road becomes progressively less distinct. You will feel like an ant, crawling across giant matchsticks of fallen lodgepole. Eventually, at a small, sloping meadow, the jeep road becomes merely a trail. Continue west northwest on this trail as long as you can; then climb uphill to an old clearcut (4800) beyond a new barbed-wire fence. There you will find the Noonday Spring and a good place to camp, complete with views east down the length of East Deer Creek and far beyond to the Abercrombie/Hooknose ridge on the horizon.

From the clearcut and spring, continue via old skid roads to the Marble Mountain Lookout Road. A sign at the open junction with the Deer Creek Summit Road says, "Marble Mountain L.O. 3 miles; Noonday Spring ¼ mile." This road switchbacks down through cattle country to East Deer Creek, the Goat Creek Road, and a good campsite. From here Deer Creek Summit is 3 miles southwest via Trail No. 13 between Dry Mountain and Rocky Mountain. Cross East Deer Creek, pass through a barbed-wire cattle gate, and climb about a mile through large fir and lodgepole. At the junction with Third Creek Road (about a mile up) continue uphill to the left. After a level mile and then a mile of easy downhill, we reach Deer Creek Summit (4600).

An all-highway alternate route from Orient to Deer Creek Summit goes south from Orient 2.7 miles on U.S. Highway 395 (the main road to Spokane). Then we follow the Boulder Deer Creek Road 11.8 miles up to the Deer Creek Summit. This road route is dry and can be very hot and dusty in summer. Beware of the high-speed logging trucks.

At the Deer Creek Summit (4600), site of a former Forest Service Guard Station, there is an unimproved campground. To find water, walk west 300 yards downhill and look and listen on the left side of the road. Cold water bubbles out of a pipe at the end of a 100-foot trail.

The north/south spine of the Kettle Range is traversed by two east/west roads, here at Deer Creek Summit and south at Sherman Pass. Although the highest mountains from Deer Creek Summit south to the Colville Indian Reservation remain as wilderness, roads have often penetrated to within a mile of them. This part of the Colville National Forest has long been used by cattlemen for summer high-country grazing. Lately it has been managed more and more intensively for timber. The very extensive logging road network both east and west of the crest provides many access points for PNWT loop trips.

From Deer Creek Summit, Kettle Crest Trail No. 13 climbs south along Taylor Ridge. We follow it 5 miles from Deer Creek Summit south onto Taylor Ridge (6050), where we exchange old roadbed for old trail. From there it is only 1.7 miles downhill to a forest campsite at Indian Creek (4600). The Forest Service will soon reroute this stretch to a new trail on Sentinel Butte and Taylor Ridge (see map). The new trail is more direct; water will be available off the trail at the beaver ponds at the headwaters of Indian Creek.

Fill your canteen at Indian Creek. The trail climbs steeply 1.8 miles to a col northwest of Profanity Peak. From the Indian Creek campsite (4500), Kettle Crest Trail No. 13 climbs steadily southwest to a pass between Profanity Peak and the ridge leading to Tenasket Mountain. In June watch for beautiful *calypso bulbosa* orchids. This section has several springs and seeps.

From the Profanity Peak Pass (5800) you will be able to look ahead to a long stretch of our route to the south. This country is heavily forested with lodgepole pine and Douglas fir and, at high elevations, subalpine fir and whitebark pine. You will see two hills (5600) ahead, Leona Mountain to your right and a long, rounded ridge blocking the left horizon leading south. Descend from Profanity Peak Pass and climb the first hill (where there are no views and water), then drop again, this time to Ryan Cabin—an historic ruin, probably a herder's shelter. A good spring is located near the cabin. Next climb out of a nearby canyon and switchback up to the summit of Ryan Hill—a good, though waterless, campsite. Ryan Hill is a good platform for reorienting yourself to the country ahead.

The PNWT (Trail No. 13) drops through fir woods before encountering a steep ascent of the south shoulder of Mount Leona. The spectacular meadows along Leona Trail No. 49 make perfect, low-impact campsites—if you have carried up water from the Satisfaction Spring 100 yards below the ridge. Trail No. 13 will soon be relocated off this ridge, but for now we have its wildflower meadows from which to view the Republic area, knobby Mount Bonaparte, and even the distant Cascades.

Along our descent south on the Mount Leona trail to a pass and the Stickpin Hill trail, we go by a good little spring and a side trail to a cabin, a corral, and a stronger spring. At the pass below Mount Leona we are 2.5 miles south of Ryan Cabin and 6 miles north of Copper Butte. From here a long, easy grade takes us up through dense forest to a paradise of open meadows and endless views, a hawks' sanctuary, a hikers' heaven, and a whitefaces' summer pasture.

Kettle Crest Trail No. 13 contours around Lambert Mountain and Midnight Mountain at an elevation of 6000' or more. At the end of a particularly lovely meadow section, we reenter the trees and find the fenced-in source and cattle trough of Neff Spring. We continue through forest and meadow to a second spring, where you should tank up if you wish to camp overnight on Copper Butte. Just ¼ mile beyond this Midnight Mountain spring, we reach a saddle between Midnight Mountain and Copper Butte; here we cross a cattle driveway road. From there we have 200 feet before intersecting with the Old Stage Road (Trail No. 1) which connects west to Belcher Mountain. Then a steady ascent of 1.3 miles on Trail No. 13 up through lodgepole forest takes us to the flat summit of Copper Butte (7135).

This highest point in Ferry County is an excellent place to camp if you have carried up adequate water from the Midnight Mountain spring. Be ready for celestial delights—for instance, a summer thunderstorm over Spokane far to the southeast. Closer by, you will be able to see the glow from Colville. On the west side of the Kettle Crest you will be able to pick out the lights of Republic, our next urban center.

From the burnt ruins of the old lookout cabin, we continue across the top of Copper Butte's massive, view-packed crest and down to the col before Scar Mountain. Here we find the North Fork Sanpoil River Trail No. 17. Next, the Crest Trail No. 13 ascends steeply up a rock face to a ridge and Wapaloosie Mountain. The Wapaloosie Mountain Trail No. 15 goes west from here 2 miles to the Albian Hill Road. At this point we can begin to see the Sherman Pass Road.

The ridge continues high, beautiful, and meadowed until its descent via the well-built path to the base of Jungle Hill. You will find a good trailside spring and campsite at a cattle-frequented tiny pond.

At the trail junction with Sherman Creek Trail No. 12 just before Jungle Hill, we are only 5 miles from Sherman Pass. The remainder of the Crest Trail to Sherman Pass is very well built. A ½-mile side trail is available to the Columbia Mountain Lookout ruin (6782), a good but waterless campsite. You will find reliable water at the 2-mile Lookout Camp (at the junction of the lookout trail with Trail No. 13) and at 1.5 miles before Sherman Pass. The total distance from Deer Creek Summit to Sherman Pass via Kettle Crest Trail No. 13 is 33 miles.

The new trailhead at Sherman Pass (5587) has a stock-loading ramp and some campsites. Water is not available there or at the Sherman Pass

Recreation Area campground a mile east down State Highway 20. However, if you walk the road fifteen minutes west beyond Sherman Pass, you will find water beside the highway.

Although our Ideal Route is still only an outline across Okanogan National Forest lands south and west of Republic, the 10 miles of Kettle Crest Trail No. 13 south from Sherman Pass to White Mountain (6921)—with their spectacular vistas—are an excellent route for immediate use. It is a dry route, however. Look for springs: (1) beyond Sherman Peak in a sloping meadow, 4 miles in; (2) at Telephone Camp near the Edds Mountain Trail; and (3) on the south side of White Mountain. From White Mountain you could reach Republic by going west on Trail No. 6, northwest on Hall Creek Road 600, and west on Trail No. 23 (past Fire Mountain, 13-Mile Mountain, and Cougar Mountain) and north on State Highway 21 along the Sanpoil River

Our Practical Route takes the easiest and most direct way to Republic from Sherman Pass—State Highway 20, a distance of 19 miles. There are occasional bivouac spots beside the road on the way to town; 1.5 miles from downtown you will reach the Republic City Park, where camping is permitted. (Perhaps a mile before this park you will pass Gib's grocery store.) There is also a park in downtown Republic, where our hikers have camped in the past. It has restrooms and water, but the legality of camping there is not known. Anyway, the laundromat has pay showers and there is a food co-op, a cobbler, and a museum on or near the high end of the main street. All in all, Republic is a very convenient stopover for PNWT pilgrims.

Beyond Republic, 9 miles on Highway 20 bring us to the end of this section at the ($4 fee) Sweat Creek Campground. On a hot summer day try to walk these blistering asphalt sections in the early morning or late afternoon. The camp's hand pump is a reliable source of water.

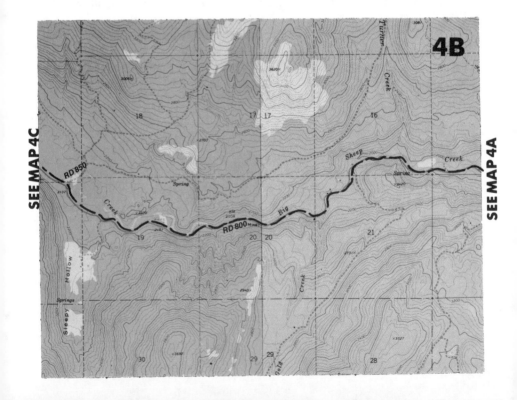

SEE MAP 4B

4A

Sheep Creek
Campground

Upper Falls

Sheep Creek
Falls

BM
1668

22 23 24 19 20

27 26 25

RD 800

Spring

36 31

34 35

Northport

SEE MAP 3U

Phillips
Lake

29

30

Steamboat
Rock

RIVER

Sand
Point

COLUMBIA

33 AQUEDUCT 34

Smelter Rock

4B

Turtsr
Creek

SEE MAP 4C

SEE MAP 4A

RD 850

Sheep Creek

Spring

RD 800 Mine

Big Creek

18 17 16

19 20 21

Sleepy Hollow

Springs

30 29 28

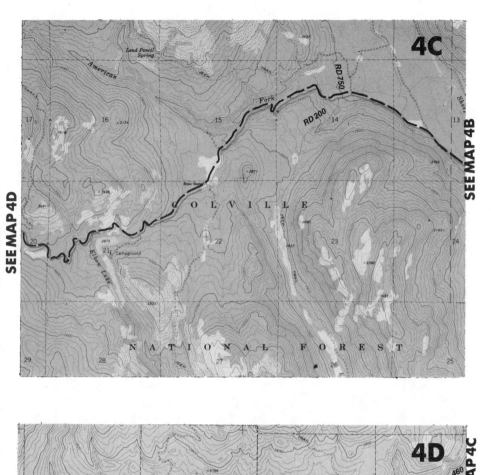

SEE MAP 4D

SEE MAP 4B

4C

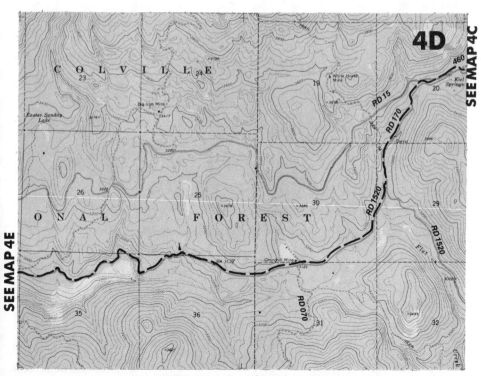

SEE MAP 4C

SEE MAP 4E

4D

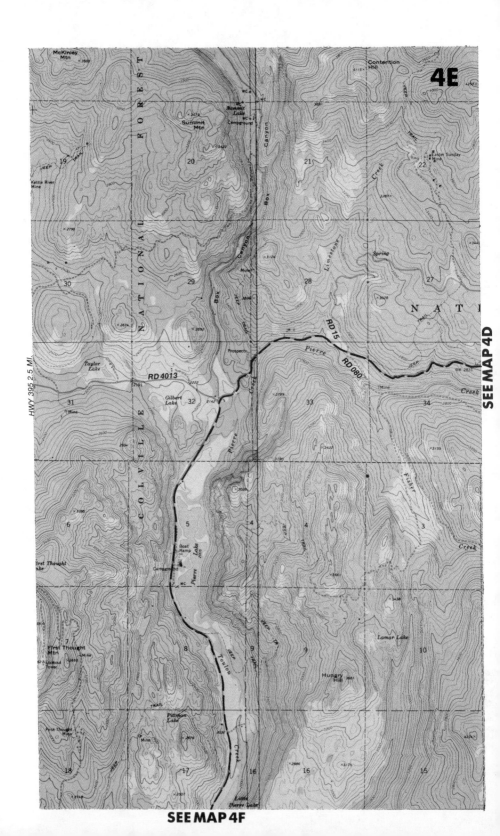

SEE MAP 4D

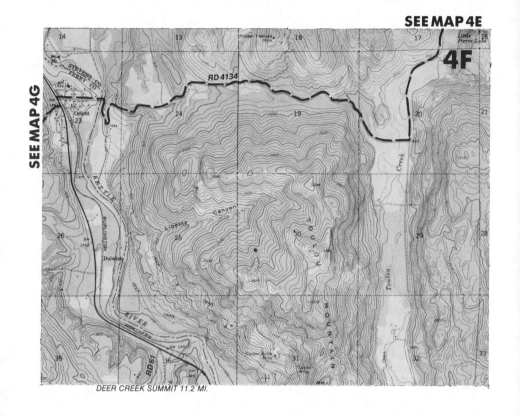

4F

RD 4134

DEER CREEK SUMMIT 11.2 MI.

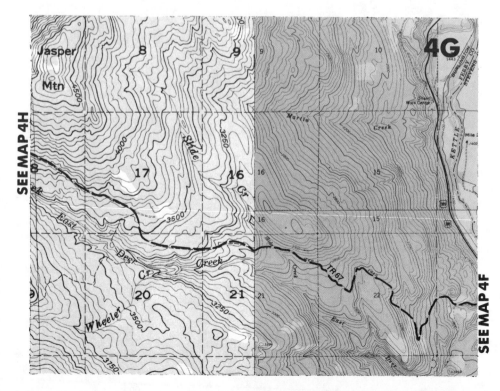

4G

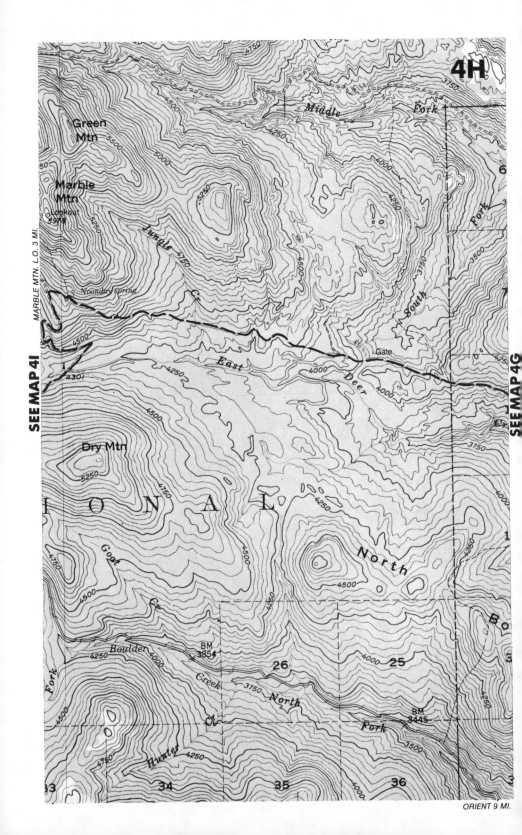

SEE MAP 4I

MARBLE MTN. L.O. 3 MI.

SEE MAP 4G

ORIENT 9 MI.

Green
Mtn

Marble
Mtn

Lookout
4978

Middle

Fork

Fork

Jungle Cr.

Noondry spring

South

Gate

East

Deer

Dry Mtn

I O N A L

Goat

North

Boulder

BM
3854

Creek

North

Fork

Cr.

BM
3445

Fork

Hunter

Bo

33

34

35

36

26

25

1

6

3

7

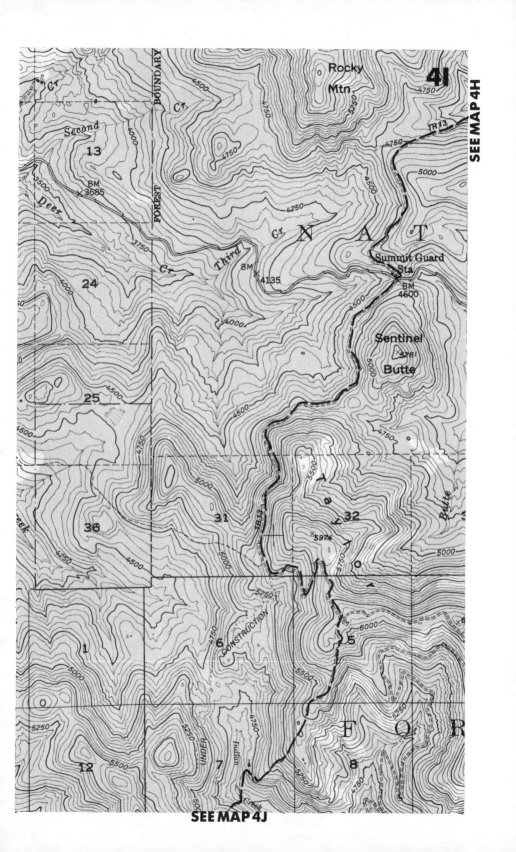

SEE MAP 4H

SEE MAP 4J

Rocky
Mtn

TR 13

Summit Guard
Sta

BM
4600

Sentinel
×5261
Butte

G N A T

F O R

Second

13

BM
×3685

FOREST BOUNDARY

Cr

Cr

Cr

Deer

Third

Cr

Cr

BM
×4135

24

25

36

31

32
×5974

1

6

5

CONSTRUCTION

12

7

8

Butte

Creek

Indian

UNDER

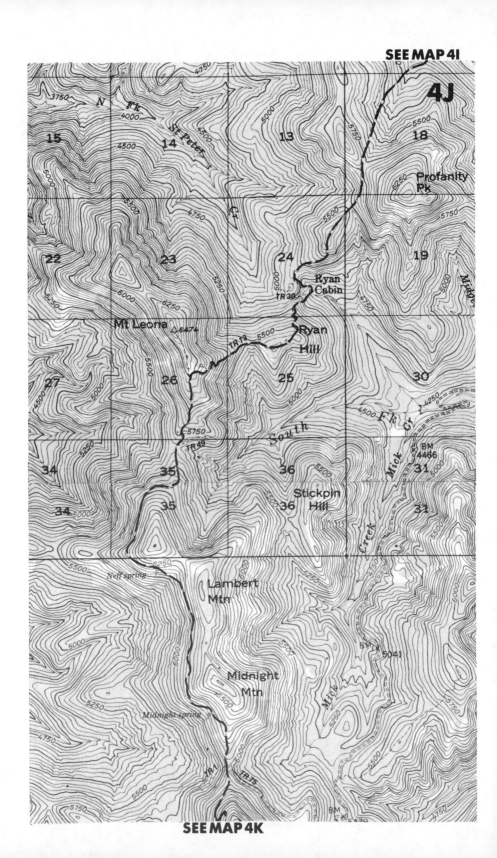

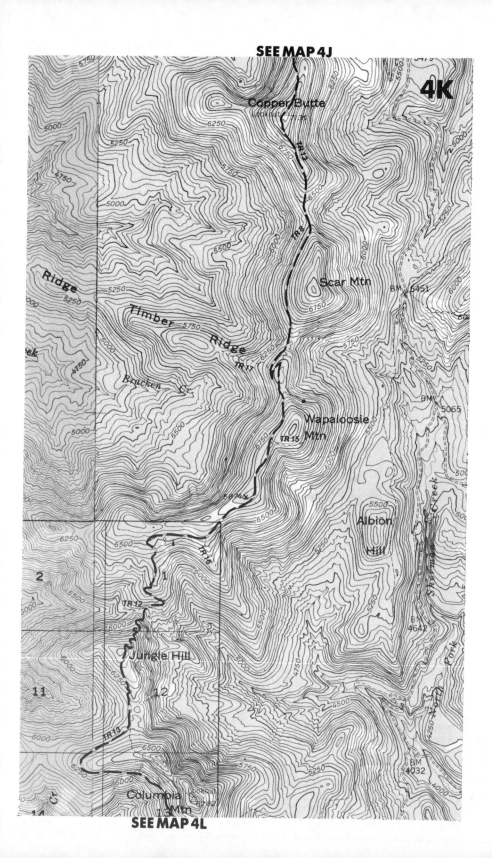

4K

Copper Butte

Scar Mtn

Ridge

Timber

Ridge

Bracken Cr.

Wapaloosie
Mtn

Albion
Hill

Jungle Hill

Columbia
Mtn

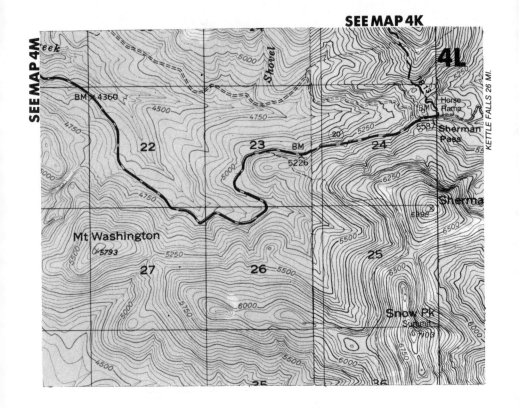

4L

KETTLE FALLS 26 MI.

BM ×4360

22

23

BM
5226

24

5582

Horse
Ramp

Sherman
Pass

20

Sherma

5898

×

Mt Washington
×5793

27

26

25

Snow Pk
Summit
7108

35

36

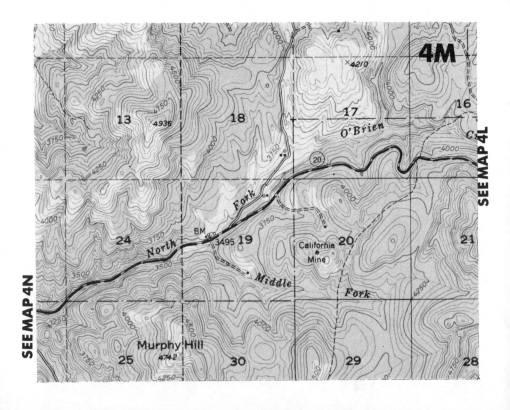

4M

×4210

13

×4936

18

17

O'Brien

16

C.

20

North   Fork

24

BM
3495

19

California
Mine

20

21

Middle

Fork

25

Murphy Hill
×4742

30

29

28

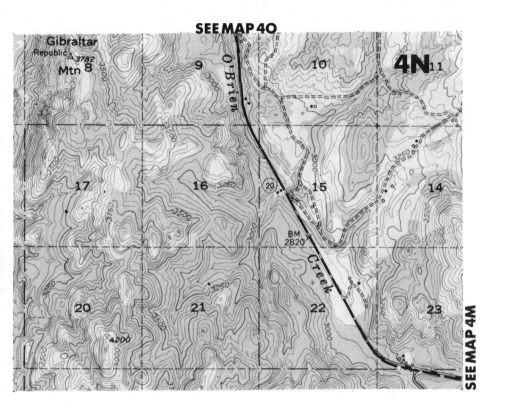

SEE MAP 4M

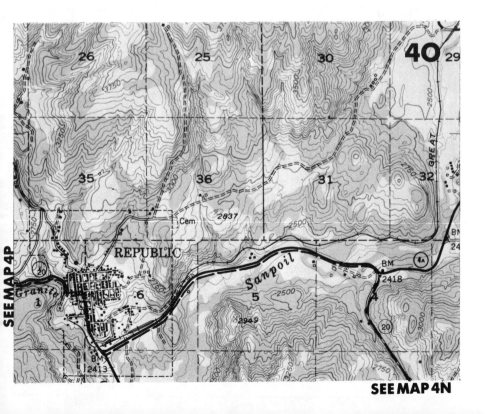

SEE MAP 4P

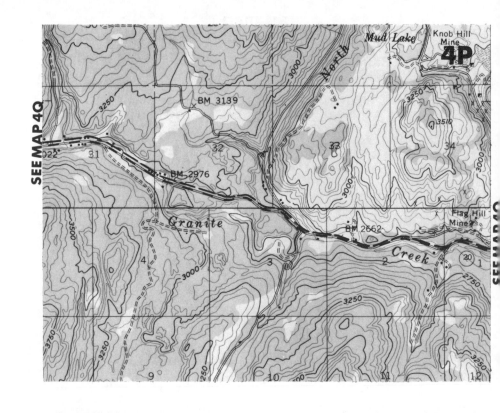

Mud Lake

Knob Hill
Mine

4P

North

BM 3139

3510

32

33

34

022 31

BM 2976

Flag Hill
Mine

Granite

BM 2662

Creek

20 1

4

3

2

9

10

11

12

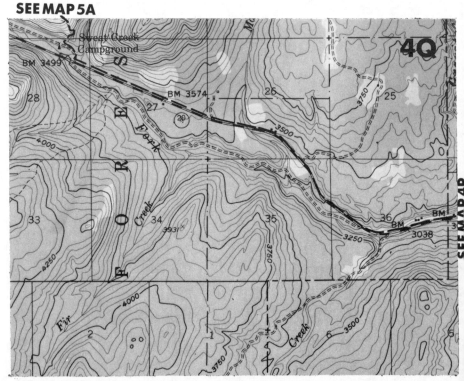

Sweat Creek
Campground

4Q

BM 3499

BM 3574

28

27

26

25

20

FOREST

Fork

33

34

Creek

35

3931

36

BM

BM
3038

Fir

2

1

Creek

6

5

THE OKANOGAN
(Sweat Creek to Cold Springs Camp)

5

Lake Osoyoos and Chopaka Mountain

INTRODUCTION

So different from the rest of the PNWT, the Okanogan is the scent of sage, the shapes of creosote bushes, and the lure of cool uplands. I have long been captivated by this dry but welcoming region. You will be, too.

Turn-of-the-century homesteaders came to the area after the cattlemen, who had followed the miners into the region in the 1860s and 1870s. Mining, cattle, wheat, and orchards are the usual measure of wealth. The Okanogan's health depends upon water—irrigation water—but the area is basically a desert. It is a region of extremes. August temperatures regularly surpass 100° F, yet high to the west snow or hail can fall in any week.

Mount Bonaparte, on the east side of the Okanogan Valley, is the highest point in this Trail section until the Cascade Mountains. From the subalpine, 7258′ summit of Mount Bonaparte, the PNWT descends to the 900′ elevations of the Okanogan Valley's parched rangelands. Spring apple-blossom time on the miles of river-bench orchards is a showy pink season of pollination and promise; in late September the groves ring with the Mexican cry of "tractor" and the steady rustle of red and golden delicious apples dropping into harvest bags and bins.

Here the PNWT goes into Oroville, a fairly large town of 1500+ people, to cross the Okanogan River bridge. After crossing the Okanogan Valley at Oroville, you again enter some Okanogan Highlands homesteading areas. Water is scarce as you trudge across the Bullfrog area, and much of the route not on county roads is privately owned. Be very careful about both water and maintaining good relations with landowners.

One of the most spectacular views on the Trail is your first introduction to the Cascade range as you descend into the Similkameen from Ellemeham Mountain. The cliffs across this narrow valley are so sharp that you wonder how a trail could possibly penetrate them. They are just your first indication of what is ahead in one of America's most fascinating wildernesses— the Pasayten.

By the way, be prepared for some ups and downs. Among the many highs and lows in this section are the 7258′ summit of Mount Bonaparte and the Oroville city elevation of only 926′. Make certain that your boots are well broken in and that you have plenty of dry socks.

This is sage-country walking at its finest.

PROBLEMS

Water supply could be a problem in this section. Be certain to carry enough between the points where you expect to find creeks, springs, etc. But remember that since this country has a relatively high cattle and human population, brookside water purity is often suspect. If in doubt about a certain source, either get your water elsewhere or boil it for an adequate time.

A problem could also exist because of the route's crossing private land in several places. Wherever possible, ask permission at nearby houses to cross such land. Close all gates, do not camp, and make no fires on private property.

Also, at Chopaka Mountain and on other warm, exposed rocks in the area, be on your guard against rattlesnakes. Bites are rarely fatal, but they can put a serious damper on your trip.

SUPPLIES

Republic, Oroville, and Loomis are the three major supply points for this section. West of the Similkameen Valley is a 137-mile stretch of supply-less hiking for which you must plan carefully. The ideal solution would be to cache a supply box in advance near the Cold Springs Campground.

Supplies and mail drops are very adequate in this section at Republic, Oroville, and Loomis. Oroville has a coin laundry and a camping goods store. The Okanogan County seat at Okanogan (50 miles south of Oroville) has an even greater selection, though highly specialized backpacking items may be hard to get.

DECLINATION   22½° to 21½° E

USGS TOPOGRAPHIC MAPS

Aeneas	15'
Bodie Mountain	15'
Mt. Bonaparte	15'
Oroville	15'
Loomis	15'

MILEAGES (total 83.6)

		Total
Highway 20, Sweat Creek Campground (3499)	0.0	0.0
West Fork of Cougar Creek via Trail No. 310 over 5482' Clackamas Mountain	6.5	6.5
Old Toroda (2958)	2.0	8.5
Forest Service Road 388 via Antoine Creek Road	3.5	12.0
Bonaparte Lake Boy Scout Camp (3554)	4.2	16.2
Mount Bonaparte (7258)	8.0	24.2
Havillah (3520)	7.0	31.2
Summit Lake Road via Fanchers Dam (3200)	2.0	33.2
Summit Lake (4320)	6.3	39.5
Tonasket Creek	4.2	43.7
Oroville (926)	8.3	52.0
Ellemeham Mountain Road	1.0	53.0
Nagy homestead (2800)	9.5	62.5
Loomis-Nighthawk Road (1162)	6.3	68.8
Chopaka Lake (2921)	9.0	77.8
Cold Springs Road junction	4.0	81.8
Cold Springs Campground (6200)	1.8	83.6

ROUTE DESCRIPTION

Sweat Creek Campground is a $4-per-site Forest Service campsite at the junction of Sweat Creek and the West Fork of Granite Creek. The campground is 9 miles west of the town of Republic on State Highway 20, a main east/west road which we will cross again several times much farther west. Be sure to fill your canteens at the campground pump before heading north.

Forest Service Trail No. 310 links the campground with the West Fork of Cougar Creek 6.5 miles due north. This trail ascends the ridge west of Sweat Creek to a wooded knob at 5388' and then Clackamas Mountain (5482). The views along this almost-obliterated first section are good of Fir Mountain, Mount Bonaparte, and Maple Mountain. This is a good place, too, to appreciate the beauty of the ponderosa pine's flaky-red bark, airy charm, and sibilant grace. Learn to recognize these fine, three-needled pines.

To follow Trail No. 310, look for the trail near the outhouses in the campground's picnic area. This trail disappears after crossing two barbed-wire fences near a power-line right-of-way. However, you should continue by bushwhacking up the slope and staying in a meadowy draw, at the top of which is a green metal stock tank and a spring. (Be sure to fill your canteen either at the campground pump or at this spring.) Follow the ridgetop through open forest and meadow until you hit the trail. You may wish to camp at this spring or at the What Spring beyond Clackamas or at any number of dry sites along the ridge.

Although this trail's condition is usually good, the way is often faint through a succession of ridgetop forests and balds. The route is usually marked with cairns or very old blazes. Occasionally you will have excellent views of the Kettle Range to the east and of our Ideal Route to the south. A series of minor highpoints precede a viewless, forested summit. Then we drop down to a saddle and climb steeply to the true summit of Clackamas Mountain (5482) in open forest. Shortly thereafter, we encounter the small sign for the Maple Mountain Trail, 4 miles north from the Sweat Creek Campground.

For an alternate ascent of Clackamas you could try Trail No. 324, which parallels Sweat Creek to the east. At about 5200' there is a good spring. Or you could reach that spring from Clackamas Mountain via the Maple Mountain Trail.

The now-excellent Trail No. 310 drops from the Maple Mountain Trail junction, steeply at first, into the valley of a tributary of the West Fork of Cougar Creek. About 1 mile down along the west side of our north-running ridge, we reach the welcome green-metal stock tank of the What Spring. Here, turn sharply left downhill toward the creek. Trail No. 310 continues 1.8 miles on the east side of the creek until finally crossing near a cabin and a barbed-wire gate. We cross from Colville National Forest land to a long road section on private land. The only good campsite between here and Bonaparte Lake is 8 miles ahead on the next section of national-forest land.

Walk downhill 2 miles on the unpaved West Fork and the Cougar Creek Roads to Old Toroda (2958), the site of a turn-of-the-century pioneer community. Today's Cougar Creek Valley is subdivided into many private holdings.

Turn west (left) on the paved Toroda Creek Road and climb 3.5 miles through range country to Bunch Road 388. (The sign points to the right toward Bonaparte Lake.) Ascend Bunch Road (sometimes called Fisher Road) through scenic ranch country to a divide 3 miles up and a small, cattle-frequented pond, the best campsite on this road.

From the divide, descend Bunch Road a mile to the South Fork Beaver Creek Road. Go right .2 mile to the Bonaparte Boy Scout Camp on Bonaparte Lake (3554). Inquire about staying overnight. If you are a long-distance hiker, the Scouts might enjoy hearing about your adventures. (Or you may wish to camp farther south at the $5-per-night Forest Service campground, connected directly by trail with our Mount Bonaparte Lookout route. A restaurant sells good hamburgers at the commercial fishing resort on the lake.)

Next, via good trail, the PNWT climbs one of its finest and most scenic vantage points. The trail begins near the Scouts' swim dock and climbs to the right up a small hogback ridge past a tenting area and, curving widely up to the left, into a decade-old burn. After a considerable rise above the lake, this trail comes out on Lost Lake Road 3934.

Turn left at this junction, pass the scenic overlook (where the Forest Service campground trail joins the road), and continue ¼ mile southwest to the signed junction with South Side Trail No. 308. Duff Spring is about ½ mile up this trail.

The 8-mile ascent from Bonaparte Lake to Mount Bonaparte's summit may seem long, especially on a hot day, but the temperature will moderate and your spirits improve with each upward step you take. And if you wish to camp in this beautiful area, there are some small campsites at Duff Spring, Myers Creek, and at the Lookout Spring.

From Lost Lake Road 3934 we ascend 3 miles to a junction (5800) with Trail No. 307. A sign at the junction points south toward the Roggow, Mill Creek, and Siwash Creek trails. However, we continue northwest on 1 wooded mile of level trail to the Bonaparte Lookout Trail.

The Bonaparte Lookout Trail zigzags 2 miles due south to the summit of Mount Bonaparte (7258). Fill your canteens at the beginning of this trail with water from the reliable Lookout Spring, reached by a 150-yard spur trail. Also, note the location of the Antoine Creek Trail a mile toward the summit.

Mount Bonaparte is the highest point in northeastern Washington. The eastern and western horizons here are framed by the Kettle River Range, Abercrombie/Hooknose, and the Cascade Mountains of the Pasayten Wilderness. This may be your best chance to sort out this immense area in your mind before the days and miles become a blur. If the weather below is hot, you may want to linger on the heights with the eagles, hawks, and the lonesome soul who's spending his or her summer watching for fires. Water is not always available at the summit, so carry up any you need from the Lookout Spring. If you have water, the top of Bonaparte makes a magnificent campsite.

If you are looking for a good circuit hike, consider a loop around Mount Bonaparte. At the aforementioned junction toward the Roggow trail, the South Side Trail No. 308 contours around the mountain at about 5600' to Fourth of July Ridge and to the Mill Creek Trail No. 304, then continues by road to rejoin our main PNWT route at Havillah, a total of 11 miles.

The PNWT descends Mount Bonaparte to the hamlet of Havillah via Antoine Creek Trail No. 305. From the summit, return to the Antoine Trail junction about ½ mile below. If the summit was at all windy, this trail through young, even-aged lodgepole will seem very calm by comparison. After a while you will get used to having spiderwebs cling to your face and body as you lope downhill. Along the way you will see much yellow sedum and occasional salt blocks for the grazing cattle. The enticements of this trail include a lovely stream, mammoth firs, coyote and other tracks, hawks, giant mushrooms, and some granddaddy larches. Though the trail may not have been maintained recently, its springy larch- and pine-needle tread is a delight to walk. Finally, the trail becomes an old road where spindly lodgepoles were thinned about a decade ago. We pass a strange shack made of lodgepole sticks nailed vertically. The lower end of this route is a confusing mix of logging roads, fields, and cattle tracks. But our route joins service road 150 to connect west to Mill Creek Road 3230, on which we continue north downstream through pastureland. Turn right on the paved county road, crossing Antoine Creek, toward Havillah. Here we encounter the true Okanogan Highlands—brown rolling hills, sage-speckled with accents of the Old West.

Tiny Havillah is recognizable from afar by the white steeple of its 75-year-old Lutheran church. No services or supplies are available in this picturesque hamlet. The PNWT does not quite enter Havillah but instead follows the Antoine Creek Road west—the sign says "STORE"—along the creek 1.5 miles. Enjoy the brook smells, flowers, and newly-plowed fields.

A beautiful trail is in the future, but for now our Practical Route must follow the roads. From the Eden Valley Road junction (3299) we go due west 1.3 miles to Fanchers Dam (a good swimming hole) and continue west .7 mile to Summit Lake Road 3525. Identify this junction in an old burn by a row of mailboxes and a sign pointing west to Tonasket. This section is hot and dry; the water available in small ponds probably needs purification.

Turn right (north) onto the Summit Lake Road, and follow it 6.3 miles across the subdivided ponderosa pine slopes of a former cattle spread. Watch out for barking dogs and "No Trespassing" signs. The road returns again to the Okanogan National Forest and continues up to Summit Lake. This lake has good camping and fishing and, in season, millions of frogs. Unfortunately, the Mount Hull lookout tower (4617) has been destroyed; without it the summit views are limited by tall trees.

Our next destination is Highway 97, which will take us into Oroville. The easiest way is simply to continue to walk the road beyond Summit Lake all the way to town. Another way would be to bushwhack a map and compass version of the Ideal Route. A third way would be to follow the old trail (often puzzling) from the lake to McDonald Mountain or as far as you can track it, and then turn downhill west and pick up the old logging roads that lead into the old Whistler Canyon Road; this way requires about 5 miles of patient groping, but you will be rewarded when you leave the forest by the beauty of Whistler Canyon. If your brains are not baking, you may be able to appreciate the charm of creosote bushes and sagebrush and of a rough and tumble arroyo landscape more typical of the Southwest than of the Pacific Northwest. Certain steep parts of the Whistler Canyon road are so heavily eroded that this route will surely not last many more years; it is not maintained. This road leads us down to the Okanogan River Valley and State Highway 97 at a point 2 miles south of Oroville.

We cross the Okanogan River bridge to enter Oroville (926). Go ahead and enjoy yourself here; Oroville has plenty of saloons, coin laundry machines, motels, campsites, grocery stores, movies, and even taxis. Clarence Wood's cobbler shop, Oroville Shoe Repair, are on the main street as you enter town. How about a swim in the warm water of Osoyoos Lake State Park? And—my own favorite—if you like English-style meat pies, be sure to visit the Canadian sister town of Osoyoos only 5½ miles north on the lake. The meat-pie bakery is downtown on the main street. Outside town, on the main road, Beans and Bread is an excellent shop for nutritious breads and for bulk flour, beans, spices, etc.

From Randall's supermarket on Highway 97 in downtown Oroville, go 1 mile west, crossing the Similkameen River bridge, and reaching the sign pointing up the unpaved Ellemeham Mountain Road. Turn right; go .1 mile to another junction, where the PNWT goes straight, uphill toward the bluff. Continue through the orchards.

In summer this Ellemeham Mountain route can be very dry and hot. But its beautiful 9 miles offer Wyoming-like vistas of the Old West. Stay on the main road. We begin a steep climb through contorted bluffs and sage range where if you walk west at dusk, you will have the warm valley breeze at your back. Just before the crest of the first bench, in a thicket on the south side of the road, there is water at a stock tank.

About 3 miles up you will come to an overlook above beautiful Blue Lake. After 2 more miles of open hills and scattered alders, you will reach a pond where a spring enters from the south end during the early part of the summer. But this is cattle country, and such unprotected water sources are always suspect.

Next, pay close attention because the PNWT leaves this road about 4½ miles past the pond. Note a corral, a covered spring, a foundation, and a log cabin converted to a cattle shed—all part of the old Nagy homestead on the right side of the road. To your left will be more corrals and a small cabin. Now just around a corner in the road from this point (i.e., ¼ mile south), you must turn right on a dirt road through a closed stock gate.

From this point it is easy to follow this new road up and over Ellenham Mountain (4430). Turn right where the road forks at a stock pond. The summit of Chopaka Mountain will be visible over the hills ahead. Continue as the road switchbacks through pasture and selectively cut fir forest to the rolling hills of Ellenham's summit. (This is all private ranch land, so be sure to close all gates along the way.) Turn right at a juncture by a group of large aspens.

This road switchbacks steeply down toward the floor of the Similkameen Valley. Recent mining activity along the way shows that the golden faith of the pioneer prospectors still lingers in these hills. The road ends in a quaking aspen grove about two-thirds of the way down the mountain (near and below the Prize Mine). Stay to the left of the aspen grove and you will find a trail to take you to the valley bottom (1162). The views here are some of the most spectacular on the entire PNWT. Ellenham

Mountain and its near neighbor Bullfrog Mountain hem in the eastern edges of Palmer Lake and the Similkameen River, while Grandview Mountain's and Chopaka Mountain's incredible cliffs mark the border of the Pasayten country across the valley.

To cross this Similkameen valley and regain the heights, walk west all the way across the valley on the road that crosses Palmer Creek. Where the road turns right (north) directly below the steep slopes of Grandview Mountain, enter the stock gate (on your left) and walk southwest at the edge of the meadow and marsh grass almost to the waters of Palmer Lake. Note a very large, divided arm of Grandview Mountain, around which the lake curves south. To climb up to that arm, we begin switchbacking up the smaller, closer ridge. Although this horse trail has not been regularly maintained, it is in surprisingly good condition. It rises from 1200' to 3600' in only 1.5 miles of horizontal distance. The views are ultra-spectacular as we switchback up the small ridge and then the first and second portions of the major ridge. And there is very welcome water where we finally cross the main ridge's great gulch. Eventually, we top out at a major saddle on Grandview Mountain.

Beyond the saddle the trail looks like a very good cattle path. Descend on it to a copse of large aspens, cut around them to the right, and follow the now-level trail to a salt lick and a grassy jeep road. Go downhill and follow this jeep road until you reach the Chopaka Lake Road.

Be on the lookout for rattlesnakes!

At Chopaka Lake (2921) you are in for a treat. Set in a meadowed trough between Grandview Mountain and Chopaka Mountain, this 1.5-mile-long lake is a barbless hook, fly-fishing paradise. Although trout fishermen are always camped at the state Department of Natural Resources campground at the south end of Chopaka Lake, a backpacker rarely will feel crowded here.

To reach Cold Springs Campground, the roadhead for the Pasayten Wilderness, follow the Chopaka Lake Road south. After rounding a turn to the right, you will notice an unmarked dirt road, which is a right turn near Chopaka Creek and a stand of trees. This is the old Beef Pasture Cabin and Tenderfoot Mine Road, the original road hereabouts, which has been replaced by the gravel highway on the slopes south of Chopaka Creek. However, the old road is perfect for us. Follow it across beautiful open pastures northwest to local drovers' old Beef Pasture Cabin and a small, rusting ore mill. A short distance beyond, cross a Chopaka Creek tributary and reach another cabin. Continue to follow the old jeep road up the lower slopes of Chopaka Mountain, sometimes in forest, sometimes in the view-rich openings. Eventually you will reach a junction with the newer, higher-quality dirt road, which upgrades our jeep trail for the rest of the way up to the dead end at the Cold Springs Campground. There is fairly frequent water along this road, but as usual in this grazing country, its potability is always suspect. At the Cold Springs Campground the upper camp has excellent views but no water; carry any you will need up the 1200-foot trail from the spring at the viewless lower campground.

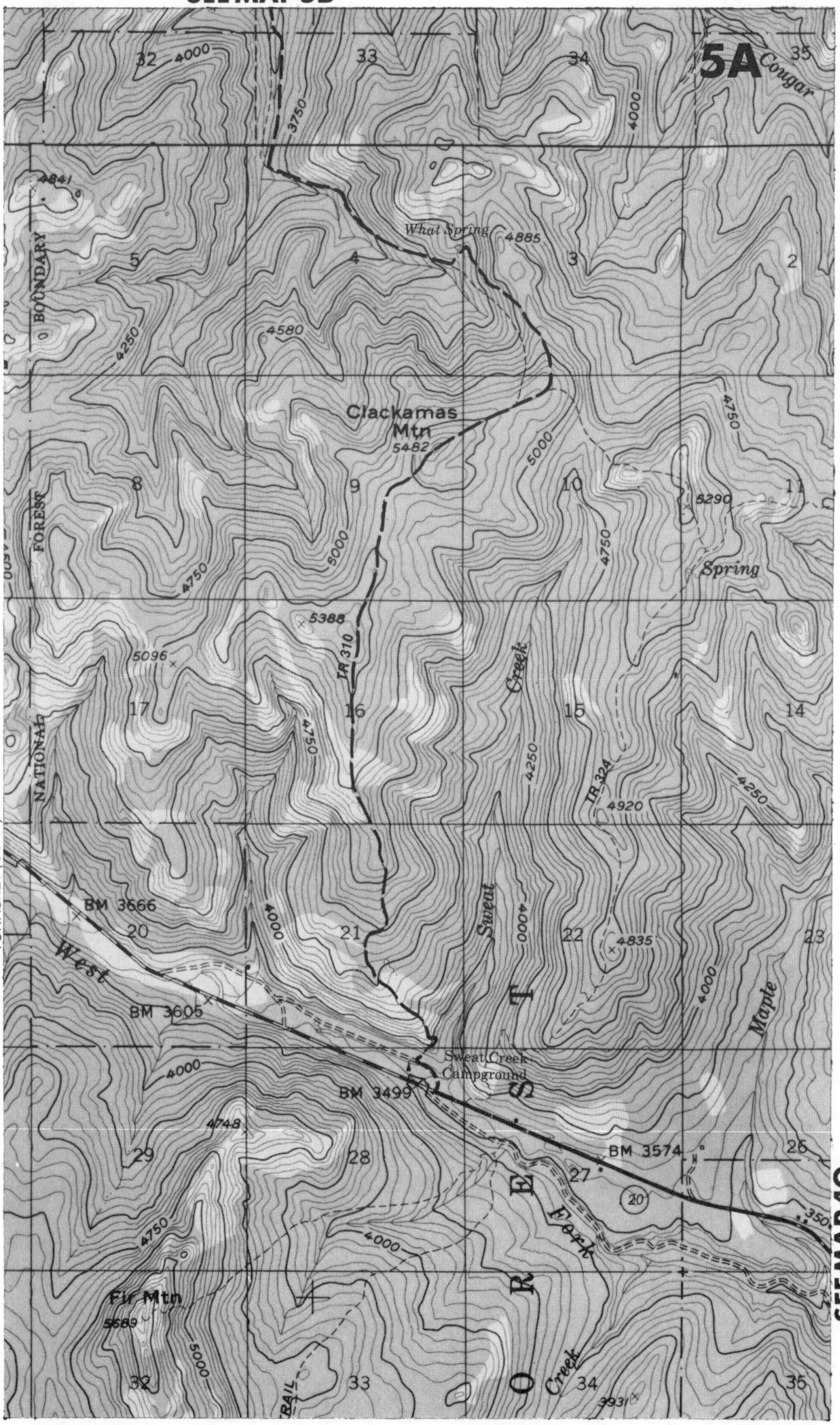

5A

Cougar

What Spring 4885

Clackamas
Mtn
5482

Spring

BOUNDARY

FOREST

NATIONAL

TONASKET (US 97) 27 MI.

4841

4580

4250

4750

5000

5388

TR 310

5096

4750

4250

5290

4750

5000

Creek

Sweat

TR 324

4920

BM 3666

West

BM 3605

4000

Sweat Creek
Campground

BM 3499

4748

4835

Maple

BM 3574

(20)

Fir Mtn
5689

4750

4000

TRAIL

4000

Creek

3931

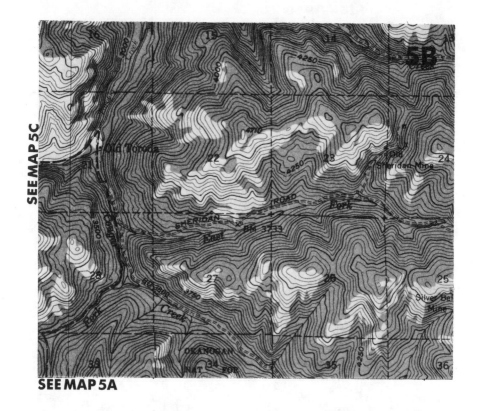

SEE MAP 5C

SEE MAP 5A

SEE MAP 5D

SEE MAP 5B

WAUCONDA (HWY 20) 2.5 MI.

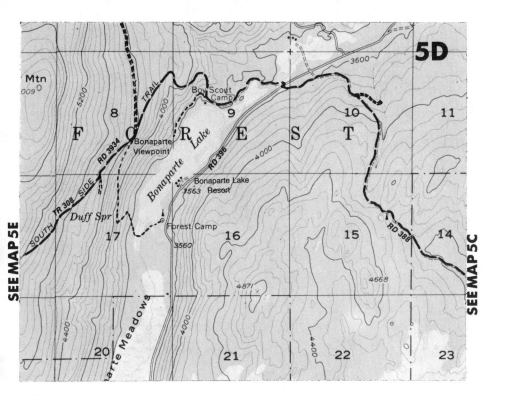

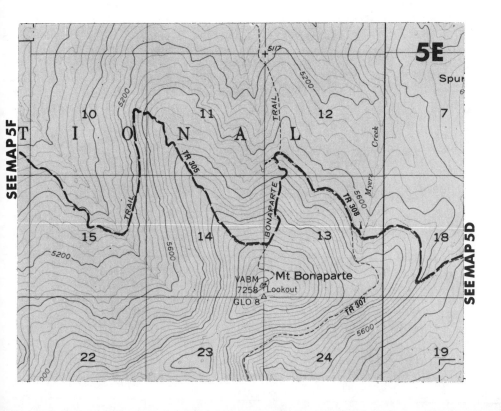

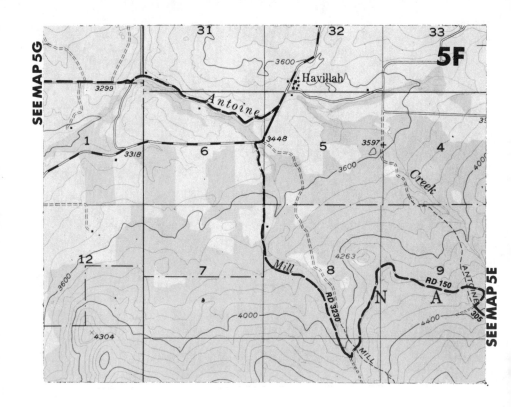

31   32   33

5F

3600

Havillah

3299   Antoine

1   6   3448   5   3597   4

3318   3600   Creek

4263

12   7   Mill   8   RD 3230   9   RD 150   N   A   305

3600   4000   4400   MILL   4304

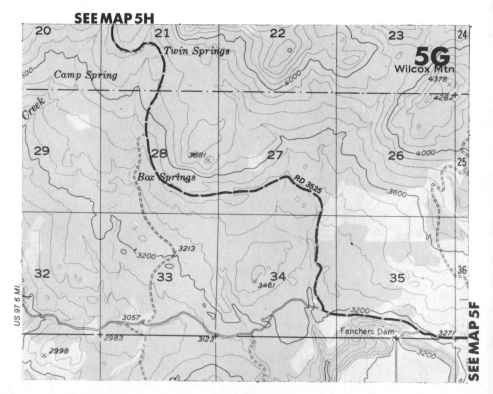

20   21   Twin Springs   22   23   24

Camp Spring   4000   Wilcox Mtn   4378   5G

Creek   4282

29   28   3681   27   26   4000   25

Box Springs   RD 3525

3600

3200   3213   3600

32   33   34   35   36

3461

3057   3200

US 97 6 MI.   2983   3123   Fanchers Dam   3271

2998   3200

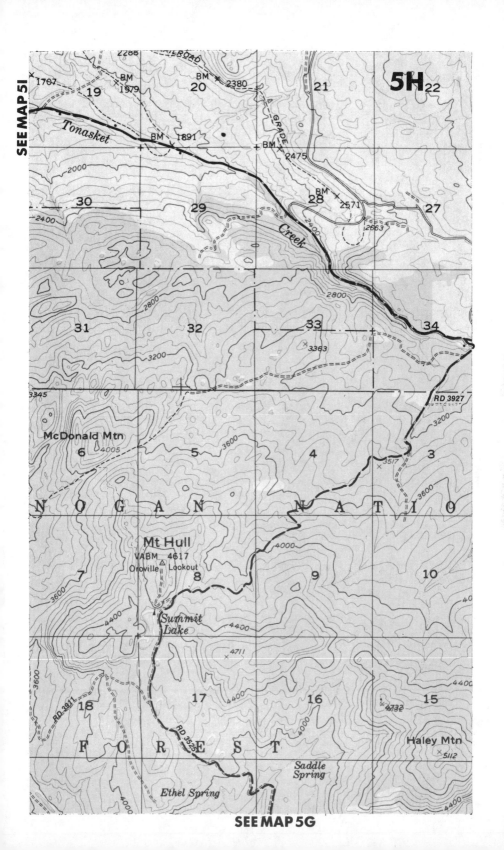

1707
19
BM 1979
20
BM 2380
21
22

Tonasket
BM 1891
BM 2475
GRADE
RAILROAD
2288

2000
30
29
Creek
BM 2571
28
2663
27

2400
2400

2800
31
32
33
3363
34
2800

3200

3345
3200
RD 3927

McDonald Mtn
6
4005
5
3600
4
3517
3

N O G A N   N A T I O

Mt Hull
VABM 4617
Oroville △ Lookout
4000
7
8
9
10

3600
Summit
Lake
4400
4400
4400
4711

RD 3911
18
17
4400
16
4732
15

RD 3525
F   O   R   E   S   T
4400
4400

Ethel Spring
Saddle
Spring
Haley Mtn
5112

4400

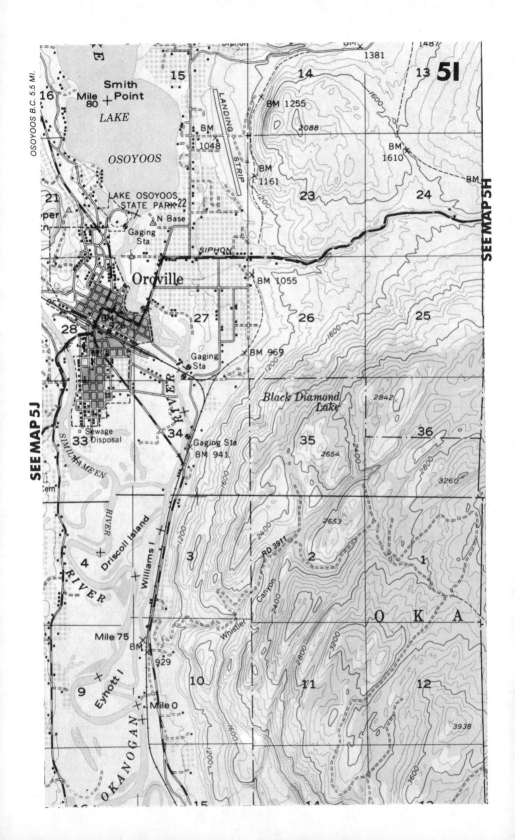

OSOYOOS B.C. 5.5 MI.

Smith
Mile +Point
80

LAKE

OSOYOOS

16

15

14

13

BM 1255

2088

BM 1381

1487

BM 1610

BM

BM
1048

BM
1161

LANDING STRIP

LAKE OSOYOOS
STATE PARK
N Base
Gaging
Sta

21

22

23

24

SIPHON

Oroville

BM 1055

28

BM
928

27

26

25

RIVER

Gaging
Sta

BM 969

1600

Black Diamond
Lake

2842

33

34

Gaging Sta
BM 941

35

36

2654

2800

3260

Sewage
Disposal

SIMILKAMEEN

2400

7653

RIVER

Driscoll Island

Williams I

3

RD 3911

2

1

4

Whistler Canyon

2400

RIVER

O K A

Mile 75
BM
929

Eyhott I

9

10

11

12

Mile 0

3938

OKANOGAN

15

14

13

SEE MAP 5H

SEE MAP 5J

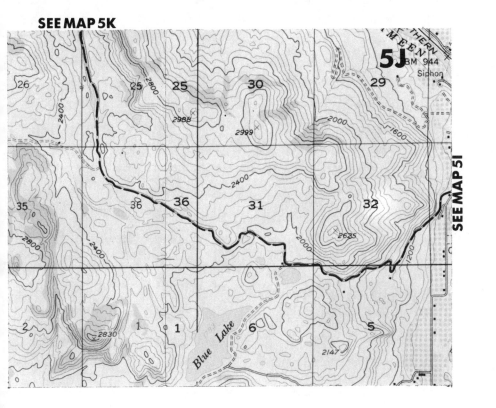

SEE MAP 5I

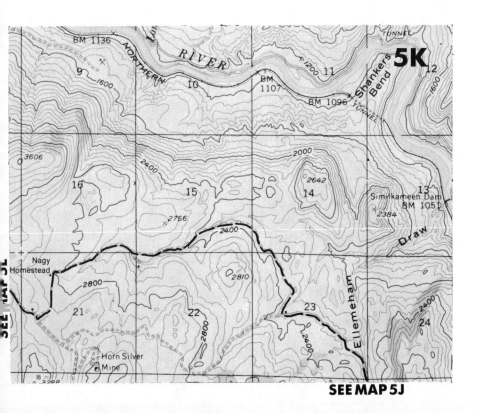

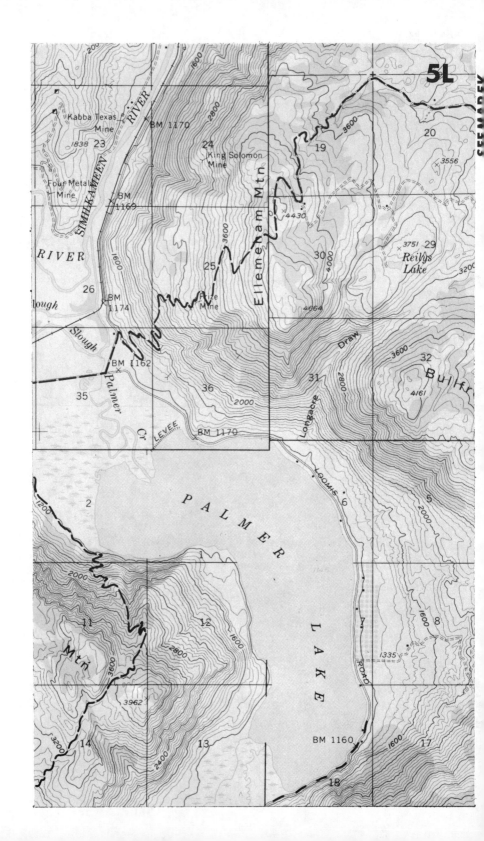

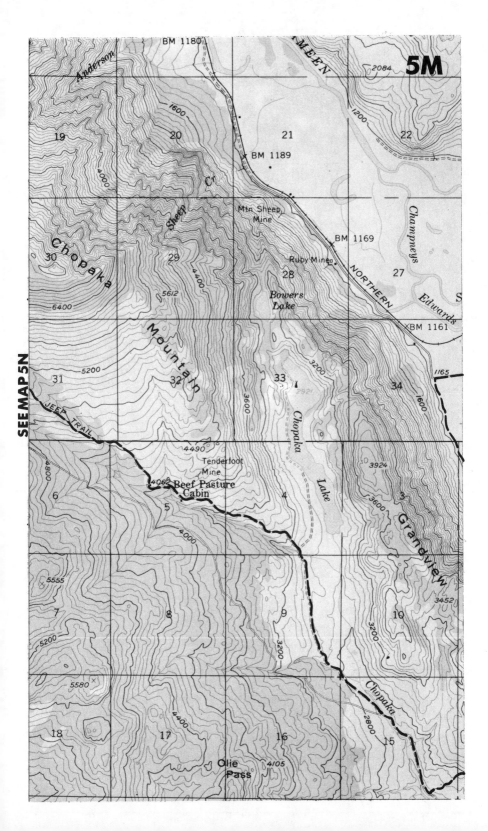

SEE MAP 5N

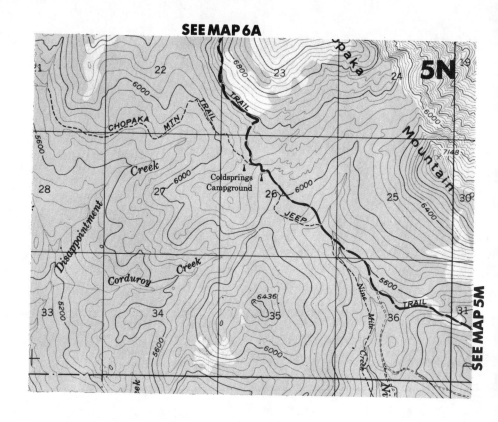

THE PASAYTEN
(Chopaka Mountain to Ross Lake)

6

Cathedral Pass

INTRODUCTION

Five hundred thousand acres of wildness is a lot—enough to get lost in, enough to cut you free from civilization, enough to teach you the meaning of the famous Wilderness Act definition, "where man is a visitor who does not remain." That five-hundred-thousand-acre figure doesn't even include the thousands and thousands of acres of contiguous wildlands or the Canadian wilderness just across the border.

Of course, man has been in the Pasayten for a very long time. Indians hunted its meadowed uplands and slopes. Early white travellers recorded its charms. If you have time, be sure to visit the Parson Smith Tree and decide if you agree with Smith's carved statement, "Of all lands she is queen."

PNWT end-to-enders always rave about the Pasayten's seven-thousand-foot-high basins and deliriously long ridges. This country *is* magnificent. And hiking and horseback conditions are excellent on its Boundary Trail, Pacific Crest Trail, Devil's Pass Trail, and Ross Lake Trail. No siwashing for us here.

The Pasayten is the most remote section of the PNWT. From near Chopaka Lake we do not see any of the usual roads and clearcuts (except at Bunker Hill) for more than one hundred miles. That that is possible at the dawn of the twenty-first century is a tribute to Congress, which in 1968 set aside this enormous area.

To get an idea of the extensiveness of this section, you should climb to a former lookout site at either end—Windy Peak in the east or Devil's Dome in the west. A side trip from Horseshoe Basin south to 8334' Windy Peak offers a superb bird's-eye view of most of the mountains and uplands in the broad, sprawling eastern Pasayten. Windy Peak's bulky spire dominates the Trail landscape all the way from Goodenough Peak to Cathedral Peak. Far to the west, 6982' Devil's Dome is in the middle of mountains that are more abrupt and less pasturelike than those at Horseshoe Basin. From Devil's Dome we can admire the rugged Picket Range across Ross Lake or the nearby Nohokomeen Glacier across Devil's Creek.

PROBLEMS

Weather. July and August are the Pasayten's most temperate months, but even in mid-summer snow and hail are daily possibilities. And if you stay into the September High Hunt season or into the snowy uncertainties of October, beware. To understand Pasayten weather expect the unexpected.

Route finding and water are not problems in this section. The trails are very good and there are usually springs, creeks, and rivers.

Because there are also hungry critters out there (even including a few grizzlies), be sure to avoid attracting them to your food and campsite.

If you travel early or late in the season when snowbanks abound, carry an ice axe to prevent bad falls.

SUPPLIES

The Pasayten is far from anywhere. Loomis (98827) is the nearest eastern source of supplies and mail. The Ross Lake Resort, Rockport, WA 98238, at the west end of this section will hold PNWT cache boxes for you.

DECLINATION   22½° E

USGS TOPOGRAPHIC MAPS

Horseshoe Basin	Castle Peak
Bauerman Ridge	Pasayten Peak
Remmel Mountain	Shull Mountain
Ashnola Pass	Jack Mountain
Ashnola Mountain	Pumpkin Mountain
Tatoosh Buttes	Ross Dam
Frosty Creek	

MILEAGES   (total 123.5)

		Total
Cold Springs Campground (6200)	0.0	0.0
Col between Knob 7160' and Joe Mills Mountain via jeep trail	2.0	2.0

Snowshoe Cabin (5600) via Olallie Creek	1.5	3.5
Long Draw Trail No. 340 (6600) via Goodenough Peak (7408)	3.0	6.5
Horseshoe Pass (7000)	3.0	9.5
Teapot Dome Camp(6880)	5.3	14.8
Scheelite Pass (6173)	5.9	20.7
Tungsten Mine, Tungsten Creek Trail No. 534 (6800)	2.6	23.3
Apex Pass (7280)	1.8	25.1
Cathedral Pass (7640)	3.0	28.1
Upper Cathedral Lake (7400)	.7	28.8
Spanish Camp, Andrews Creek Trail No. 504	4.1	32.9
Ashnola River(5040)	7.1	40.0
Martina Creek (5863)	1.7	41.7
Junction before Barker Brown Cabin basin (6600)	1.7	43.4
Peeve Pass (6840), Larch Creek Trail No. 502	1.5	44.9
Park Pass Trail No. 506 (6640)	.5	45.4
Whistler Pass/Sand Ridge Trail (6900)	1.0	46.4
Quartz Lake Trail (6840)	.3	46.7
Dean Creek Camp (6400)	3.0	49.7
Bunker Hill (7239)	2.9	52.6
Dean Creek Trail No. 456 (7085)	.2	52.8
East Fork Pasayten River (3960), Hidden Lakes Trail No. 477	6.5	59.3
Pasayten River Bridge (3920)	.7	60.0
Harrison Creek (4000) via Pasayten River	1.2	61.2
Pasayten Airfield (4279)	3.8	65.0
Chuchuwanteen Creek (4600)	4.0	69.0
Frosty Lake (5343)	3.0	72.0
Pacific Crest Trail No. 2000, Castle Pass (5451)	3.6	75.6
Hopkins Pass (6122) via PCT	3.3	78.9
Woody Pass (6624)	5.1	84.0
Holman Pass (5050)	5.9	89.9
Canyon Creek (4910)	.7	90.6
Sky Pilot Pass (6280)	2.5	93.1
Devil's Pass (6060)	4.8	97.9
Devil's Dome (6982)	3.2	101.1
Devil's Junction Campsite (1800)	5.5	106.6
Ruby Creek Bridge	12.2	118.8

State Highway 20	.2	119.0
Ross Dam (1617)	4.5	123.5

ROUTE DESCRIPTION

From the Cold Springs upper camp roadhead, go due north on the old prospecting jeep trail. You will climb steeply through lodgepole and fir. Where this jeep trail traverses open, grassy slopes, you will have noted from the campground a long, receding wooded valley, north-bordered by a large, mostly bare hill; beyond this valley (North Draw) you will see massive mountain abutments. Keep this view in mind because the cleft at the end of Long Draw is our first Pasayten Wilderness destination, Horseshoe Basin. Most of our route will be across the fabulous mountain meadows east of Long Draw.

The jeep trail introduces us to the broad, open-basin country so typical of the Pasayten. After a 2-mile climb via jeep trail across the northwest slopes of Chopaka, we reach a col between Knob 7160' and Joe Mills Mountain (7716). The latter is actually a subsidiary peak of Chopaka (7882). (The water available on these slopes may or may not be good to drink; leaching cow pies are everywhere.)

From the col an old cattle driveway continues northwest, away from the jeep trail, behind Knob 7160' down to Olallie (berry) Creek. To follow this steep, rocky, viewless trail, turn off the jeep road at the col. This unattractive driveway emerges in the cheery little valley of Olallie Creek at the ruins of a drovers' cabin. The treeless south slope here is creased by decades of cattle hooves, and sometimes it is hard to tell the difference between the trail and the animal paths. But make your way along the Olallie Creek Trail 1.5 miles downstream to its junction at 5700' with an unnamed tributary of the North Fork Toats Coulee Creek. The broken-down remains of the cattlemen's Snowshoe Cabin mark this junction. Fill your canteens here.

There is a much better route west from the col between Knob 7160' and Joe Mills Mountain. However, it involves some cross-country forest hiking. It initially follows cattle trails to contour through incredibly beautiful meadows between the summit of Knob 7160' and the vast lodgepole-pine forest below. (There is at least one seep as you cross these pastures.) Continue contouring the south-exposure meadows until you reach the steep, forested drop to Olallie Creek opposite Goodenough Park. Follow your compass west northwest (280-290°) down to the stream and trail junction at Snowshoe Cabin. Because this cross-country route has no trail indicators, do not attempt it in bad weather.

A sign at the cabin ruins indicates the direction of the trail to Horseshoe Basin. Go .3 mile north on this trail (i.e., in the direction of Snowshoe Mountain) and look for an old trail departing southwest. Note the cairn and the initials "P.N.W.T." on an old blaze. Follow this unmaintained trail up the south side of Goodenough Park and along the ridge which peaks out, so to speak, at Goodenough Peak (7408), a very scenic gateway into the Pasayten. From it we have a grandstand view of Arnold Peak's mellow pastures, Horseshoe Basin's open spaces, and Horseshoe Mountain's curved bulk. Beyond to the southwest is pointy, enormous Windy Peak.

The distance from the unnamed creek across Goodenough Park and Goodenough Peak to the Long Draw Trail is 3 miles. Long Draw Trail No. 340 contours 3 miles along the lower slopes of 8076' Arnold Peak to a major trail junction at Horseshoe Creek at Horseshoe Pass (7000). An excellent creek is located about halfway, at Lone Wolf Camp.

At Horseshoe Pass, side trail 533D goes one mile to Smith Lake. Also, from the pass you can go south to Windy Peak 5.7 miles via Trail No. 533 and Windy Trail No. 342. Don't miss this memorable side-trip goal at 8384' elevation.

So far all of our efforts have been directed merely at reaching the Pasayten Wilderness. We have arrived in this scenic parkland, and now the fabulous Cascade Crest is calling from 65 miles west across Boundary Trail No. 533. Plus, we have 52.2 miles more after that to the end of this chapter at Ross Dam. And, as you will discover, this is not exactly level walking.

The Boundary Trail is a heavy-duty, easy-to-follow, superbly scenic route. Nowadays the size of stock parties is restricted to twelve animals; everyone must obtain a wilderness permit.

The Boundary Trail has many spectacular views. The reason is simple —long Cascade upland ridges and many summit crossings. Even where the trail is not crowding the edge of some great gulf like here at Horseshoe Basin and beyond, we can see plenty of near and distant peaks. The view at Louden Lake is typical. This shallow pond occupies part of a flat between aptly named Rock Mountain and the western, outer slopes of Arnold Peak. Meadow Grass is the predominant vegetation. Isolated subalpine firs grow singly or in threes, fours, and fives nearby or straggle up the slopes. A pretty scene. And despite at least a half century of use by large horse parties and by cattle herds and sheep flocks and recently by a few back-packers, Louden Lake, like the rest of the Boundary Trail, is in excellent, natural condition. Let's keep it that way.

From Horseshoe Pass (7000) to the south end of Haig Mountain at Dome Camp (6880), we travel 5.3 miles with constantly changing views of Windy Peak. The terrain has no radical elevation changes—just great adventure. We pass Wagon Track Camp and Fireplace Camp. Dome Camp, located among widely scattered lodgepole pines, has a picnic table and flat spot for a tent.

The next convenient stopping place is 8.5 miles west at the old Tungsten Mine. This claim was developed during World War I by teenaged Paul Louden and his older partners. PNWT hikers alway stay in the long cookhouse or the cozy cabin above it. Look for the large iron bathtub (rechristened a horse trough in 1983) that Paul Louden packed in about seventy years ago on his mule Jack.

Haig Mountain and Bauerman Ridge make excellent cross-country routes. Instead of following the trail across their south slopes, you could make an excellent high traverse across the open, inviting summit ridges to Scheelite Pass.

From the Tungsten Mine at Wolframite Mountain, the trail makes a swing north up the headwaters of Tungsten Creek and around south to Apex Pass. The trail crosses here into the upper Chewack River watershed. Apex Pass (7280) is between Apex Mountain (8297) and the long, northwesterly ridge that connects north to Cathedral Peak and the Canadian border. The Chewack River tributary named Cathedral Creek drains the great basin between Apex Pass and Cathedral Pass. Like so much of the eastern Pasayten, this area was burned in the great forest fires of the late 1920s. For decades the silvery, standing snags from those conflagrations were a characteristic Pasayten sight. Now most of them crisscross the ground with their ant-bait trunks. The height of the few standing veterans is already beginning to be equalled by the lodgepoles growing up all around them. At Cathedral Pass you can see a fascinating souvenir of the Cathedral Creek fire of more than fifty years ago. Especially on cool, mid-September autumnal days you will notice a vibrant band of yellow just below the pass. These larches were spared by the fire, perhaps because of a backdraft coming through the cleft between Cathedral Peak (8601) and Amphitheater Mountain (8269, 8358).

One of the nice things about the 3-mile approach to Cathedral Pass is that from just beyond Apex Pass you can see the trail contouring around to the head of the creek gully and then climb directly up to the bare, rocky col. Another nice thing is the surprise view up there of a flat basin dotted with scattered fir copses. Upper Cathedral Lake is nestled below the abrupt walls of Amphitheater Mountain's Knob 8252' offshoot ridge. We descend .7 mile to the lake, a good campsite, and continue to the Lower Cathedral Lake junction across a dramatic slope of enormous boulders.

Although no place here is more than a two- or three-day walk out to civilization, we are definitely well beyond the range of most travellers. You might meet a trailriding party at Barker Brown Cabin or Dean Creek, or perhaps some Canadians on a day trip. But, in general, this north central wilderness is the province of the dedicated distance traveller. If you want to guarantee yourself maximum solitude, come here in the off-season. Then you will be unlikely to meet anyone but your shadow—and probably not even him.

Spanish Camp, named for the area's Basque shepherds, is 4.1 miles farther. The old cabin is at the edge of a wood just below Rock Mountain. About a mile beyond the Lower Cathedral Lake junction, we pass a boggy flat and a reflecting pool, beyond which Remmel Mountain seems to rise out of thin air.

Next we pass two branches of the Remmel Lake Trail. And finally, after a relatively long time in the trees, we come to the cabin at Spanish Camp (6850). This ranger patrol station is one of the very few remaining cabins scattered throughout this prime grazing country. Spanish Camp cabin is securely locked against men and critters, but you could release your mount in its corral or feed your own hunger on its porch. Bald Mountain

(7931) makes a bare, rounded backdrop to the functional, sturdy cabin.

Leave the cabin's multiple stock trails behind and cross the creek on the Boundary Trail west toward Bald Mountain. This soon becomes another long, horizon-filled ridge trip. The broad, open, grassy upland northwest of Bald Mountain's bare summit is as fine a stroll as you could wish for. We are consistently at elevations here above seven thousand feet. However, to enjoy this upland to the maximum, follow the old Boundary Trail route (as marked on the USGS map) up Bald Mountain from the cabin. Between the cabin and the Ashnola River, the relocated, easier-grade version contours below the most spectacular parts of this ridge. Whichever route you choose, you may wish in good weather to camp on the ridge to enjoy its superb 360-degree views of this remote country. Carry up water or search for some in the boggy meadows located above the forested Ashnola River Valley.

The last part of this 7.1-mile, Spanish Camp–Ashnola River day is an interminable series of switchbacks on newly reconstructed trail. Looking ahead at the flood-scoured mouth of Timber Wolf Creek or at Sand Ridge and Sheep Mountain makes you realize what a big country this really is and what a healthy chunk of elevation you must soon regain.

The old shelter at the Ashnola River (5040) is in good condition, but there are also many fine places to set up your tent. This bottom country is beautiful for fishing, relaxing, or soaking in the sun. In bad weather it's a good layover until the heights have cleared. West of the Ashnola the trail ascends rapidly, jogging north 1.7 miles to the Martina Creek/Ramon Lakes trail (5863). Before Martina Creek we cross the scenic, rocky gorge of an unnamed Ashnola River tributary.

The Park Pass/Ramon Lakes trail is an excellent loop trip up into the Basque sheepherding country. The trail loops entirely around Sheep Mountain and rejoins the Boundary Trail beyond Peeve Pass.

Once we are up out of the Ashnola, it's high country for many miles amidst the open spaces to which PNWT pilgrims are usually accustomed. Not far out of the trees, where the route opens up into long views of sky, grass, and Sand Ridge, we reach a junction (6600) where we turn right uphill to contour around the edge of the unnamed creek basin. The other way crosses through the basin and past the ruins of the Barker Brown Cabin, an old prospecting site, which is often used in summer by a local outfitter for his dudes and their riding mounts and pack stock.

Peeve Pass (6840), between Sheep Mountain and Sand Ridge, offers a side trip south on Sand Ridge to Whistler Basin and more prime meadowlands. Or from a junction a mile north of Peeve Pass, we could connect with the Sheep Mountain/Park Pass/Ramon Lakes Trail No. 506 mentioned earlier. Descend from Peeve Pass to a meadow basin, a good camping place with plenty of water and natural horse feed.

Next we contour up through woods to Quartz Mountain. At the head of the North Fork of Mayo Creek, we meet a ½-mile side trail to Quartz Lake. This classic high-country lake makes a charming campsite.

Quartz Mountain itself is a grandstand viewing platform for our best views yet of the Cascade Crest. Because the Boundary Trail contours along the treeless slopes for almost three miles at about 7100', we behold a most fascinating puzzle of peaks stretching across the western horizon, the many mountains where the Pacific Crest Trail threads its way from Canada toward Mexico, two thousand miles south. Very soon we will be over on the Crest exploring those famous mountains, including volcanic-glacier-clad Mount Baker, which we first glimpse from Quartz Mountain.

Nearer at hand we have progressively better views of the long, mostly treeless ridge known as Bunker Hill (7239). To reach it, we descend from Quartz Mountain's pole- and cairn-marked upland trail to the divide at the main headwaters of Dean Creek. At the bottom of this draw, look upstream a short distance for an old horse camp hidden away on the right bank of the stream. The next reliable water west from here (except for snowbanks) is beyond Bunker Hill summit.

Before climbing the Bunker Hill ridge, the Boundary Trail first crosses the 1.5 mile length of Knob 6671', a mostly wooded trail with excellent views north and east of a decade-old burn and of Sheep Mountain's inviting meadows.

Bunker Hill repeats and magnifies our Quartz Mountain views of the Cascade Crest. Follow the forest trail up to the ridge-line approach to the summit. A skirmish line of firs defends the ridge's relatively gentle south slope. The trail passes through these trees and into the open not far from the burnt remains of the old lookout cabin.

In the broad meadowland west of the summit, we are joined by Dean Creek Trail No. 456. Then, crossing a beautiful greensward, the Boundary Trail swings below and west of Bunker Hill's north ridge to an excellent, grassy campsite on the headwaters of Bunker Hill Creek. From here the Pasayten River (6½ miles) is all downhill through thick forest. This can be a long stretch, and the first water is not until we cross Bunker Hill Creek, almost at the bottom. The trail, however, does not drop straight to the river but curves to parallel it to the East Fork Pasayten River. This part is pleasant, level walking.

There is a good, forested campsite on the East Fork, but only .7 mile farther will bring you to the Pasayten River Bridge (3920). Immediately across the bridge is a riverside campsite. You can find a better one, more open to the sun, by following the trail inland a short distance to the Pasayten River Trail. From there you will find an excellent riverside camp a short distance north and/or the Harrison Camp one mile south.

The Pasayten River, north or south, is an excellent link with the outside world. Two miles north, not far beyond the Canadian border, the river crosses a rickety swaying bridge, which is unsteadily suspended from two long cables. At this point you could hike part of British Columbia's Centennial Trail, a rather incomplete path between the Cathedral Lakes country (just north of the PNWT's Cathedral Pass) and Vancouver, B.C. Or from the large clearcut that was visible from Bunker Hill, you could follow the logging road about 20 miles north to British Columbia Highway 3. From there you can reach pay showers, dining, lodging, and regular bus service at Manning Park Lodge, about 5 miles west. There is no food store at the Lodge, but they will hold mailed packages for long-distance hikers. (Write: Manning Park Lodge, Manning Provincial Park, British Columbia, VOX IRO Canada.) And if you walk north to the border, be sure to look for the little side trail to the Parson Smith Tree.

From the trail junction west of the Pasayten River bridge, go southwest 1.2 miles along the river trail to the Harrison Creek Trail junction (4000), an access route to this area via Monument 83 and Manning Park. A short distance later we reach delightful Harrison Camp on the Pasayten River.

The entire 5-mile southwesterly route from the Pasayten River bridge to the old Pasayten Landing Field follows pleasant woodland corridors with rare river views, occasional creek crossings, and easy, undulating terrain. There is a good campsite at Soda Creek (4200). Because of current Forest Service wilderness regulations, the Pasayten Landing Field is no longer maintained as an emergency airstrip, and small trees are beginning to cover the north end of the runway. However, the sturdy, log Guard Station cabin and the barn and horse corral are still in good condition. The runway now serves as good pasture for stock parties.

The PNWT goes directly across the north end of the airstrip into the woods for the ascent up Soda Creek. After contouring above a pretty forested gorge, the trail crosses to the north bank and follows the North Fork of Soda Creek to a spruce and fir divide, where murky Dead Lake is a good swimming hole in hot weather. There is no good camping at Dead Lake (5062), but you can find a spot a mile downhill at the Chuchuwanteen River (4560). The distance from the airstrip to the Chuchuwanteen River is 4 miles; from the river to Frosty Pass totals 6 miles.

The heavily forested, wide valley of Frosty Creek is our dramatic entrance to the heights of the Cascade Crest. The first 5 miles in thick timber accentuate the final climb out of the vividly stratified upper basin to Frosty Pass. Before the series of sharp switchbacks begins, we reach the unattractive Frosty Lake horse camp (5343). Much nicer, but less protected, campsites exist in the high basin below Mount Winthrop and at Frosty Pass; the former has water but the latter requires a long water-carry uphill.

To reach Frosty Pass the Boundary Trail switchbacks steadily up from Frosty Lake northwest onto the open slopes of Mount Winthrop. At about 6200' we loop around a high tributary of Frosty Creek and contour out west to the pass.

At Frosty Pass (6500) we finally leave the vast Columbia River drainage, which we have been following ever since Brown Pass on the Continental Divide. From Frosty Pass we drop very steeply .6 mile west down to Castle Pass (5451) and Pacific Crest Trail No. 2000.

Castle Pass is a rather swampy area between Route Creek, which flows north and joins Castle Creek going into Canada and the Castle Fork of Big Face Creek. The Okanogan/Whatcom County ridge divides these two west-of-the-Crest drainages. In fact, Castle Pass Trail No. 749 goes west along this divide, eventually to reach Ross Lake via either the Willow Lake

Trail or the Lightning Creek Trail. From Castle Pass, Manning Park Lodge and Highway 3 are only 11.3 miles north.

Our next destination, however, is Holman Pass, 14.3 miles south across what is generally considered to be the best scenery in the entire 2500 miles of the Crest Trail. From Castle Pass we go south on the combined PCT/PNWT national scenic trails. We traverse the west slopes of Blizzard Peak for 3.3 miles above the Castle Fork to rise gradually to 6122' at Hopkins Pass. This route is mostly through forest, but there are occasional openings, especially the avalanche chute where a high branch of the Castle Fork tumbles across the trail from below the summit.

At Hopkins Pass a sign describes the Chuchuwanteen Creek Trail as "abandoned." This trail would be a convenient loop trip back to our earlier Chuchuwanteen River crossing. From Hopkins Pass we switchback up almost to the top of Knob 6873', where we regain the Crest. A little way up from this pass we meet a side trail to Hopkins Lake, a good place to camp.

The scenic 5.1-mile passage from Hopkins Pass to Woody Pass contours south mostly between 6600' and 6800', except where it is higher, between Hopkins Lake and halfway along Lakeview Ridge. This is a superb route and offers outstanding views from the Devil's Stairway, Knob 7126', and the PCT section that temporarily follows the top of Lakeview Ridge. Beyond, where the trail drops west off the ridgetop, we come to a side trail down a gully to a good campsite with pasture and water at Mountain Home Camp. The PCT/PNWT continues south across open slopes to Woody Pass (6624).

At this pass between Knob 7381' and Powder Mountain (7714) we cross over to continue our southward course on the east side of the Cascade Crest, now above the headwaters of U-shaped, avalanche-chuted Rock Creek Valley. Woody Pass, as befits its name, does have weatherbeaten larches and subalpine firs, but dominant is the enormous, beetling rock massif of Powder Mountain, which looms weightily over PNWT and PCT pilgrims. There we cross back to the west side of the Crest. Beyond Woody Pass the currently maintained trail switchbacks below the conglomerate and slate scree slopes and up again to Rock Pass (6491). Two higher scree-slope routes have been abandoned. Several seeps, springs, and creeks exist between Woody Pass and Holman Pass.

The trail crosses the Crest about 300 yards southeast of Rock Pass and contours south below Holman Peak at the 6400' level before dropping down to a good spring and campsite at 6200'. The view here is spectacular of the Canyon Creek Valley, which we will soon cross after following an easy grade down to Holman Pass. The Goat Lakes are an off-trail, potential stopping place southeast of the spring and are reached by following the meadow uphill to their picturesque basin.

Holman Pass (5050) is the heavily wooded, viewless junction where the Pacific Crest Trail is bisected by Holman Creek Trail No. 472A (from the West Fork Pasayten River) and by Devil's Ridge Trail No. 752. Here the PNWT leaves the PCT and we descend steeply .7 mile to Canyon Creek, where there is a fine, small campsite in old-growth subalpine-fir forest. A short distance down from Holman Pass we go by the low-roofed Yon Dodge Cabin. Yon Dodge (1911–1971) was a sheepherder, and his cabin is very low because he was only five feet two inches tall.

About a mile up from Canyon Creek at about 5720', there is an excellent campsite with a fine creek. We then contour south up to Sky Pilot Pass via Devil's Ridge Trail No. 752. A good side trip at Sky Pilot Pass (6280) is to climb the Chancellor Trail No. 754 south to Knob 6711' (Chancellor Campground is 7 miles south via this trail). From its open, grassy summit, Canyon Creek Valley spreads out before us, showing the way we have come across the Crest. Also, while you're here, be sure to look for flat-topped, lookout-towered Slate Peak to the south and for the long western sweep of our trail to Devil's Pass and Devil's Dome via the classic U-shaped valley of the North Fork of Canyon Creek.

From Sky Pilot Pass we drop down 1.3 miles to 5280' Deception Pass (between Shull Creek and the North Fork of Canyon Creek). This gloomy, aptly named minor pass lacks both campsites and reliable water. From it we gradually climb 3.5 miles west below the unnamed ridge of Knob 7514' to the head of the valley and Devil's Pass. The beautiful, open second-half of this climb is notable for broad valley views, snow patches, and sharply tilted sedimentary rocks.

There is a very fine spring 800 feet before grassy Devil's Pass on a side trail down to a shelter in a little basin. An interesting side trip is the popular loop trail south to Devil's Park, Macmillan Park, and Canyon Creek (the same Canyon Creek we crossed earlier). Our next high-country traverse is the best part of this end of the Pasayten Wilderness and here, once again, we enjoy mile after mile of ridgetop views.

Devil's Dome at 6982' is the center of this splendid, stop-and-stare scenery along the direct route. After 1.9 miles we come to a good potential camping area southeast of Knob 6881' on an arm above a basin—where, by the way, there is likely to be plenty of snowmelt water. After crossing that arm, we contour up Devil's Ridge and switchback sharply to the windy summit of Devil's Dome. Note especially Mount Baker and the Pickets to the west, Valhalla-like Skagit Peak to the North, and our Cascade Crest route to the northeast. Here we also begin to be conscious of Ross Lake, which, although nearby, is a full mile lower in elevation. If there is a highlight to the wonders here it must be the yawning gulf that separates the 9066' summit of Jack Mountain from the valley floor beneath its glaciers.

Across more beautiful upland trail, 1.6 miles farther west, there is a short side trail to the Bear Skull Shelter, a good place to camp, especially in bad weather or huckleberry season. (The lookout cabin on Devil's Dome no longer exists.)

Ross Lake is 5.5 miles west down the very steep, wooded Devil's Dome Trail. Although this trail is in good condition, your knees won't be when you have finished it. Or when it has finished with you. The first two-thirds of the trail offers incomparable views of the greatest vertical mountain face on the entire PNWT—Jack Mountain. We contour down, steeply at first, from heather meadows to dry slopes of white pine, lodgepole pine, and fir and then to cool woods of vine maple, alder, and sword fern. Eventually, after many switchbacks in thick cedar and fir forest, we reach the lakeside trail and a way trail to the excellent Devil's Junction campsite. (During the summer Park Service reservations are required at all the *established* lakeside campsites.)

You may wish to arrange in advance for a Ross Lake Resort boat to carry you over to the west bank. This would not only be shorter, avoiding State Highway 20, but would help to maintain your Pasayten Wilderness feelings of remoteness into the adjacent North Cascades National Park.

Ross Lake's level, excellent East Bank Trail is a delightful contrast to the radical elevation changes we have just experienced. The alders give it a sweet lowland smell, but there are also beautiful birches, vine and bigleaf maples, western red cedars, Douglas firs and a ground cover of Oregon grape and ferns.

We cross a long suspension bridge (suitable for pack stock) over precipitous Devil's Creek gorge. We pass a mossy seep where the trail has been blasted into the devil's-food-cake swirls of the lakeside rock. There are so many things to see here—the fir-tipped points, the misty cliffs, and the blinding-white glaciers. In addition to the lake itself, other water sources are never too far away.

The East Bank Trail passes several good campsites: Devil's Junction; Rainbow Point (3.7 miles); May Creek (.9 mile); and Roland Point (1.3 miles). Then it contours inland 3.7 miles on the lowest slopes of Jack Mountain, south over Hidden Hand Pass (2520), and past Ruby Horse Pasture to the Ruby Creek Trail No. 736. You will be amidst mosses, ferns, hermit thrushes, cedars, mushrooms, and Douglas firs. In 2.6 more miles, via the old placer mining route, we reach 1950-vintage Ruby Creek Bridge, where there is a small campsite.

From the bridge go .2 mile up to 12-year-old State Highway 20, along which water is available but not good camping. Before this blasted-out-of-the-rock speedway was built, the North Cascades were an unbroken two-hundred-mile skein of wilderness valleys, ridges, creeks, mountains, and glaciers. Perhaps a way to regain the illusion of what was before would be to construct a new lakeshore trail here, at water's edge below the road.

During your 4.5-mile road walk, don't let the whizzing cars and trucks distract you from the occasional scenic vistas of the south end of the lake. Late summer and early autumn are pretty times to visit because the water level is likely to be up and the old stumps will not be visible. (The state of Washington does not plough this road after the first heavy snows.)

There is no official camping at the Ross Dam parking lot, but for a person on foot the seclusion of the forest is everywhere. From the Ross Dam parking lot, an .8-mile tourist trail takes us down to the great concrete impoundment. We pass a fine creek, which splashes by enormous trees and the mosses, devil's club, and ferns that make this moist, enchanted west end of our Pasayten trip so different from its east end's sagebrush meadows and upland ridges.

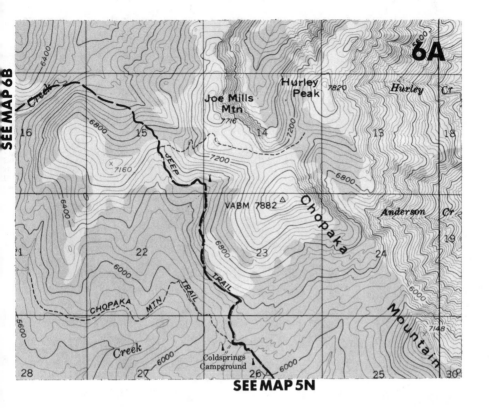

SEE MAP 6B

6A

Hurley Peak 7820

Joe Mills Mtn 7716

Hurley Cr

Creek

16

15

14

7200

13

18

6400

6800

JEEP

7200

7160

6800

VABM 7882

Chopaka

Anderson Cr

21

22

6800

23

24

19

6400

6000

TRAIL

6800

7148

5600

CHOPAKA MTN TRAIL

6000

Mountain

6000

Creek

6000

28

27

Coldsprings Campground

26

6000

25

30

SEE MAP 5N

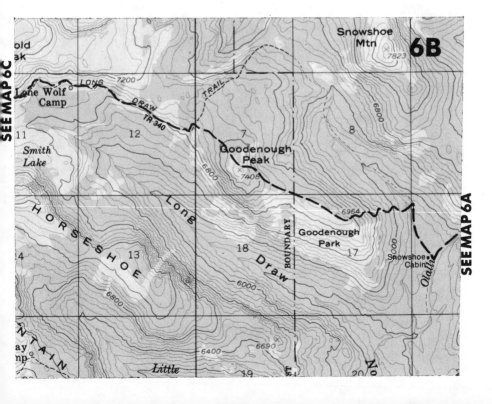

Snowshoe Mtn

6B

old ak

7823

SEE MAP 6C

LONG

7200

TRAIL

Lone Wolf Camp

DRAW

TR 340

6800

11

12

7

8

Smith Lake

Goodenough Peak

6800

7408

6964

H O R S E S H O E

Long

BOUNDARY

Goodenough Park

SEE MAP 6A

4

13

18

17

Draw

Snowshoe Cabin

6000

Olalla

6000

N T A I N

ay np

6400

6690

Little

19

20

No

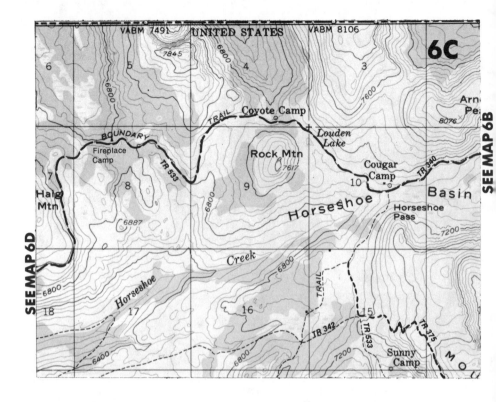

VABM 7491   UNITED STATES   VABM 8106

7845

6   5   4   3

6800

7600

Arn
Pe

8076

TRAIL   Coyote Camp

Louden
Lake

BOUNDARY

Fireplace
Camp

Rock Mtn

7617

Cougar
Camp

TR 340

Basin

7   8   9   10

TR 533

Haig
Mtn

6887

6800

Horseshoe

Horseshoe
Pass

7200

Creek

6800

TRAIL

6800

18   17   16   15

Horseshoe

6800

TR 342

TR 533

TR 375

6400   6800   7200

Sunny
Camp

M O U

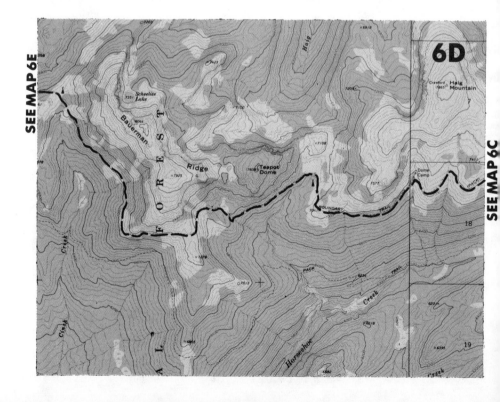

Haig

7461

Scheelite
Lake

7100

Crawford

Haig
Mountain

7

Bauerman

FOREST

7108

Ridge

Teapot
Dome

7571

Dome
Camp

BOUNDARY

TRAIL

18

PACK

Creek

Creek

Horseshoe

Creek

19

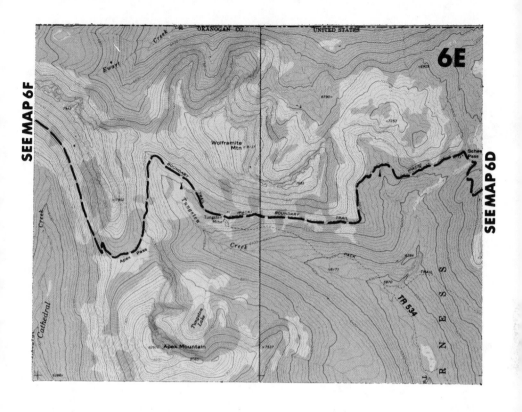

SEE MAP 6F

6E

SEE MAP 6D

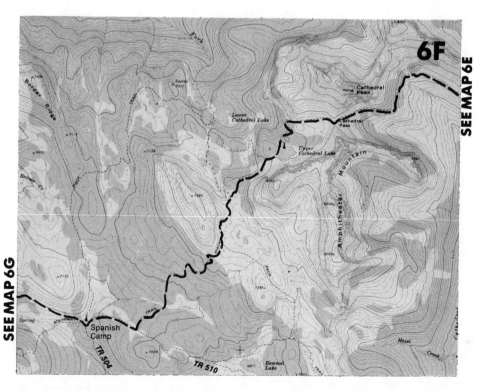

SEE MAP 6G

6F

SEE MAP 6E

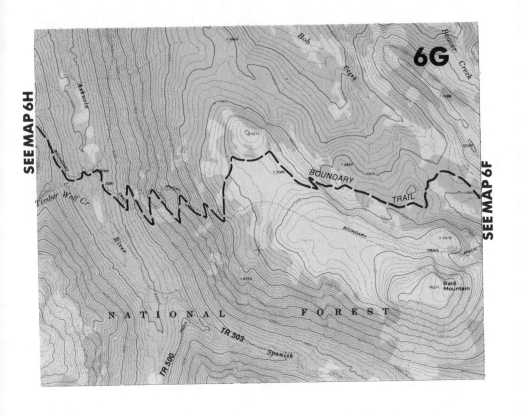

SEE MAP 6H

SEE MAP 6F

6G

Bob
Creek

Beaver
Creek

Ashnola

Timber Wolf Cr.

River

BOUNDARY   TRAIL

BOUNDARY

TRAIL   (PACK)

Bald
Mountain

N A T I O N A L   F O R E S T

TR 503

TR 500

Spanish

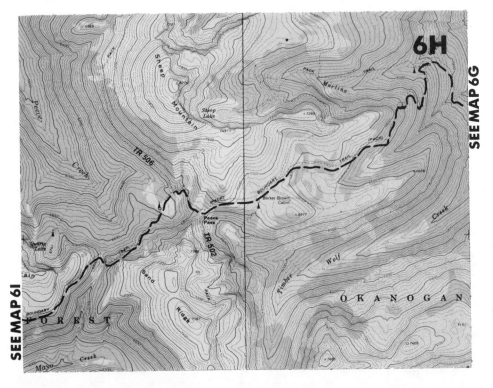

6H

SEE MAP 6G

SEE MAP 6I

Sheep
Mountain

Sheep
Lake

Martina

PACK

TRAIL

TR 506

Peeve
Creek

Quartz
Lake

BOUNDARY   Barker Brown
Cabin

TRAIL   (PACK)

Timber   Wolf   Creek

TR 502

Peeve
Pass

Sand

Ridge

BOUNDARY

F O R E S T   O K A N O G A N

Mayo   Creek

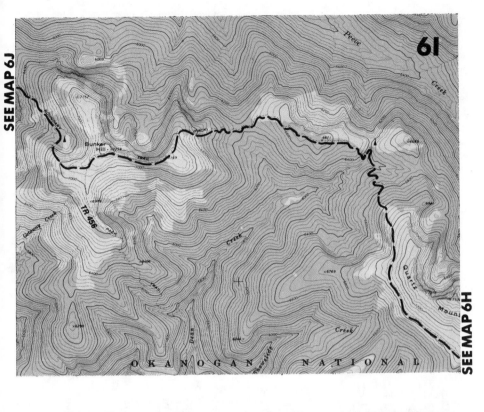

SEE MAP 6J

6I

SEE MAP 6H

OKANOGAN   NATIONAL

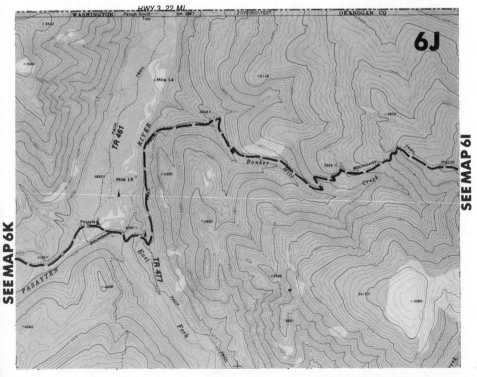

SEE MAP 6K

6J

SEE MAP 6I

WASHINGTON   OKANOGAN CO

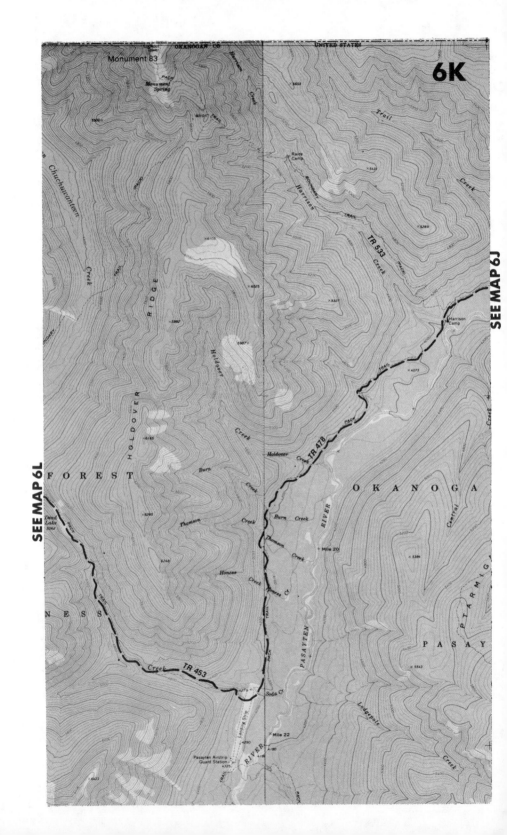

SEE MAP 6J

SEE MAP 6L

Tungsten Mine

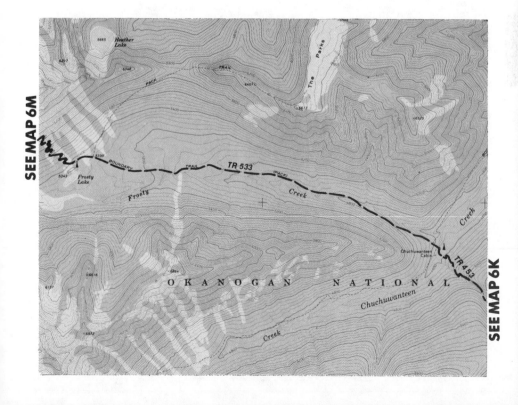

SEE MAP 6M

SEE MAP 6K

HWY 3 9.7 MI

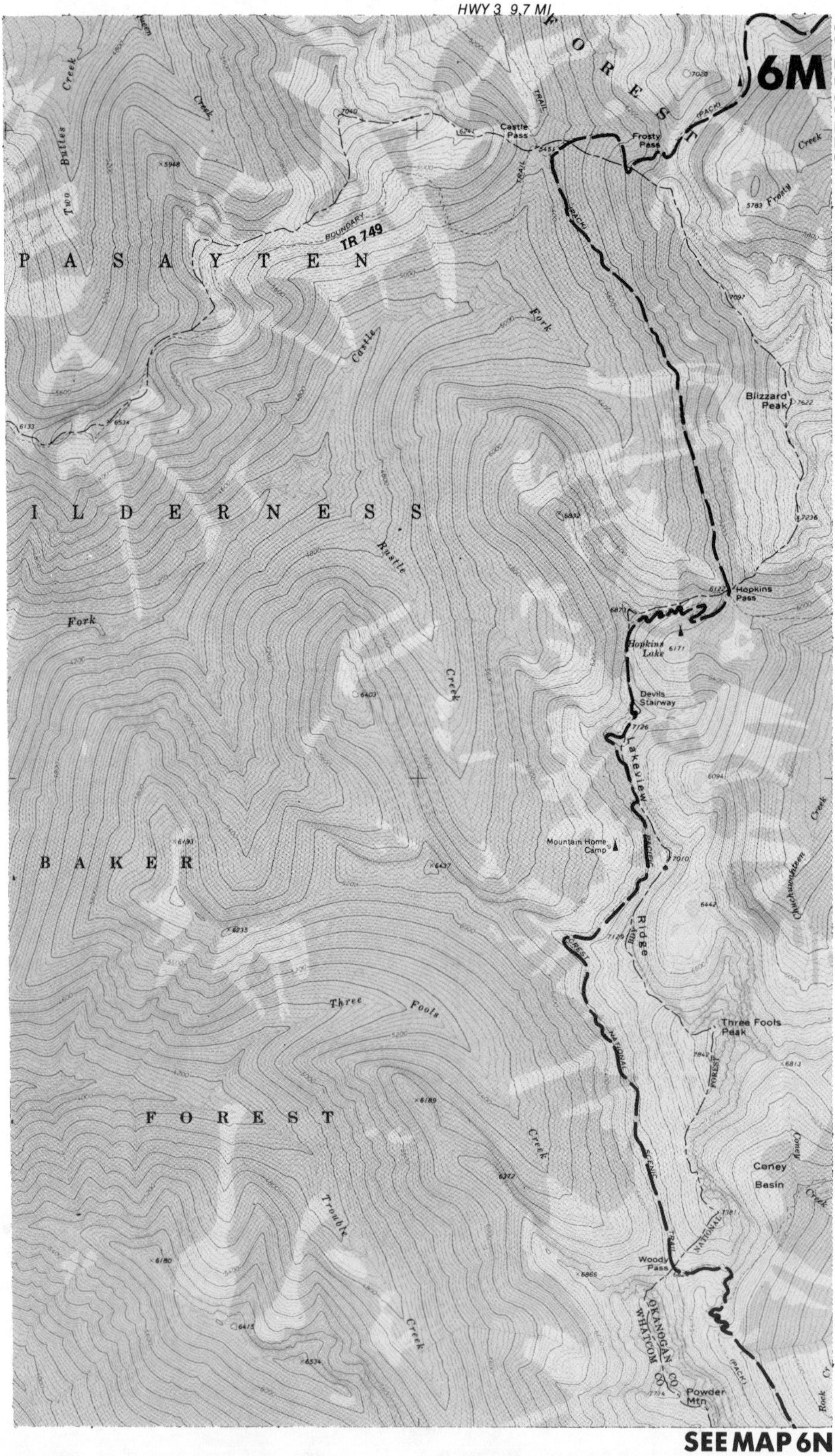
6M
P A S A Y T E N
ILDERNESS
B A K E R
F O R E S T
FOREST
BOUNDARY
TR 749
Castle Pass
Frosty Pass
Hopkins Pass
Blizzard Peak
Hopkins Lake
Devils Stairway
Lakeview
Ridge
Mountain Home Camp
Three Fools Peak
Coney Basin
Woody Pass
Powder Mtn
OKANOGAN CO
WHATCOM CO
Two Buttes Creek
Castle Fork
Rustle Creek
Three Fools Creek
Trouble Creek
Frosty Creek
Chuchuwanteen Creek
Coney Creek
TRAIL
(PACK)
NATIONAL SCENIC TRAIL

SEE MAP 6L

SEE MAP 6N

SEE MAP 6M

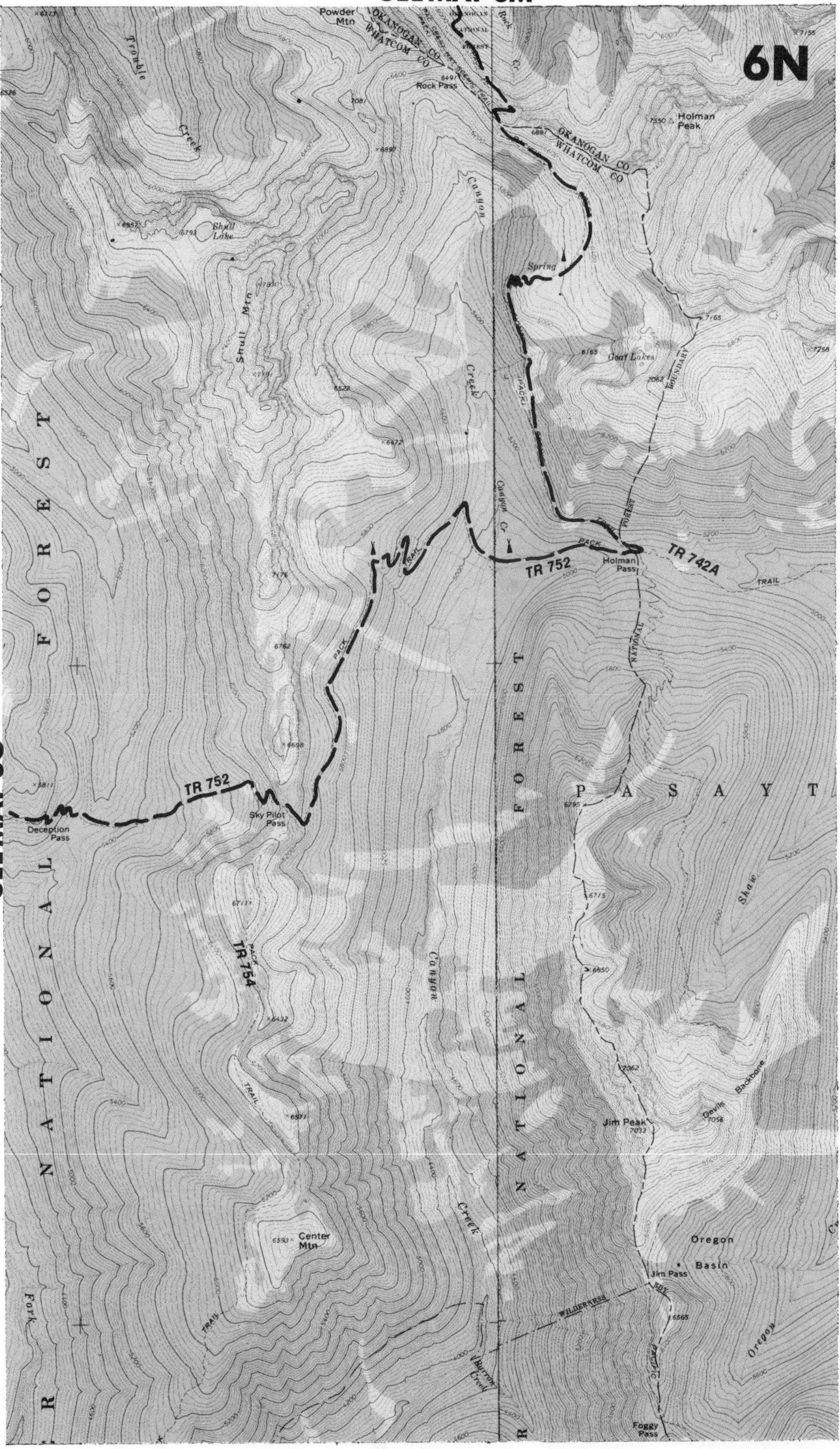
6N
Powder Mtn
OKANOGAN CO
WHATCOM CO
Rock Pass
Holman Peak
Trouble Creek
Shull Lake
Shull Mtn
Canyon Creek
Spring
Goat Lakes
BOUNDARY
PACK
Canyon Cr.
TR 752
Holman Pass
TR 742A
TRAIL
NATIONAL FOREST
Deception Pass
Sky Pilot Pass
TR 754
P A S A Y T
Shaw
Jim Peak
Devils Backbone
Center Mtn
Oregon Basin
Jim Pass
WILDERNESS
PACIFIC
Foggy Pass
Oregon
Fork
Barron Creek

SEE MAP 6O

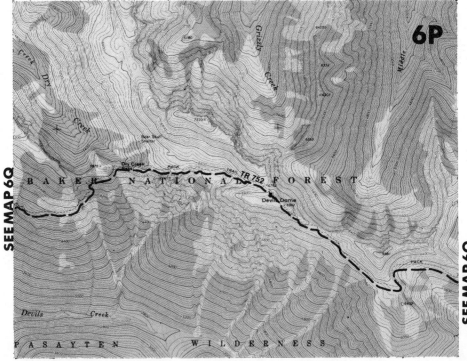

SEE MAP 6P
SEE MAP 6N
SEE MAP 6Q
SEE MAP 6O

6O

6P

Cinnamon

W I L D E R N E S S

TR 752

TRAIL

PACK TRAIL

North Fork Canyon Creek

North

Devils Pass

Spring

PACK

Trail

North Fork

Devils Cr.

PACK

Grizzly Creek

Middle

Dry Creek

Creek

Bear Skull Shelter

Dry Creek Pass

PACK

TRAIL

TR 752

Devils Dome

B A K E R   N A T I O N A L   F O R E S T

PACK

Devils   Creek

P A S A Y T E N   W I L D E R N E S S

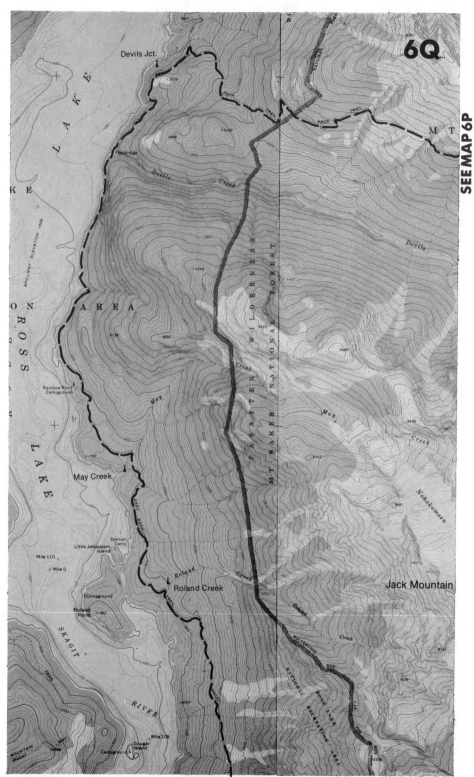

SEE MAP 6P

Devils Jct.

Footbridge

Devils Creek

PASAYTEN WILDERNESS

MT BAKER NATIONAL FOREST

Devils

May Creek

Creek

Rainbow Point Campground

Rainbow Point Campground

Spencer Camp

Little Jerusalem Island

Mile 110

Mile 0

Campground

Roland Creek

Roland Point

May Creek

Roland Creek

Jack Mountain

Nohokomeen

SKAGIT

RIVER

Mile 108

Cougar Island

Campground

WILDERNESS

NATIONAL

RECREATION AREA

MOUNTAIN

SEE MAP 6R

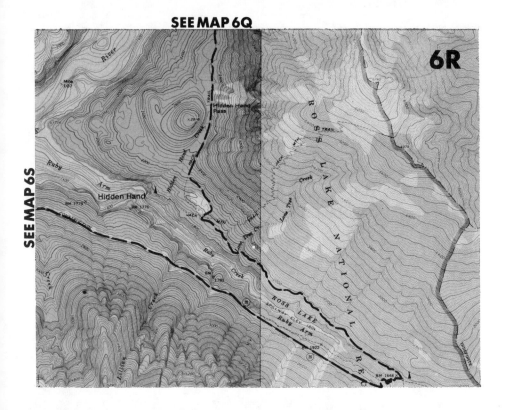

SEE MAP 6S

SEE MAP 7A

SEE MAP 6R

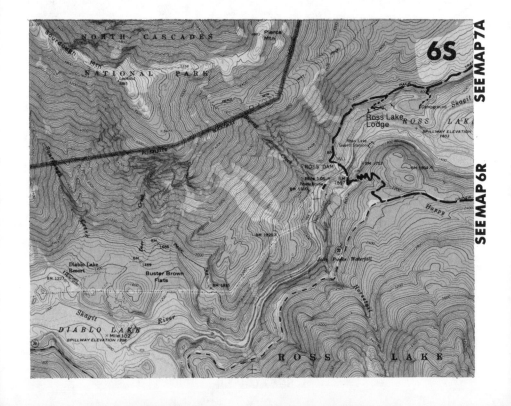

NORTH CASCADES TO SALT WATER
(The Upper Skagit to Chuckanut Drive)

Little Beaver Creek Valley

INTRODUCTION

This section is an excellent sample of the enormous variety to be found along the entire Pacific Northwest Trail. It includes both high alpine country and salt water, lakes and rivers, wilderness and towns. It crosses one national park and one national forest. Unlike most of the PNWT, it also includes much private and state land. This is the mountainous part of the Trail closest to the region's major population center in the metropolitan corridor between Olympia, Washington, and Vancouver, B.C. Thus there is some justification for considering these 137.5 miles as the PNWT's flagship section.

This chapter's Practical PNWT, however, is not yet as close to the Ideal Route as we would like. Getting the most out of the PNWT in the Mt. Baker area now involves considerable cross-country hiking. And at the western end of the Lookout Mountain/Chuckanut Mountain traverse (where we finally see our long-awaited views of salt water bays and islands), several years of volunteer trail-building are necessary to get the route off the low roads and onto the heights. As of this writing, we have completed construction of the first 5 miles of the Ideal Route east from Chuckanut Drive.

With *your* support this chapter's Ideal Route could become a reality in a relatively short time. Please help us to make the Mt. Baker-to-salt-water section a model for the entire Trail.

PROBLEMS

You may encounter unexpected changes because of new developments along both the Practical and Ideal Routes. Most of this section is being continually logged; trails are often obscured by new clearcuts.

Also, the trail ahead may be closed because you have arrived during the peak forest-fire season (unpredictable from year to year). Or you may be trying to get through in a year or season of exceptionally deep snow or heavy flooding. Contact our Association or public agency officials for the latest Trail condition reports.

To avoid potential difficulty in reserving campsites in North Cascades National Park and Ross Lake National Recreation Area, try writing in advance for a reservation and a wilderness permit to Backcountry Information, North Cascades National Park, Marblemount, WA 98267 (206/673-4590). During the summer there is usually a ranger, from whom permits are available, at the eastside boat ramp near Ross Dam.

SUPPLIES

Supplies both are and are not a problem in this section. They are not a problem because you are never very far from a small town, especially those along the Skagit River. However, supplies on the route itself are rather scarce. Packages may be sent ahead to the Ross Lake Resort at Rockport, WA 98283 (206/397-7735). Soda pop, candy bars, fishing tackle, and bait are sold at the resort but nothing else; the Barnetts have no restaurant there. They operate a taxi service for water transportation on Ross Lake. If you wish to be picked up somewhere up the lake, you must make a paid reservation in advance. There is no public transportation to or from Ross Dam.

The Diablo Lake Resort has a grocery store with a small selection of expensive supplies. Much better is the Marblemount store, 28 miles down the Skagit River from Ross Dam, on State Highway 20. In 1983 the Acme Grocery in Acme had a good selection of foodstuffs.

From North Chuckanut Mountain the Trail is within sight of the city of Bellingham. But because Bellingham is a confusing hodgepodge of non-parallel streets, be sure to stick to the following two, relatively easy access routes. First, Chuckanut Drive is a very scenic, long highway up the coast to town. Second, beginning at the PNWT between Lookout Mountain and Chuckanut Mountain a few hundred feet north of the I-5 crossing, walk northwest 2 miles on Samish Way to the bus stop at the Lake Padden Golf Course and City Park. (Catch it at 23 minutes after the hour between 6 a.m. and 6 p.m.; there are no Sunday buses.) Pay your 25 cents and get a transfer. Bellingham Mall (another 2¼ miles down the road) has a laundromat, a grocery store, a self-service postal station, and numerous other stores. Or ask your bus driver how to continue to downtown. There the bus station coin lockers are across the street from the YMCA, you could stash your gear in a coin locker while taking the YMCA's $1.50 shower. (If you meet a friendly student up the hill at Western Washington University, you might be able to shower at the university's gym.) There are two backpacking stores downtown; the Basecamp is located on Holly Street. The Friday *Bellingham Herald* has an events section about happenings in town and at the university. And, if you want to eat someone else's cooking, try the Mexican Village (5–8 p.m.), Jacques' Cafe (6 a.m.–2 p.m.), and Pauline's Cafe. The main post office is on Prospect Street downtown; it's the best place to pick up general delivery packages. Two blocks northeast is the library (open until 9 p.m. Mon.–Wed., otherwise until 6 p.m.) There is a free museum near the main post office; behind the P.O. look for the Maritime Heritage Center, and if you are an end-to-ender, ask to see the salmon hatchery and spawning channels for insight on a true long-distance trip.

DECLINATION   22½° E

USGS TOPOGRAPHIC MAPS

Ross Dam	Hamilton	15'
Pumpkin Mountain	Wickersham	15'
Mt. Prophet	Lake Whatcom	
Mt. Challenger 15'	Bellingham South	
Mt. Shuksan 15'	Alger	
Mt. Baker 15'	Bow	

MILEAGES   (total 138.5)

		Total
Ross Dam (1614)	0.0	0.0
Green Point Campground (1680)	.9	.9
Mouth of Beaver Creek (1618)	4.8	5.7
39 Mile Camp (1680)	5.0	10.7
Luna Camp (2480)	5.1	15.8
Beaver Pass (3620)	6.0	21.8
Stillwell Camp (Little Beaver Creek Junction) (2468)	1.8	23.6
Twin Rocks Camp (2647)	2.6	26.2
Whatcom Pass (5206)	5.0	31.2
Chilliwack River (2468)	3.9	35.1
Hannegan Pass (5066)	7.8	42.9
Ruth Creek Roadhead (3110)	3.6	46.5
Mt. Baker Highway junction (2011)	5.2	51.7
Mt. Baker Lodge (4034)	7.5	59.2

Trailhead on Austin Pass Road (4742)	1.0	60.2
Lake Ann Trail junction (3930)	3.0	63.2
Baker Lake Road 1144 (1440) via Swift Creek Trail No. 607	8.0	71.2
Boulder Creek Campground (1056) via Park Creek Camp Route	5.2	76.4
Cutoff Road 1114 (1002) via Baker Lake Road 11	3.1	79.5
Road 12 (2000) via Cutoff Road 1114	1.3	80.8
Wanlick Creek trail (2300) via Road 12	9.0	89.8
South Fork Nooksack River Road (1900) via Wanlick Trail	1.8	91.6
Lyman Pass (800) via South Fork Nooksack Road	14.0	105.6
Saxon (321) via Larson Bridge and Dyes Ranch site along South Fork Nooksack River	10.0	115.6
Wickersham (314) via Road 9 (the Deming-Wickersham Road)	1.5	117.1
Park (319) via Park-Wickersham Road	2.0	119.1
Lake Whatcom Boulevard (347)	.8	119.9
Cain Lake Road (401) via Camp No. 2 Road	2.8	122.7
I-5 (280) via Cain Lake, Palmer Lake, and Squires Lake	2.2	124.9
Lake Samish Road (290) via Nulle Road	1.0	125.9
D.N.R. Road SWC-1200 (1150) via Sutherland Road, Bear Creek Road, and bushwhacking	1.4	127.3
Lizard-Lily Lake Trail (1900)	1.8	129.1
Lizard Lake Campsite (2000)	.5	129.6
North Butte (2200)	1.0	130.6
Lily Lake Campsite (2010)	1.0	131.6
Samish Overlook Trail (1300)	2.3	133.9
Samish Overlook (1300)	1.5	135.4
Chuckanut Drive (120)	2.25	137.65
Samish Bay (0)	.1	137.75
Colony Creek's outlet on Samish Bay (0)	.75	138.5

ROUTE DESCRIPTION

From Highway 20 follow a well-trod tourist trail .8 mile from the parking lot down to Ross Dam (1617). From Ross Dam go 5.6 miles to the mouth of Big Beaver Creek (1618) along a good trail. After a side trail down to the floating cabins of the Ross Lake Resort, we stay high above the lake and enjoy fine views of Ruby Mountain, Ruby Arm, and Hidden Hand Pass. Later, halfway along this trail near the boating campground on Cougar Island, is the junction of the Pierce Mountain/Sourdough Mountain Lookout trail.

The Lookout (5985) makes an excellent 4.5-mile side trip from which the steep canyon of the Upper Skagit and its impressive hydropower works are dramatically laid out. This lookout was first located by the late Glee Davis (1885-1982), our Association's first honorary member. Glee had homesteaded with his mother, Lucinda Davis (for whom nearby Davis Mountain is named), in the 1890s. The family ran a roadhouse where Diablo Lake is today.

More woods walking brings us to the dramatic gorge and waterfall of Pierce Creek. We then switchback down sharply to lake level.

Just before a heavy-duty-steel stock bridge crosses the mouth of Big Beaver Creek, a short side trail takes us to the hikers-only Pumpkin Mountain Camp. Boaters' and horsemen's sites are located across the Big Beaver Creek bridge and ¼ mile toward the lake. Permits and reservations are required from the U.S. Park Service to camp in both the Ross Lake National Recreation Area and the North Cascades National Park. Permits for the campsites of your choice could be difficult to obtain during the height of the backcountry visitation season in August. "Primitive" camping permits (i.e., for camping away from the designated camps and shelters) are another possibility. We have not yet arranged for the creation of PNWT through-permits, valid in all parks and wildernesses along the Trail, such as those available to Pacific Crest Trail pilgrims.

Not long ago there was an excellent system of shelters in this area, but current Park Service policy generally restricts our camping to deep woods, non-shelter sites. All of the shelters and cabins have been dismantled except Beaver Pass ("emergency use only") and Graybeal.

Big Beaver and Little Beaver Creeks are the take-off points for some of America's most challenging mountain routes, particularly the very difficult Picket Traverse, and the one from Whatcom Pass north to Mt. Redoubt. In these valleys it is occasionally possible to see heavily laden Everest types weighted down with tons of carabiners, pitons, chocks, nuts, ropes, crampons, and ice axes. However, you do not need to be Sir Edmund Hillary to enjoy plentiful views of glaciers and permanent snowfields along this route.

Beaver Pass (3620), at the northern headwaters of Big Beaver Creek, is 16.1 miles from Ross Lake. The trail climbs very gradually for most of its length, passing several campsites and many immense cedars and hemlocks. We skirt beaver ponds, glimpse the icy heights of the Pickets, and finally ease up through silver-fir forest to the pass. Numerous cascades from the unseen, icy heights above intersect the main creek along its length. Here you will understand why these mountains are called the North *Cascades*.

From Beaver Pass go 1.8 wooded miles northwest down to the junction with the Little Beaver Creek trail at the site of the demolished Stillwell Shelter (2468). This trail, too, is excellent; the switchbacks have recently been relocated. Vistas of the sharply glaciated Little Beaver Creek Valley

Ross Lake's West Shore Trail

begin to open up. The trail goes westward 4.7 miles, climbing slowly, and has reached an elevation of 2947' by the time we arrive at the site of the demolished Twin Rocks Shelter. This enchanting spot at the head of the valley—where the trail begins to switchback up—is surrounded by massive walls, water the color of glacier-ground powder, water ouzels, alder thickets, and gravel bars. Falling, coursing, flashing water is the predominant sensation, but one punctuated from time to time by the artillery-shell report of massive ice blocks chunking off the edge of the Challenger Glacier into the valley below.

Whatcom Pass at 5206' is 2259 feet higher than the old Twin Rocks Shelter site, a height gained in less than one mile of a crow's-flight distance. The original prospectors' trail here was almost straight up. The more than one hundred switchbacks on the current trail are a model of the trail builder's art, but most people are too distracted by huckleberries (in season), long vistas, and wildly beating hearts to notice how beautifully constructed these switchbacks are.

Camping is no longer permitted at Whatcom Pass, but if you have time and good weather, be sure to take a short side trip out toward Challenger Glacier. (The distance over is deceivingly far and the glacier itself is for experts; Challenger got its name because it is a definite climbing challenge.)

Beyond the pass, water is available at Tapto Camp and at several points down Brush Creek to the Chilliwack River (2468). The Graybeal Shelter (built by the Forest Service in 1961) is available for camping 1.7 miles lower down this route. This wooded descent from Whatcom Pass's alpine beauty is only slightly less arduous and scenic than the climb.

Fording the Chilliwack River can be tricky in high-water times; people have drowned here. But the Park Service has recently built an excellent cable car, reached via a trail just up from the ford.

A highly scenic good-weather alternate route would be to go north

3.5 miles to the Fire Camp Shelter ford and journey west to regain the PNWT Chilliwack route via Copper Ridge, an additional distance of only 11.3 miles. The extra zillions of switchbacks are worth the effort, and the sunrise views from the Copper Mountain lookout (6260) of Bear Mountain, Indian Mountain, Mt. Redoubt, and Middle Peak are something you are unlikely to forget.

From the Brush Creek/Chilliwack River junction it is 1.7 miles, including the Chilliwack ford, west to the U.S. Cabin Camp.

Hannegan Pass (5066) is 7.8 miles up the Chilliwack River beyond its junction with the Brush Creek trail. The Chilliwack Trail alternates deep forest with avalanche chute openings. Until Copper Creek (2.6 miles from U.S. Cabin Camp) the ascent is gradual, with no surprises. But beyond the Copper Creek campsite, it climbs steadily past Hells Gulch to the Copper Ridge trail junction. The Boundary Camp is located at this junction (where we also pass from the North Cascades National Park into the Mount Baker-Snoqualmie National Forest).

Hannegan Pass separates the Skagit Range and Hannegan Peak (6186) and the Nooksack Ridge and Ruth Mountain (7106). The Ruth Creek trail descends 3.6 miles down the north side of lovely, steeply glaciated Ruth Creek to a roadhead (3110) where there is a shelter and many picnic-table-equipped campsites. After 5.2 miles of road walking on the Ruth Creek Road, we reach the Mt. Baker Highway on the North Fork of the Nooksack River. Camping is available at a historic cabin just before this junction and at the Silver Fir Campground.

Follow the Mt. Baker Highway 7.5 miles to the Mt. Baker Ski Area. Mail drops may not be sent to the Mount Baker Lodge (popular in winter but closed in summer) and supplies are not available there.

At Hannegan Pass, the Ideal Route to Baker starts out by contouring south around the east shoulder of Ruth Mountain, above tree line and below the present glacier line and past a high tarn to the gap between Ruth Mountain and Icy Peak (Incredible Passage, 5600'). From here we look across south to the white shoulders of Icy Peak and the Northeast Cirque headwaters of the Nooksack River. The headwall of this amazing cirque (Jagged Ridge) averages almost 8000 feet in elevation. The Nooksack Tower (8268) to the west sticks up like a grand rampart, with the summit of Mt. Shuksan (9127) peeping up behind. This southerly and westerly view is one of the greatest life has to offer, but turn around, peer back east, and behold the dazzling wildness of the Picket Range (Whatcom Peak, 7874; Challenger, 8236; Crooked Thumb, 8120; Phantom, 8045; Mt. Fury, 8299; and Mt. Terror, 8181). Uncle! Uncle!

The Incredible Passage gap is 5 miles from Hannegan Pass. Descend cross-country 3 more miles down to the Nooksack River (3360). In 5½ more miles we reach Price Lake (3895), after which another 6 miles of bushwhacking bring us to Galena Basin and Heather Meadows.

This bushwhacking on the west slopes of the Cascades involves (until this new trail section is built) steep talus, potential ice fields, thick Douglas-fir forest, briars, devil's club, and generally harder slogging than any PNWT bushwhacking section east of here, including the worst you have experienced in Montana and Idaho. But although your progress on the PNWT's Incredible Passage/Nooksack Cirque route may be painfully slow, the rewards will be correspondingly great.

The Practical Route from Mount Baker Lodge to Lyman Pass follows a paved road south, climbing 500 feet in 1 mile to our Austin Pass trailhead (4742). This is the divide between Mt. Shuksan's Shuksan Arm and Mt. Baker's Ptarmigan Ridge. The area is justly famous as a car-tourist destination; watch out for the gawking drivers as you walk. (Actually, the road climbs ½ mile farther to Artist Point and a close-up photograph vantage point of Mt. Baker's all-white volcanic cone.) A trail from the Lodge picnic area effectively shortcuts some of this road's switchbacks to our trailhead.

From the Austin Pass parking lot, the Lake Ann Trail No. 600 drops 3 miles into the headwaters of Swift Creek, descends southeasterly, and makes a large swing east to the junction (3930) of the Swift Creek Trail. The Lake Ann Trail is well travelled since it is a popular daytripper destination and since it is the main Shuksan climbing route from the Lodge. In good weather (Hah!) don't miss the many-switchbacks side trip to the Lower Curtis Glacier via Lake Ann, a typical high Cascades tarn.

The 8-mile Swift Creek Trail No. 607 is an unmaintained, extremely brushy route with two very uncertain river crossings at the lower end. Early in the season, beware of rotting snow bridges, which may collapse under your weight and dump you into glacial streams. And be prepared for nettles, devil's club, huckleberry brush, vine maple jungles, and other treats. Swift Creek can be very tiring, but it is also a dramatic, wild valley with high bluffs, a roaring tributary creek, and waterfalls. In just a few miles from the Mount Baker Lodge, we are back in the remote Cascades.

A few small campsites (with water) are available at the junction of the Lake Ann and Swift Creek trails. And about 2 miles down the latter, on a wooded moraine before a rushing glacial stream, there is another. Just 4 miles from the junction we pass a side trail to the old Morovits Stamp Mill ¼ mile away. Here the trail's tread is very brushy and eroded, but easily identifiable. The real problem lies ahead—the washed-out Swift Creek bridge. When the trail finally descends into a large talus area, you may be tempted to ford immediately where the creekside trail has washed out. However, climb over this large, eroded section and continue on the trail another ¼ mile to the real crossing. There, there is no longer a bridge, but you should be able to improvise a late-season crossing. Next we leave Swift Creek, travelling through deep forest to Rainbow Creek—and another washed-out bridge. After this last obstacle it is an easy hop to the road.

If you wish to visit Baker Hot Springs, turn right at the road and walk ⅛ mile uphill. There are no facilities at the refreshing little hot-water pool, but you will often come upon an assortment of visitors, even dusk-to-dawn parties. Be sure to bring your own drinking and cooking water. There is a small, flat campsite within 100 feet of the hot spring and separated from it by a screen of trees.

From where the Swift Creek trail intersects the road, turn left on Road 1144. We pass Morovits Campground and, 3.2 miles from the Swift Creek Trail, arrive at Park Creek Campground and Road 11, the main valley road. From here a short side road leads to the Baker Lake Resort, where candy, lodging, meals, and washing machines are available. However, at this junction the PNWT turns right and goes 2 miles to the Boulder Creek Campground. Early on we pass our only view of Baker Lake—and a possible overnight spot on an old road which leads to this relatively new reservoir.

From the Boulder Creek Campground, travel south 3.1 miles through the forest along Baker Lake Road 11 to the Sulphur Creek Cutoff road 1114 (950). (This junction is about 100 yards beyond a small knoll past the "In The Shadow Of The Sentinels" nature trail.) If you wish to rejoin the Ideal Route here, take Road 12 to Road 13, and then 13 to the 3-mile-long Schreibers Meadow trail to 4962′ Baker Pass.

The Practical Route follows Road 12 for 9 miles. (Road 12 is a winter ski-touring route unsuitable for hiking or horse use until summer-use improvements are made.) We pass Schreibers Meadow Road 13, cross Rocky Creek, and climb to Wanlick Pass with good views of Mt. Baker on the way up. There is a very small campsite (with water) 100 yards before the pass's road junction.

We descend the scenic Wanlick Creek Road west until at a flat clearcut we reach the South Fork Nooksack River Valley. There the road finally deviates northwest from Wanlick Creek, but instead we follow the logging track southwest, directly across the flat clearcut, ¼ mile to its junction with the excellent Wanlick Creek Trail. There is good camping at the roadhead in the clearcut and at the trail's crossing of Wanlick Creek (at its junction with the river). Continue to follow the trail to the South Fork Nooksack River Road (1900). The trail ends at a bridge—which we do *not* cross. Instead, we turn left on the road.

The South Fork of the Nooksack River flows westerly between the Mt. Baker country (including Twin Sisters Mountain) and the hills to the south, such as Mt. Josephine, which form the divide with the Skagit River. Here we follow the South Fork river valley by road through heavily logged country for 14 miles on a private logging road to Lyman Pass (800). Beware of seasonal road closures in this area during dry periods of peak forest-fire danger. Also, because of heavy logging traffic you should travel this road only on weekends or after 6 p.m. There are no campsites along this 14-mile road section.

To follow the Ideal Route from Baker Lodge to Lyman Pass hike 9 miles from Heather Meadows via a good trail past Bagley Lakes (4240), Chain Lakes, and out along Ptarmigan Ridge to Camp Kiser (6000). Camp Kiser—a small, undeveloped campsite—is at this writing the end of the developed trail until we reach Baker Pass, 17 miles farther. This cross-country section meets many glacial streams, which should be forded in the early morning when the water level is lowest. Mt. Baker is one of the West Coast's major glacier-clad volcanic peaks. Conditions are unpredictable—

including occasional "Red Zone" closure by the Forest Service at Boulder Creek because of volcanic danger. And late or early in the season, beware of potential snow, mud, and rock slides in every gorge. This route crosses Avalanche Gorge, Lava Divide, Park Creek, Boulder Creek, Crater Moraine, and Sulphur Moraine.

On a beautiful sunny summer day, however, you are unlikely to be thinking about such dangers. Just enjoy the scenery from Baker Pass to Wanlick Pass, a 7-mile bushwhack across the South Divide and Loomis Mountain.

From Wanlick Pass, head southwest on Road 1230, then east, and curve southwesterly 3.5 miles to the Blue Lake/Dock Butte trailhead (3800). Trail 604A goes southwesterly 1.5 miles to Dock Butte (5210) with an initial ½-mile side trail to Blue Lake. Dock Butte has excellent views of Mt. Baker and all the mountains beyond Baker Lake. Plus, we can begin to view the fabulous Skagit country. From Dock Butte, ridgerun to Washington Monument (4811) and descend northwesterly to Springsteen Lake (3500)—a total of 5 miles, and a top trail-construction priority of the PNWTA. An existing trail from Springsteen Lake goes 4 miles to the junction of the Mt. Josephine Truck Road (2988). For now, travel the Truck Road 6 miles to the Mt. Josephine Lookout (3956). Eventually, the Ideal Route will be on the south side of the heights. (The Josephine Lakes are a potential campsite/water source south of the Truck Road almost a mile before you reach the Lookout.)

Continue on the Truck Road 9 miles to the junction with the Camp 17 Road. Turn right; go northwest on the Camp 17 Road 3 miles to Lyman Pass and the junction with the South Fork Nooksack River Road.

Lyman Pass (800), between Mt. Josephine and Wickersham Hill, was once the site of the old Soundview Logging Camp No. 17. Today there is no regular campsite there, but there is a very large clearing (and an unknown water supply).

Because the road is inland (south) from the South Fork, we must loop north from Lyman Pass to rejoin the river before heading downstream (northwest) on the east bank.

To reach salt water, the Practical Route goes north from Lyman Pass about two miles to Larson's Bridge. There is a scenic but waterless roadside campsite on the bluff above the river. The bridge itself has a good camp spot, with only river water available.

Cross the bridge and follow the logging road along the clearcut slopes above the east bank of the river. Early on, at the first junction along this road, we turn left to contour down the valley. About a mile later we see a side road dropping left down beside a recently clearcut and burned small knoll between us and the river. Take this side road; if you continue straight on the level-to-uphill route, you will soon reach a dead end. Descend this side road into an alder, maple, fir, and Sitka-spruce woods. Motorcyclists have created a maze of bottomland tracks through these forests and creeks, but if you continue on whatever looks like the main track, you will be following the old logging railroad/road route to the Dyes Ranch and on down the South Fork. There are numerous possible campsites along this often wet and muddy way. Nothing remains of the Dyes Ranch; near there a plankless cable bridge still crosses Cavanaugh Creek about 100 yards upstream from the present ford. Much of this South Fork route is a very pretty tour of the river's banks, but more of it is a series of mud puddles as the road wends northwest through low hills and swamps.

We emerge from the riverine woods at the Lummi Indian tribe's Skookum Hatchery on Skookum Creek. (Skookum means strong in the Chinook jargon.) This hatchery was built in 1969 and now releases annually three million coho salmon and four million fall chinook salmon.

Informal camp spots are available along the river, which the paved road crosses a mile later on the iron Saxon Bridge. A shake mill is about ½ mile farther on the right side of the road. Just before we reach the hamlet of Saxon, we see the Doran Road go steeply uphill to the left. At the top of that short rise there is a cemetery. This is the Practical Route, but if you plan to buy supplies at the Acme store or to pick up a cache box at the Acme post office across the street from the store, go straight ahead here instead of turning left toward the cemetery. After ¼ mile, turn left on the Maleng Road. In another ¼ mile, turn right and go 2 miles north on the Deming Road.

Our Practical Route goes south from the cemetery on the Doran Road and south onto the Innis Creek Road past open fields and buildings covered with moss. We can see the gap through the hills that we will follow to Park. Finally, after 2.8 miles we arrive at Wickersham (314). Although Wickersham was once prosperous enough to have two hotels but now cannot even support a post office, it does have rail passenger service of a sort. Call the Lake Whatcom Railway for its schedule of weekly steam-train excursion runs to Park on Lake Whatcom (206/595-2218).

To proceed to Park on the trail, cross the bridge at Wickersham and go north .5 mile on the Deming Road to Park Road. From uninviting Mirror Lake we follow the level, bucolic Park-Wickersham Road 3 miles west to Park (319) on Lake Whatcom (307), northwest Washington's largest lake. At the turn of the century, when the logging camps were booming, Park had one thousand residents. Today you will find a hamlet with a burger and milkshake stand, a Lake Whatcom Railway trail shed, and a new Whatcom County park on the lake.

From Park we continue southwest on Lake Whatcom Boulevard as if we were going to Bellingham. However, in .75 mile we reach a junction (347) at the Hovde Tree Farm. Follow the old logging road behind the big "Road Closed" sign. Go 2.8 miles on this Camp No. 2 Road southwest around 1000' Iowa Heights to the junction (401) of the north/south Cain Lake Road. No supplies are available at Cain Lake, but the Glenhaven Grocery is located about a mile north.

Continue to the south end of Cain Lake on the Camp 2 Road. We go past fields and houses and enjoy views of Knob 1315', which will be immediately south of our Palmer Lake route. At the southwest corner of Cain Lake, we reach a state Public Fishing Access, a potential campsite.

At this access, turn left up an obscure jeep road. Then, at a junction 100 feet farther, bear up to the left and keep going to a right switchback in the road. Turn left there (above a small lily pond) onto the Palmer Lake Trail. Continue by dirt road past Squires Lake to a paved road. Turn downhill (right) at the houses onto Squires Road. Then go left on Pacific Highway and you will come immediately to the Burlington-Alger Road, which takes us downhill and right in ¼ mile to the I-5 Freeway underpass (280).

Go under the freeway and travel 1 mile west on Nulle Road, crossing Friday Creek and passing an Indian Camp and a government water facility, to the Lake Samish Road (290).

From the junction (292) of the Nulle, Lake Samish, and Sutherland roads, take the Sutherland Road west, then northwest, and finally north to just over ½ mile. Turn left onto the Bear Creek Road, which heads west and then southwest .2 mile to its end. Next go cross-country across logged-off terrain growing up in small trees and brush. Go approximately 300 feet southwest, then 600 feet west, then 200 feet south to a crossing of Bear Creek at an elevation of 508'. From this crossing proceed right up the fall line (quite steep) on a compass bearing of 190° for approximately .5 mile to intersect Department of Natural Resources Road No. SWC-1200 (1150). Turn left on this dirt road and proceed just a dab over a mile in a southeasterly curve to well-marked Lily Lake Incline Trail (980).

Turn right and go up the fairly steep trail (an old incline railway bed) approximately .75 mile to join the Lizard-Lily Lake Trail (1900). Turn left and go .2 mile to a different (second) trail to Lizard Lake (2000).

Then turn right and go .25 mile to Lizard Lake (where there are fire grills and a toilet). From the campsite (1862) near the toilet, follow red and white candy-striped tapes along a brushed out, newly located trail 1 mile to North Butte, at 2200' the highest rock summit in the entire Chuckanut Range. Then continue for another mile along the view-packed palisades on the southwest shoulder of South Chuckanut to the Lily Lake campsite (2010).

From Lily Lake take the trail east .3 mile to regain the Lily Lake-Lizzard Lake Trail (1800). Turn right and descend this trail 2 miles, crossing the headwaters of South Bear Creek and then Whitehall Creek to intersect the new Samish Overlook Trail (1300). Turn right.

The ultimate goal of the Pacific Northwest Trail Association is to replace any inadequate parts of the Practical Route with new trail constructed as an Ideal Route. In 1983 the Samish Overlook Trail was our first effort in that direction. It provides direct trail access between the back side of Chuckanut Mountain and the western side at Samish Bay. This has added significance as the first place where PNWT pilgrims from the Continental Divide actually touch salt water!

The first 1.5 miles of this new trail contour westward at about 1300' elevation through alder and fir woods, passing two small gaps. This mountainside was logged in 1911, and the old sawmill site is our destination. We go there via five long switchbacks down the steep mountainside above Samish Bay. The first scenic overlook (near the foot and horse camps at

1300′ elevation) has views of the Anacortes refineries, Samish Bay, and the incredibly beautiful San Juan Islands. The lower, second overlook (about .5 mile north at the end of the first switchback) looks out over Oyster Creek and Lummi Island.

The Samish Overlook Trail has water near the Railway Incline Gap and at a seep 1.25 miles down from the hiker and horse camps (on the second switchback leg). There is no water at the Samish Overlook's developed camps themselves. We switchback in 2.25 miles from the camps down to Chuckanut Drive, a famous scenic highway created by the Civilian Conservation Corps during the Great Depression.

The PNWT continues directly across this paved road and descends through the trees .1 mile to the railroad tracks at the edge of Samish Bay. Turn left there and in .75 mile you will reach the Colony Creek railway bridge and the end of this PNWT section. From the tracks look for seals, bay ducks, great blue herons, eagles, and sunsets.

The purpose of this future Ideal Route from Lyman Pass to salt water is to get away from the roads and lowlands where so much of today's Practical Route is located. We take the much more exciting (and strenuous) way of going over 4257′ Lyman Hill (Wickersham Hill), 3364′ Anderson (Alger) Mountain, 2677′ Lookout Mountain, across Samish Pass, and onto 1577′ Chuckanut Mountain. Lookout and Chuckanut are long ridges rich in island and sunset views. Though its elevations are lower, this section will be no less dramatic than the rest of our incredible Pacific Northwest Trail.

From Lyman Pass we go northwest on the South Fork Road about 1000 feet to a left turn onto the Roaring Creek Road. We continue 9 miles on the Roaring Creek Road to the highpoint of the Samish/South Fork Nooksack Divide. Once we top this Lyman Hill, we bushwhack southwest 1 mile to the old Thunder Creek Trail and follow that to the hamlet of Prairie (250) on the Samish River.

From Prairie go 1.6 miles north on the Wickersham Road to the Anderson Mountain Road. Follow this up and over extensively clearcut Anderson Mountain. From the west slopes at about the 1800′ level we must bushwhack from the road west to a trail that takes us to the midpoint of the Camp 2 Road between Park and Cain Lake. Then we reach Cain Lake along the Practical Route.

However, we quickly depart from the Practical Route ½ mile beyond the Public Fishing Access. Turn right and climb to the end of the .2-mile-long logging road. Then start bushwhacking up along the Lookout Mountain divide. Siwash 2.1 miles north to join the Barnes Creek Road, which comes in from the west. Go north .3 mile on the Barnes Creek Road to where it crosses the divide and then bushwhack .2 mile to Knob 2676′— with potential views of this area's two jewels, Lake Whatcom and Samish Lake. At this point we can finally see salt water (northwest across the city of Bellingham) and will soon be even closer to our long-sought marine views.

From Knob 2676′ bushwhack the divide .2 mile to Tower Road. Continue north on Tower Road .7 mile to the tower on Knob 2677′. Then bushwhack .3 mile north down to a junction with the Entwhistle Road. Follow the Entwhistle Road 3.6 miles west to about where the Samish Road crosses I-5. There is a grocery store just across I-5. Turn right past the store on the Samish Highway .4 mile to a junction with a logging road. Bear off to the west 1.8 miles to the end of this road (past the power line).

From the end of the power-line road, take an old trail west .8 mile until where it turns south. We continue west, bushwhacking .5 mile to Pine Lake. Bushwhack around the south end of the lake and continue west .2 mile to a Whatcom County Park trail. Follow this trail northwest 1 mile, initially passing Cedar Lake, to where it turns sharply north. At that point we bushwhack west ½ mile to the Cleator Road. (The map shows the way this part of the Ideal Route will ultimately be constructed to allow for the proper grade.)

From the Cleator Road we climb about 500 feet due west to the brink of Chuckanut Mountain. There Chuckanut Bay and a legion of beautiful salt-water islands greet us after our long trek from the interior of the continent.

Follow the Cleator Road 1.2 miles south to its dead end. Bushwhack around Lost Lake to its south end to pick up the Larrabee State Park trail and continue south for 1 mile. At the point where the Larrabee State Park trail goes west, we bushwhack due east .1 mile to a logging road. Follow this road 1.8 miles, crossing Oyster Creek about two-thirds of the way through. PNWTA volunteers are now developing a route here south, then southwest, that takes in the highpoints. First we bushwhack 2 miles to Lizard Lake. Then we bushwhack south .6 mile via Knob 2085' to the existing east/west Lily Lake Trail. (Note: you can use the existing trail from Lizard Lake east, then south, then west past Lily Lake to the point where we bushwhack the divide down to the Chuckanut Manor Restaurant).

Finally, from the Lily Lake Trail we follow our Association's brand new trail section south 4.8 miles to Chuckanut Drive and salt water.

The mileage from the Cain Lake junction to salt water via this future route totals 24.8 miles. Converting these bushwhacking sections to volunteer-built trail is the top priority of the Pacific Northwest Trail Association.

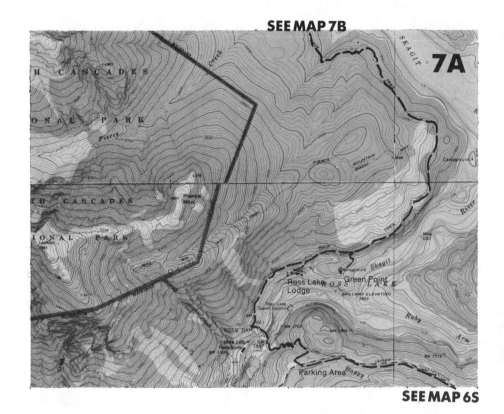

SEE MAP 6S

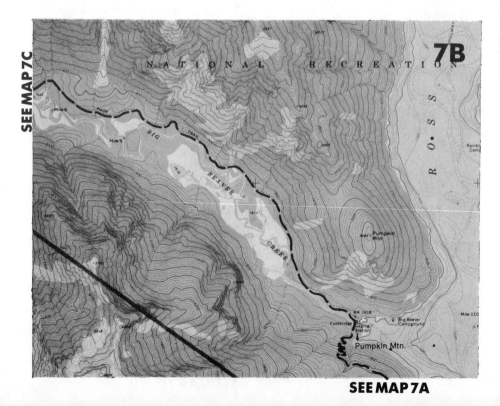

SEE MAP 7A

SEE MAP 7D

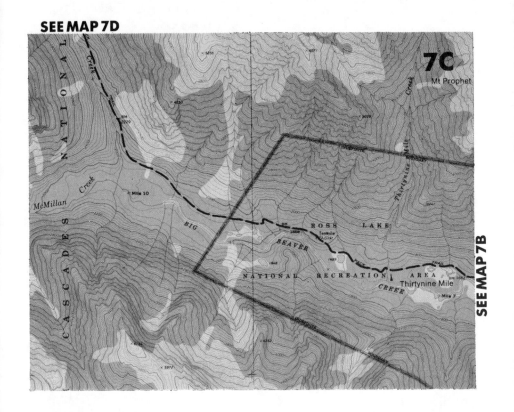

SEE MAP 7B

SEE MAP 7E

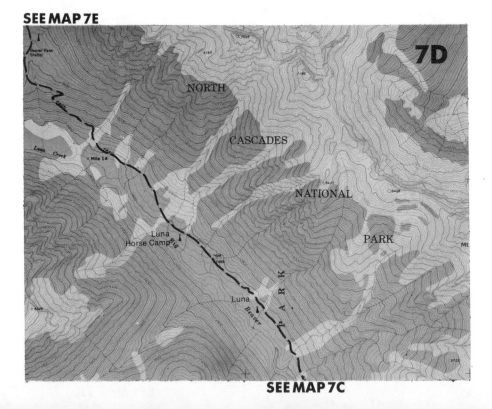

SEE MAP 7C

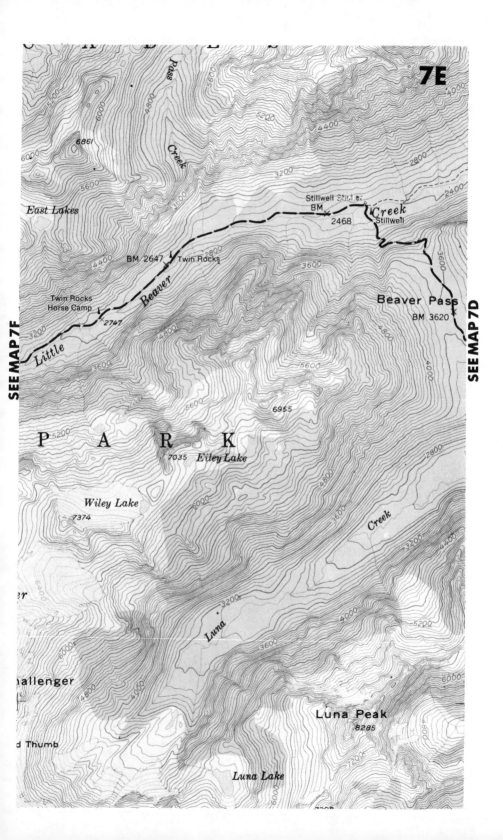

Pass

Creek

6861

East Lakes

Stillwell Shelter
BM
2468

Creek
Stillwell

BM 2647 Twin Rocks

Beaver

Beaver Pass
BM 3620

Twin Rocks
Horse Camp
2747

SEE MAP 7F

Little

SEE MAP 7D

P A R K

6955

7035 Eiley Lake

Wiley Lake
7374

Creek

Luna

allenger

Luna Peak
8285

d Thumb

Luna Lake

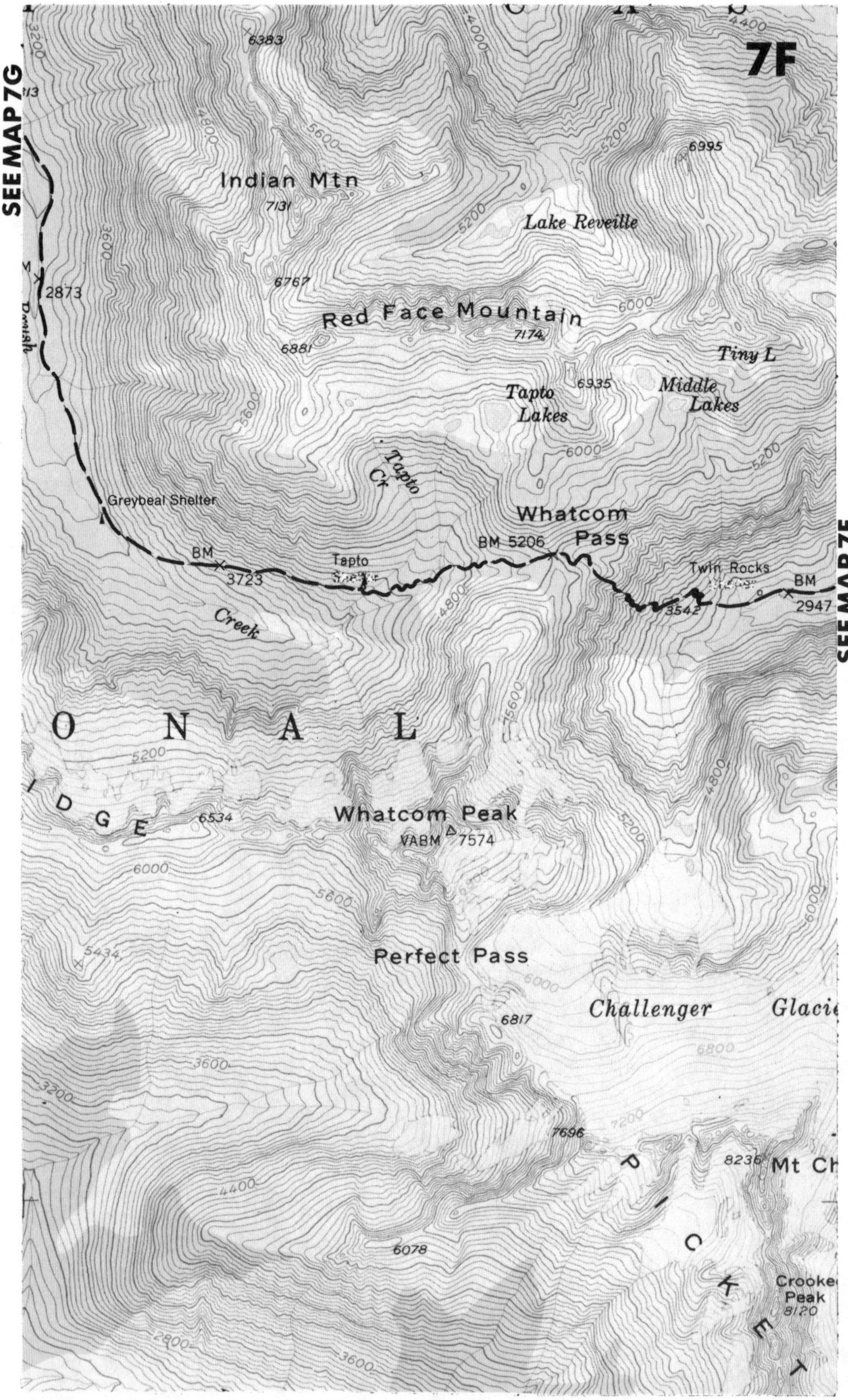

SEE MAP 7G

SEE MAP 7E

6383

6995

Indian Mtn
7131

Lake Reveille

2873

6767

Red Face Mountain
7174

6881

Tiny L

Tapto
Lakes
6935

Middle
Lakes

Tapto
Cr

Greybeal Shelter

Whatcom
Pass

BM 5206

Twin Rocks

BM
X
3723

Tapto
Shelter

BM
2947

Creek

3542

O N A L

5200

I D G E
6534

Whatcom Peak
VABM 7574

6000

5434

Perfect Pass

Challenger Glacie

6817

6800

3600

7696

7200

P

8236 Mt Ch

4400

Crooked
Peak
8120

6078

2900

3600

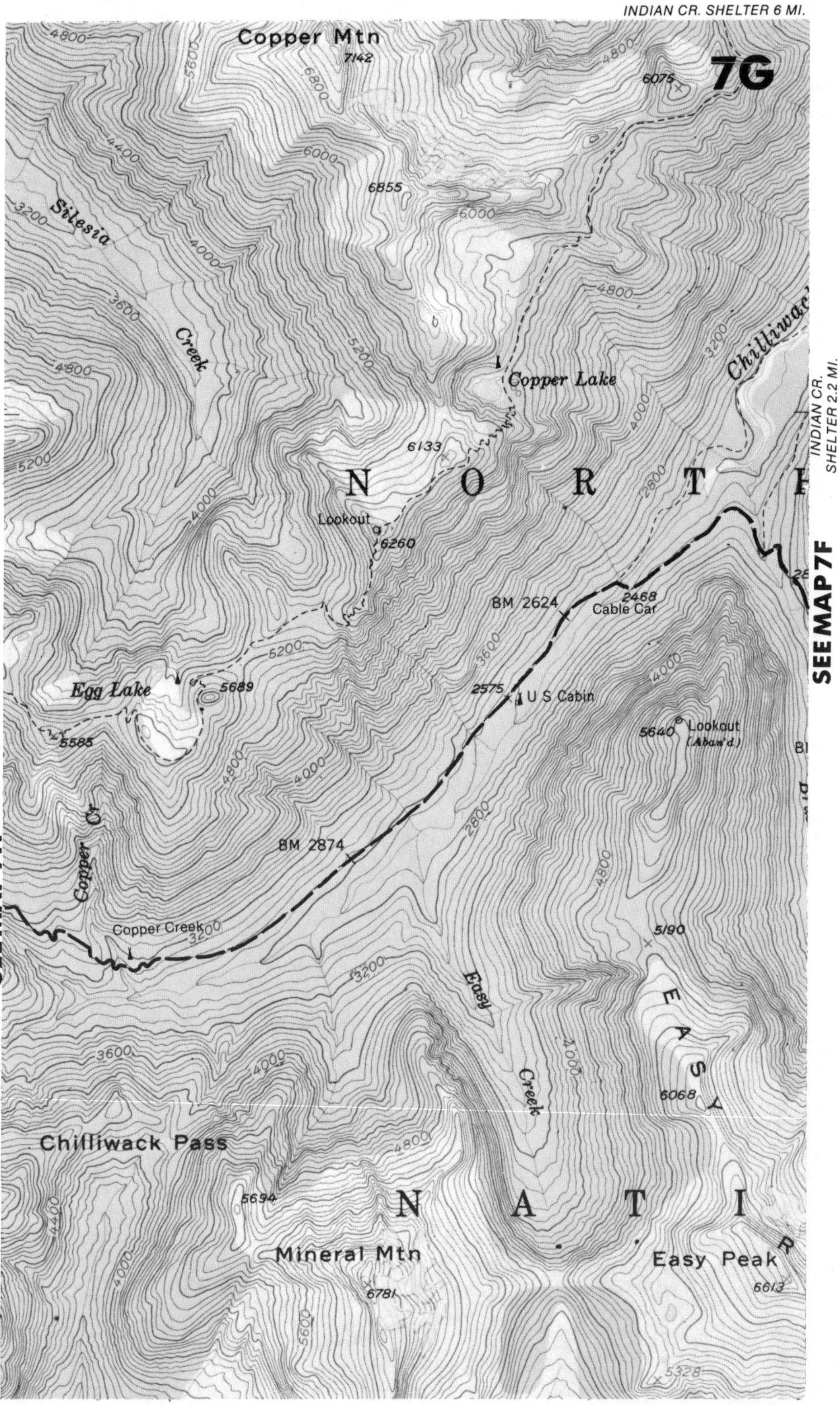

Copper Mtn
7142

6075

7G

6855

Silesia

Creek

Copper Lake

6133

N O R T H

Lookout
6260

BM 2624

2468
Cable Car

2575

U S Cabin

5640

Lookout
(Aban'd)

Egg Lake

5689

5585

Copper Cr

5200

BM 2874

5/90

Copper Creek

Easy

Creek

E A S Y

6068

SEE MAP 7H

SEE MAP 7F

Chilliwack

Chilliwack Pass

5694

N A T I

Mineral Mtn

6781

Easy Peak

6613

5328

Creek

Granite Mtn

6688

3600

5600

BM 3857

6138

rit

TR 674

Hannegan
Peak

6186

4800

4000

4424

Chilliwack

BM 3673

Boundary

River

6966

Hannegan
Pass

BM 5066

4400

5200

6301

5963

4000

6765

4000

6565

RIDGE

3600

5200

Ruth Mtn

VABM 7106

6148

5200

4800

6309

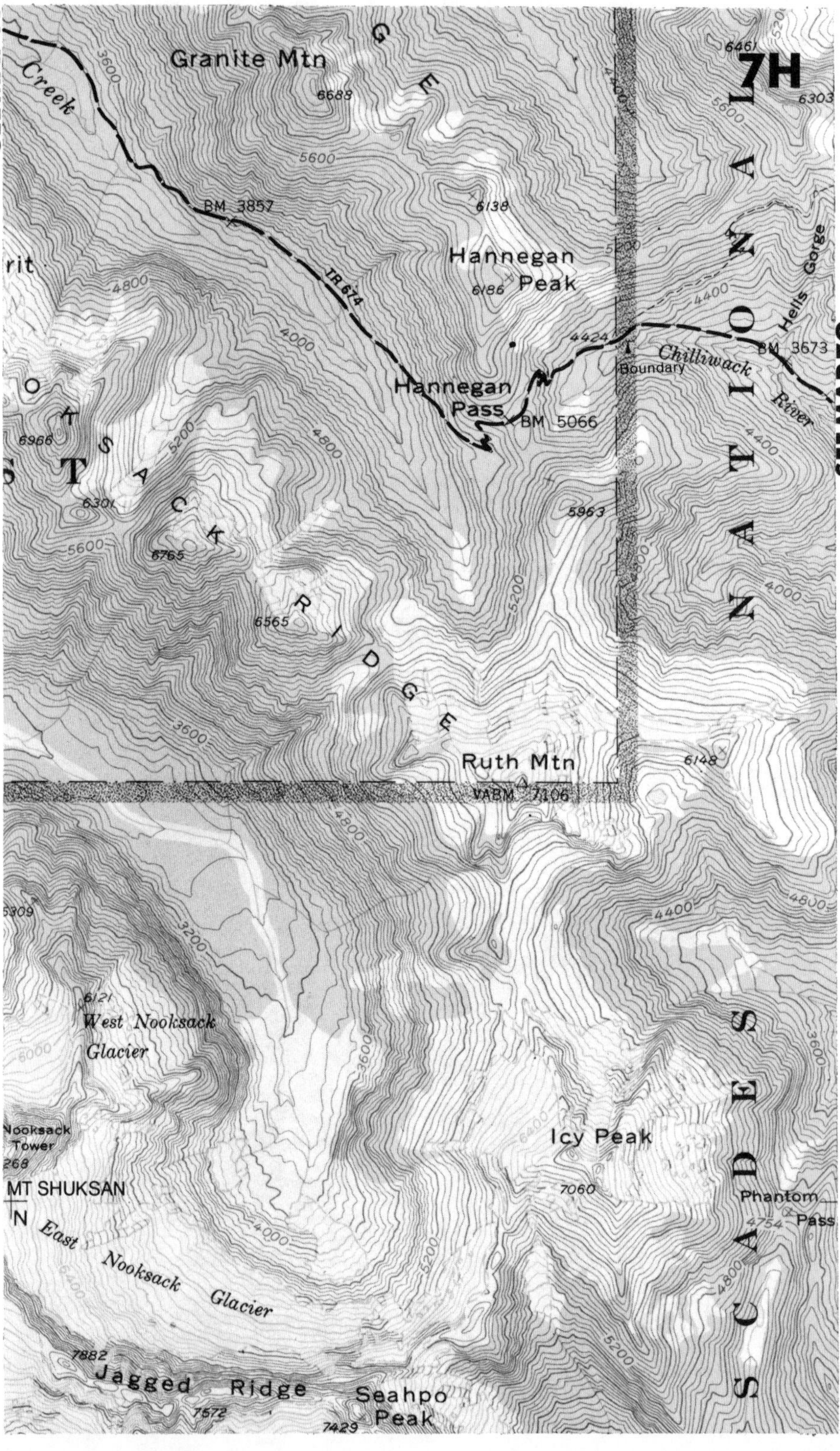

4400

4800

4800

3200

6121

West Nooksack
Glacier

3600

5000

Icy Peak

Nooksack
Tower
268

7060

Phantom
Pass
4754

MT SHUKSAN

N

East

4000

5200

5500

Nooksack

Glacier

4800

7882

Jagged Ridge

7572

Seahpo
Peak

7429

5500

CASCADES

NOOKSACK

NATIONAL

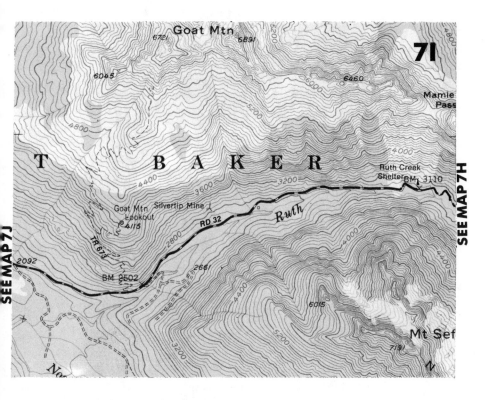

SEE MAP 7J

SEE MAP 7H

7I

Goat Mtn

6721

5891

6045

6460

Mamie
Pass

5200

4800

4000

T   B A K E R

Ruth Creek
Shelter BM 3110

4400

3600

3200

Ruth

Goat Mtn
Lookout
4115

Silvertip Mine

RD 32

2800

TR 673

2092

BM 2502

2661

4400

4000

4400

6015

Mt Sef

5200

7191

N

3200

No

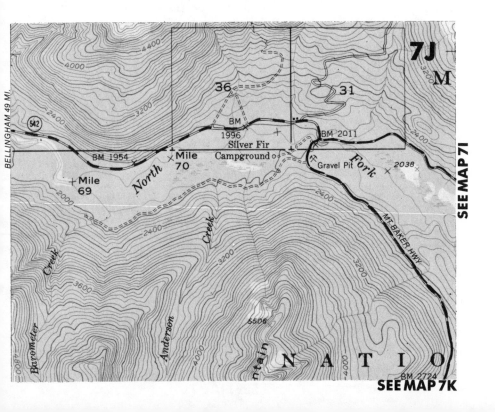

SEE MAP 7I

7J

M

4400

4000

2400

3200

36

31

BELLINGHAM 49 MI.

542

BM
1996

BM 2011

2400

3200

BM 1954

Mile
70

Silver Fir
Campground

Gravel Pit

Fork

2038

Mile
69

North

MT BAKER HWY

2000

Creek

2400

2400

3600

Anderson

Creek

3200

3200

Baromèter

4800

4000

4000

ntain

5506

N A T I O

BM 2724

SEE MAP 7K

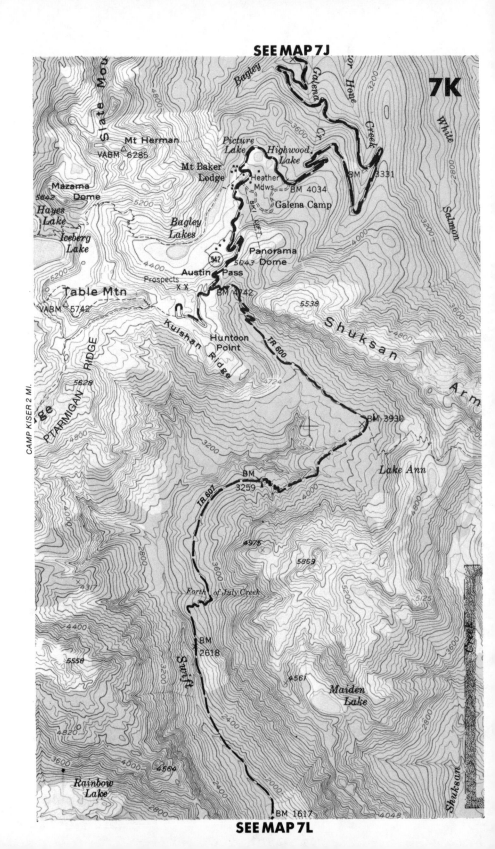

7K

SEE MAP 7L

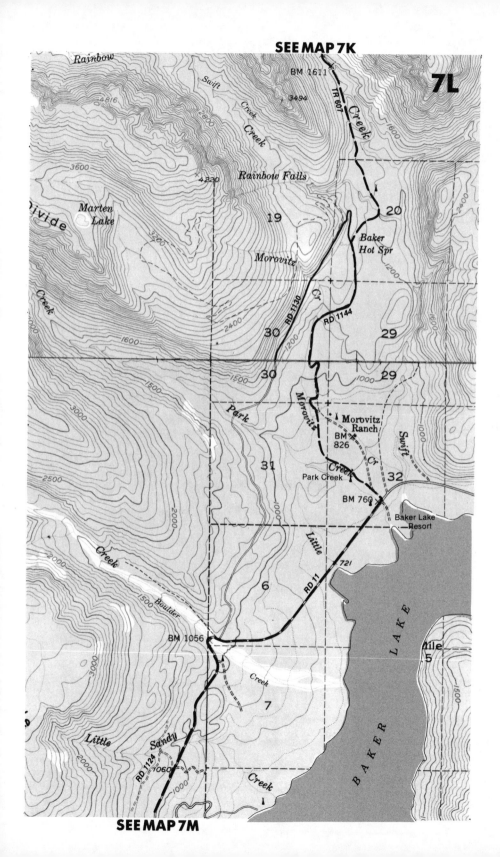

7L

Rainbow

BM 1611

TR 607

Swift

Creek

Creek

3494

4816

1600

Creek

1600

3600

4320

Rainbow Falls

Baker
Hot Spr

20

Divide

Marten
Lake

19

Morovitz

1200

3200

Cr

RD 1130

RD 1144

29

30

Creek

2400

1200

1600

1600

1000

Park

1500

30

29

3000

Morovitz

Morovitz
Ranch

BM
826

Swift

1000

2500

31

Cr

Creek

32

Park Creek

BM 760

Baker Lake
Resort

2000

Creek

Little

721

RD 11

6

1500

Boulder

BM 1056

L A K E

3000

2000

ile
5

1500

7

Creek

B A K E R

Little

Sandy

RD 1124

1060

Creek

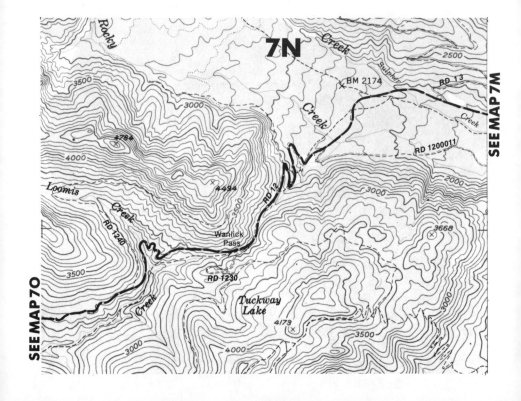

Dillard Creek

Sandy

Creek

RD 1120

Creek

RD 11

7M

Horseshoe Cove

RD 1122

898

19

BAKER LAKE

Diversion Dam

BM 1619

RD 1200011

RD 12

Sulphur

RD 1114

BM

1002

Sulphur Point 2262° Lookout

Rocky

Komo Kulshan Guard Sta

BM 856

800

30

Creek

1799

CONCRETE 13 MI.

7N

Rocky

Creek

Sulpher

2500

3500

3000

BM 2174

RD 13

RD 1200011

Creek

4784

4494

Loomis

Creek

RD 1240

RD 12

2000

3000

3668

Warrick Pass

3500

RD 1230

Tuckway Lake

Creek

4173

3500

4000

3000

3500

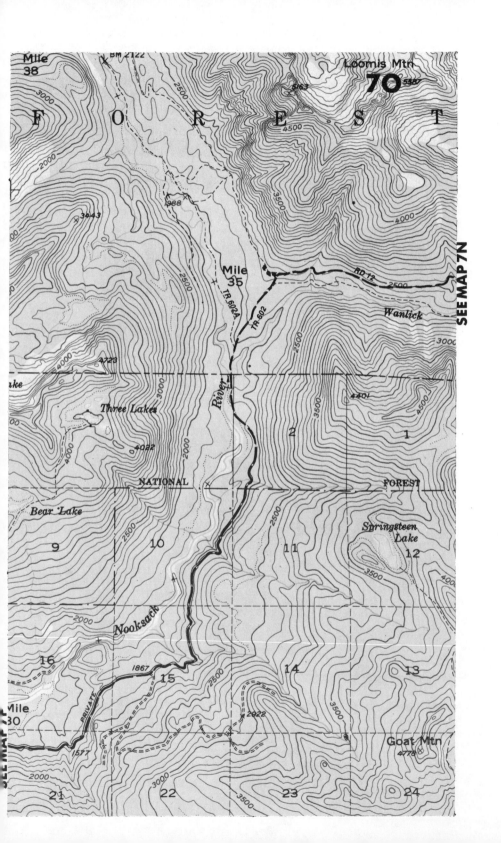

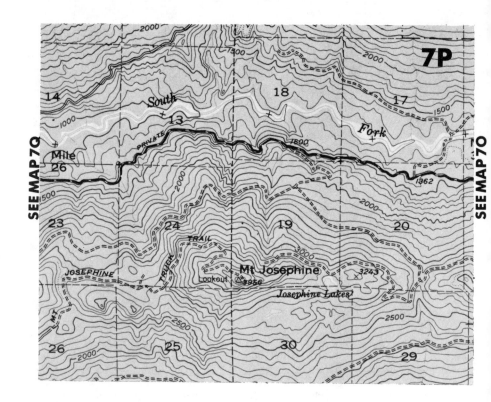

SEE MAP 7Q

SEE MAP 7O

14
South
+ 13
18
17
2000
1500
2000
1000
1600
Fork
1500
Mile
26
1362
1500
2000
2000
23
24
19
20
TRAIL
TRAIL
PRIVATE
JOSEPHINE
Mt Josephine
3243
Lookout
3956
Josephine Lakes
MT
2500
2500
26
25
30
29
2000

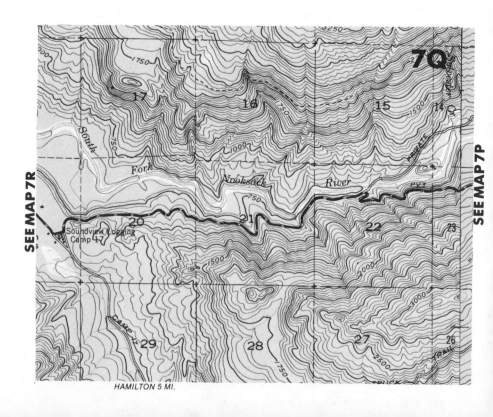

SEE MAP 7R

SEE MAP 7P

3250
2000
1750
17
16
15
14
1500
750
750
1000
South
750
Fork
Nooksack
River
PRIVATE
PVT
750
20
21
22
23
Soundview Logging
Camp 17
1500
2000
3000
CAMP
29
28
27
26
2500
750
TRAIL
TRUCK

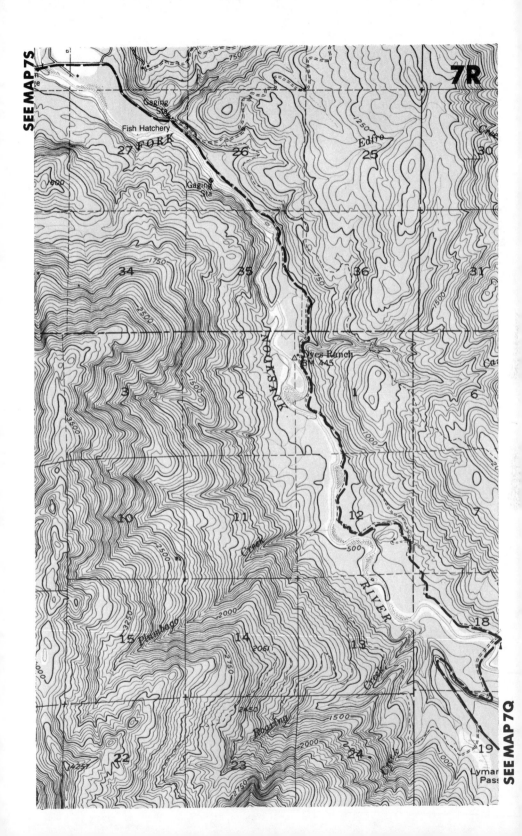

Gaging
Sta.

Fish Hatchery

FORK

27

26

Edith

25

30

600

1750

34

35

36

31

2500

1500

NOOKSACK

1000

Dyes Ranch
BM 445

3

2

1

6

Cas

3500

1500

1000

Creek

10

11

12

7

2500

500

500

RIVER

18

Plumbago

2000

15

14

13

Creek

2051

2250

3257

22

23

24

19

1500

Roaring

2000

Lyman
Pass

1750

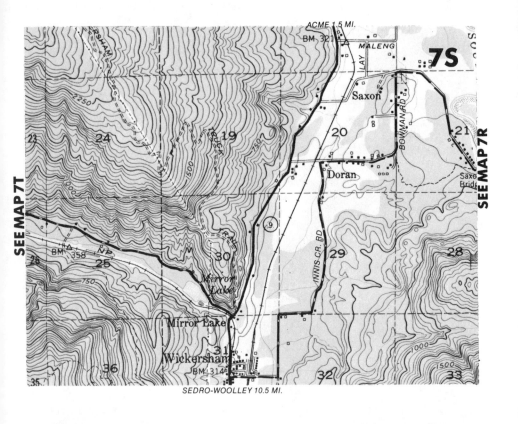

ACME 1.5 MI.

BM 321

MALENG

LAY

7S

Saxon

BOWMAN RD

SEE MAP 7R

23

24

19

20

21

Saxo
Brid

SEE MAP 7T

Doran

INNIS CR. RD

9

BM △
358

26

25

30

29

28

Mirror
Lake

Mirror Lake

Wickersham

31

BM 314

32

33

36

35

SEDRO-WOOLLEY 10.5 MI.

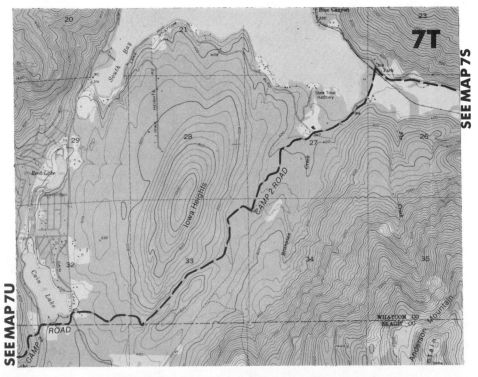

Blue Canyon

20

21

23

7T

South Bay

WHATCOM

Park

State Trout
Hatchery

SEE MAP 7S

29

28

CAMP 2 ROAD

27

26

Reed Lake

Iowa Heights

Creek

32

33

34

35

SEE MAP 7U

Cain Lake

CAMP 2
ROAD

WHATCOM CO
SKAGIT CO

Anderson Mountain

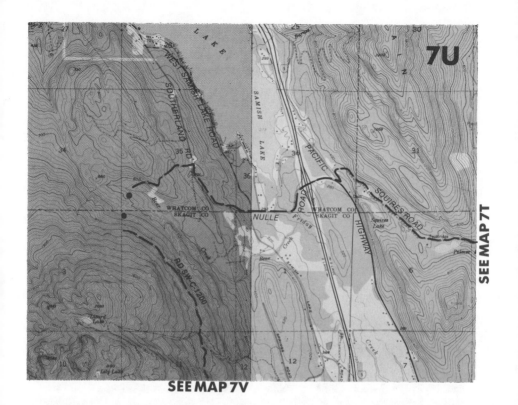

SEE MAP 7T

SEE MAP 7V

SEE MAP 7U

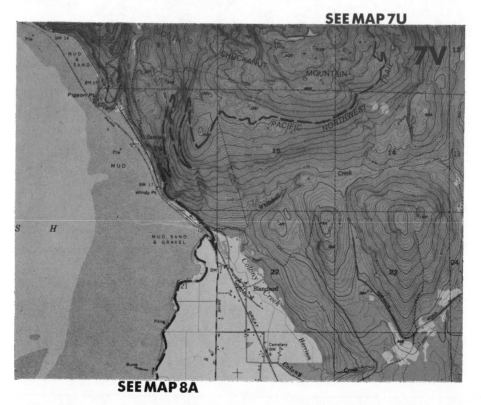

SEE MAP 8A

DIKES AND ISLANDS
(Samish Bay to Admiralty Head)

Skagit Game Range

INTRODUCTION

This is a sea-level section, a long, long stretch of beaches, bluffs, and breaking waves. Here the trail fronts Samish Bay, Padilla Bay, Similk Bay, Fidalgo Bay, Lake Campbell, Lake Erie, Bowman Bay, Canoe Pass, Deception Pass, Dugalla Bay, Rosario Strait, the Strait of Juan de Fuca, and Admiralty Inlet. That adds up to a lot of oysters, gulls, and sunsets.

Unlike much of the PNWT, this section offers year-round, snow-free hiking. You will, however, need good rain gear during the drizzly winter and spring months. In addition, because most of the PNWT here follows roads or offers nearby road alternates, the Chuckanut Drive/Keystone Ferry route is highly recommended for bicycle touring. A fine loop tour is possible by biking via Discovery Bay, the Hood Canal Bridge, and the Winslow Ferry to Seattle and by back roads to Fidalgo Island or the Edmonds Ferry to Whidbey Island.

Don't miss this section's stunning views of Mt. Baker, the San Juan Islands, and the rapidly approaching Olympic Mountains. Pungent sea smells suggest a world of mysteries and adventures. Enjoy blossom, grass, and alder scents, and push through thick, fragrant dike-top patches of tall colt's foot and showy thistles. Sit down to feast on summer blackberries while watching killdeer antics along the shore. You may see a seagull repeatedly drop a mollusk shell to crack it open. The drainage channels will be full of cattails and the roadside covered with California poppies and purple chicory. Rich polder-like fields will stretch away warmly to the east and sun-splashed waters will glitter in the west. In migration season the bays will resound with bird cries. In mid-winter the gray rains and mists promise a more solitary world. You will want to return again and again to this PNWT section.

PROBLEMS

Many of the dike and beach portions of the PNWT here cross or touch private land. So in this section, even more than in most others, you are an ambassador for our Association. Of course, on any private land do not pick flowers, cacti, clams, etc. Be diplomatic.

The Whidbey Naval Air Station is presently off limits to civilian hikers. You could try writing the commanding captain for permission to cross his long beach, but don't get your hopes up. Yes, it is a long way around.

Two types of problems concern tides. First, the moon's two-cycle, daily tides must be allowed for as you time your trek down most of the beaches. Otherwise, you may be dangerously squeezed against bluffs, logs, and oblivion. Second, red tide (a biological poison) can end your trip permanently if you eat contaminated clams, oysters, mussels, etc., from affected waters. Check with local authorities and old-timers for the current situation. (Don't assume that everything is OK merely because the water is not red; the toxins involved are measured in parts per million and are invisible.) The red tide information number is 1-800-562-5632.

Beware of such problems as seashore-intensified sunburn—should you somehow hit a sunny spell—and mosquitoes, which can be very friendly when you visit their drainage-canal breeding grounds along the dikes.

Much of this route is not ideal for horse travel because stopping places along the beaches do not provide stock facilities and because the dikes are often poorly maintained and full of rocky detours around dense briar patches. Leave old Dobbin home. Your bicycle would fare better, but if you pedal, you may want to follow the nearby country lanes to avoid dike-top punctures and beach-sand delays.

SUPPLIES

The following post offices are located on or near the PNWT: Blanchard (98231), Bow (98232), Anacortes (98221), Oak Harbor (98277), and Coupeville (98239). For grocery stores try: Bow, the junction of Christiansen Road and Highway 20, Anacortes, Lake Erie, Oak Harbor, and Coupeville (Prairie Center Mercantile). Only the Lake Erie Grocery is right on the route. However, because this section is relatively easy, you may be moving ahead faster and consuming less food per mile than usual.

DECLINATION   22½° E

USGS TOPOGRAPHIC MAPS

Bow	Oak Harbor
La Conner	Smith Island
Anacortes South	Port Townsend North
Deception Pass	Coupeville

MILEAGES (total 52.7)

		Total
Colony Creek bridge (Chuckanut Drive)	0.0	0.0
Dirt road to the mouth of Colony Creek	.2	.2
Levee on Samish Bay and Gun Club road to Edison bridge	3.4	3.6
Edison on Road 537 to Bay View—Edison Road junction	.5	4.1
Samish River bridge	.5	4.6
Padilla Bay Interpretive Center	4.6	9.2
Bay View State Park	.6	9.8
Lower Padilla Bay dikes	.7	10.5
Memorial Highway (State Hwy. 20) at Whitney	2.9	13.4
Junction with Padilla Heights Road	2.6	16.0
Similk Beach via Padilla Heights Road, Stevenson Road, Summit Park Road, and Christiansen Road	3.5	19.5
Junction of Gibralter Road, Highway 20, and Miller Road	.8	20.3
Campbell Lake Road	1.2	21.5
Sharpe Road/Ginnett Road junction	1.9	23.4
Deception Pass bridge	3.0	26.4
West Point (Whidbey Island)	1.2	27.6
Powell Road via West Beach	2.0	29.6
Joseph Whidbey State Park via Powell Road, Moran Road, Highway 20, Ault Field Road, Golf Course Road, and Crosby Road	9.4	39.0
Libbey Beach Park via the beach at low tide	5.4	44.4
Cedar Gulch (DNR walk-in campsites beyond Point Partridge)	1.9	46.3
The Keystone Ferry Landing at Admiralty Head	6.4	52.7

ROUTE DESCRIPTION

After crossing the two-lane Chuckanut Drive bridge over the wide mouth of Colony Creek on Samish Bay, turn northwest on a dirt road back beside the bridge. This ¼-mile road ends at a tiny spit of land (a possible campsite but lacking in potable water).

Begin walking the dike southwesterly at water's edge. This levee runs 2.4 miles to a site marked "ruins" on the topographic map, though nothing in particular is visible there. Next follow a road 1 mile beside a dike and telephone lines south to a gun club and into Edison, on Edison Slough. At low tide the incredible mud flats of Samish Bay frame the first part of this route. At high tide waterfowl abound here during the migration season, as attested by the many hunting blinds along the levee. Remains of the old wooden pilings still follow the shore, now a strong earth and riprap structure. Until about a century ago this whole region was heavily forested with massive, primeval Douglas firs. Logging and diking quickly changed this landscape from forest to agriculture. Enjoy the bountiful produce of the Skagit Valley. Forget about freeze-dried food and load up on ice cream, cheese, milk, berries, fruits and fresh green things.

Drinking water is scarce or non-existent along this part of the PNWT. Fill your canteens at the Chuckanut Manor Restaurant near Colony Creek or perhaps when you get your mail drop at the Blanchard or Bow post offices.

As you cross a short bridge to enter Edison, you will see one of the most welcome commercial signboards on the entire PNWT: "Homemade Pies and Soup." The letters are white, big, and bold against a barn red wall. Ask the owner about her free dip of ice cream for PNWT pie eaters.

Edison has no post office, but to find groceries you must travel east 1 mile to Bow, where the store is opposite the post office. Immediately south of Edison there is a state liquor store on county road 537.

Go due south from Edison on 537 for ½ mile to a junction with the Bay View–Edison Road. Go west through open fields on this road ½ mile to the Samish River bridge. Here is a splendid view of Chuckanut Mountain and all the country of your last few days on the PNWT. In the foreground of this bucolic scene are many moored fishing vessels, reminders of the bounteous local fishing a century earlier. In 1880 Edison's commercial salmon fishery began, but overfishing, large-scale trapping, and rapid habitat changes drastically depleted the resource.

Continue west ½ mile beyond the river to a junction at an old barn. Turn left; continue 4.1 miles south through farm fields and across wooded Bay View Ridge to the Padilla Bay Interpretive Center. This free-admission facility is a must for PNWT travellers—and not only because it has drinking water and fine rest rooms. Its excellent displays and programs have been operated by the Washington State Department of Ecology since the building opened in 1982. The site was the gift of Edna Breazeale of the pioneer Breazeale family. (Now if only we could obtain a similar gift for a Pacific Northwest Trail Association headquarters!)

Bay View Recreation Area's camping and beach facilities are only .6 mile farther down the road. (Water and 108 campsites are available, but no groceries or mail service.) Continue south .7 mile through the hamlet of Bay View (no facilities) to the beginning of another dike section. If you are a bicyclist or someone in a hurry, keep to this La Conner and Samish Road 2.9 miles south to Highway 20. Otherwise, experience the more roundabout pleasures of the levees.

Padilla Bay is one of only eight "national estuarine sanctuaries" and is one of Puget Sound's largest relatively undisturbed tideflat areas. The 11,600 acres of tidelands have been protected from earlier plans to convert the bay into industrial and residential land. The bay hosts 57 different fish species as well as 50,000 wintering ducks; it is especially rich in black brant. Add to that a spectacular wealth of eagles, herons, hawks, and even the American peregrine falcon. The bay's environment includes: open marine waters, subtidal sand and mud, eelgrass beds, exposed mudflats, salt marshes, beaches, rocky shores, dredge spoil sites, and nonforested and forested uplands. Along the PNWT be on the lookout for harbor seals in the tidal channels and mudflats.

Both the dike and road route and the La Conner and Samish Road route measure 2.9 miles to the Memorial Highway at the Whitney railroad stop and Ortho Fertilizer facility. The dike route begins near some trailer houses at the La Conner and Samish road, passes pea fields, curves southward to an Indian site (with no visible artifacts), passes a big drainage channel, enters Indian Slough, passes a jetty and an abandoned barge and cannery, and returns to the road. A mile of road walking brings us to the main highway. This whole Padilla Bay section offers great views of the PNWT ahead, especially Mt. Erie, of the Highway 20 twin curved bridges, and of the Shell and Texaco oil refineries at Anacortes.

A large restaurant (the Farm House Inn) and a farm produce stand are immediately across Highway 20. However, remain on the north side of the highway as you head 2.6 miles west to a junction with the first road beyond the Swinomish Channel bridge, the Padilla Heights Road. (An "Indian Smoke Shop" sign is across the highway from this junction.) From where you begin this part at Whitney, Anacortes is 8 miles and Whidbey Island 11 miles ahead via main roads. You will be off the mainland here on Fidalgo Island.

At the heavily travelled Swinomish Channel bridge, keep to the pedestrian walkway on the north side. From this bridge there is an excellent view, in season, of tulips, daffodils, and other blossoms as well as of the bays and sloughs that separate Fidalgo Island from the mainland of North America.

An interesting side trip is available south to La Conner, where many services are available as well as a unique Swinomish Indian Reservation WPA totem pole from the Great Depression. La Conner is a colorful tourist and boating town and sometime artist colony. From Whitney go due south on the La Conner and Samish Road to La Conner, and return to the PNWT by crossing the bridge south of town and going northwest along Reservation Road, a PNWT detour of only 9 miles.

The Fidalgo Island section of the PNWT is currently on roads because of the difficulty of finding a route across private lands. From the intersection of Highway 20 and the Padilla Heights Road, go .8 mile west up a long grade to a sharp right turn in the road. Bicyclists continue right and downhill left to join Reservation Road and along it to the bottom of the hill. Walkers and horsemen can shortcut this .7-mile loop by following a dirt continuation of the Padilla Heights Road straight down the hill for .1 mile. Continue west on the Stevenson Road past small homesteads and a grange hall to Summit Park. At 697 Stevenson Road, seafood lovers will want to visit Ken Thibert's crab market for fresh crabs, oysters, and fish.

The route jogs right at a Puget Power substation, then immediately left at a church. Go west on Summit Park Road to a junction with the Christiansen Road near a veterinarian's office. Parallel the golf course south on the Christiansen Road to Similk Beach. By road it's 3.5 miles from Highway 20 to Similk Beach. Camping and stores are not available along these roads. However, with a ⅛-mile detour to the Christiansen Road/Highway 20 junction, you can hit a restaurant and a grocery store at the foot of Fidalgo Bay. A drive-in theater is handy nearby.

Similk Beach and its golf course front scenic Similk Bay. Ordinary supplies are not available here, but one glorious treat is. Visit the unpretentious Oyster Shed on the beach—its hours are irregular—for delicious oysters on the half shell or unopened. (The Pacific Northwest Trail is the only long-distance trail that can boast of fresh oysters!) If the water level were to rise a tiny bit here, the beach and the whole golf course valley behind it would be flooded and Fidalgo Bay joined to Similk Bay.

We climb from this flat valley about 200 feet (and .8 mile), past many houses that hug the west slope of the golf course, and ascend to Howards Corner and the junction of Gibralter Road, Highway 20, and Miller Road.

It is only a 3-mile side trip to Anacortes, with its complete facilities plus a ferry connection to the San Juan Islands and Vancouver Island, one of the greatest travel bargains anywhere. (The San Juans make an excellent bicycle tour.) Anacortes was founded in 1890 as a railroad boom town for the hoped-for Northwest terminus of the transcontinental railroad.

Follow Miller Road (past the Fern Hill commercial campground) to where it rejoins Highway 20, and travel downhill on 20 to a right turn onto the Campbell Lake Road (1.2 miles). Lake Campbell is a 40-acre fresh-water fishing hole. Its low elevation (44) contrasts with nearby, forested Whistle Lake (432).

Near a picturesque old barn with a fading, painted advertisement for Centennial flour, there is a public access road to Lake Campbell, providing fishing, swimming, boating, and latrines, but no camping or supplies or water. Go 1.5 miles west on the Campbell Lake Road to its junction with the Heart Lake Road and Donnell Road. A few hundred feet north of this junction is the Lake Erie Grocery (and commercial campground).

For a fine side trip to the spectacular summmit of Mt. Erie (1273), the highest point in the area, go ¼ mile farther north up the Heart Lake Road from the Mt. Erie Grocery to a "Gallery 10" sign (and a power line to the top of the mountain). From the sign follow a climbers' trail to the summit.

Our next major destination is Deception Pass, so named because Captain George Vancouver in 1792 mistook it for merely a narrow Y rather than the end of the 48 states' second largest island. Our own PNWT passage follows the roads here. Continue west to the Devil's Elbow U-turn on Sharpe Road and continue southwest to Ginnett Road, a total of 1.9 miles. Follow Ginnett Road west to Rosario Road and then the latter south to Rosario Beach. (Sharpe County Park is a new 70-acre natural area along the way; it has no water or developed campsites.) Next go by trail and shore around Sharpe Cove, Bowman Bay, and Lottie Bay to the Deception Pass Bridge. This is a scenic area of countless sea birds, foggy headlands, and peeling-red-bark madrona trees. A side trip on good trails will take you to Lighthouse Point and excellent views of Deception Pass, Deception Island, and on clear days, the snowy Olympics. (For people who prefer an all-road route via Cougar Gap and Pass Lake, the distance from the Sharpe Road/Ginnett Road junction to the Deception Pass bridge is 3 miles.) Camping and water are available at Deception Pass State Park; and you can find groceries a mile south on Highway 20.

Whidbey Island is a sandy relic of the great glaciers. Famous in pioneer times for its rich soils, it later supported many potato farmers and turkey growers. Today its economy is geared to tourism and to the U.S. Navy. The Navy may be good for the local economy, but its Whidbey Naval Air Station is very inconvenient for PNWT hikers. The Trail follows saltwater beaches all the way from Deception Pass to the Keystone Ferry, where we leave Whidbey Island for the Olympic Peninsula. However, the Navy's beach is off limits to civilians without a pass. So we must go around the Naval Air Station, double the Navy's beach distance of 4.5 miles.

Bicyclists can attempt our beach route, especially bicyclists with wide tires. However, we recommend a scenic road alternate via Highway 20 (which recently acquired a right-lane shoulder for this purpose) to the Scenic Heights Road immediately south of Oak Harbor. The Scenic Heights Road provides great views of Oak Harbor Bay, Flower's Heights, Blower's Bluff, and Penn Cove. Continue past the old inn to Coupeville, a touristy but pleasant Penn Cove town founded in 1852, a very long time ago by Northwest standards. Go south from Coupeville to Ebey's Landing and the marked scenic route to the ferry.

PNWT hikers should follow the trail 1.2 miles from the south end of the Deception Pass bridge parallel to North Beach out to West Point. At most places, except Gun Point, you can easily walk the sandy crescent beaches. A very large campground (with water and rest rooms) is available near West Point. There are several picnic shelters along this scenic route.

From North Beach you can observe the brisk 7-knot tidal current in and out of Deception Pass, but from West Beach you will be facing the open reaches of the Strait of Juan de Fuca, where winds often roar in straight from the distant horizons of the vast Pacific.

Hike south from the West Point picnic area and Cranberry Lake's fascinating dunes 2 miles along the beach. This is an excellent birding area as well as an opportunity to explore special desert-like dune vegetation, including saxifrages, stonecrops, vetches, etc. For camping, a practical strategy would be to camp at West Point and next at the town beach in Oak Harbor (Whidbey Island's major center for all services). Our route around Navy property does take us close to Oak Harbor, so such a supply stop would not be a problem. However, visiting that city would break the spell that develops when you spend mile after mile on the beach, away from civilization. Hiking the PNWT on Whidbey's beaches is like sailing into the unknown with a fair wind astern. Try to sail around all distractions as best you can, and keep a weather eye on the alluring Olympics ahead.

Our West Beach walk runs smack into the Whidbey Island Naval Air Station's restricted 4.5-mile section at the Island County Park known as Moran's Beach. You will recognize it by the Navy's "keep out" sign and by their runway approach lights, which extend out into the water on pilings. Strangely enough, no fence blocks access to Navy property. Unfortunately, Moran's Beach is a no-camping and no-water facility.

Leave the shore at Moran's Beach and go east .2 mile on Powell Road to a right on Moran Road. Trek past fields .5 mile to a right onto good old Highway 20 at a G & O Real Estate office and Northgate Terrace. Continue south on that busy road through woods, fields, and cabbage patches, and continue around the Clover Valley part of the Air Station while enjoying views of Dugalla Bay and tramping southwesterly. After 4.3 tense miles on 20, turn right at Ault Field Road and pass: a junk yard, the main entrance to the Air Station, the NCO Club, and the skeet shooting range (2.4 miles total). Turn left (south) onto Golf Course Road and go 1 mile, passing the golf course and firing range, to a right (west) onto Crosby Road (past the radio towers, which communicate with the ships and subs at sea). Crosby Road zig zags south, then west, around a plot of undeveloped land to join with West Beach Road. (This former Navy property has been converted into Joseph Whidbey State Park, which has outhouses, but neither camping nor water.)

Our route around the U.S. Navy has taken 9.4 miles of road pounding. Ear pounding, too, if the carrier jets have been practicing their touch-and-gos and if engine tests have been roaring away while you were in the vicinity. If you are tempted to trespass across the unfenced beach perimeter, remember that not only would that be illegal, but also it would be dangerous because of the low-flying aircraft, jet-test blasts, and firing-range bullets.

South beyond the state park, many houses have been built on Sunset (west) Beach land so low that one giant storm will surely wash the whole place clean overnight. Some recently built bulkheads have already been destroyed by beach erosion. Anyway, walk south on the road past this scene of folly .8 mile to a county parking area, which provides beach access (but no water or camping). From here a romantic campsite (with no water) is halfway up the bluff road to the south. Look carefully on the right side of the road for a pathway that has been blocked off by a mound of dirt. Abandoned behind this in the trees is a cliff-top military observation bunker, the grassy roof of which makes one of the most scenic and unusual tent platforms anywhere. An ideal vantage point for incredible sunsets.

From the county parking area at Sunset Beach, walk 5.4 miles on the low-tide beach to another Island County beach access, Libbey Beach Park. This one is also a no-camping, no-water site; it does have an outhouse. Libbey Beach Park is completely surrounded by suburban-type houses in a little defile where Libbey Road comes down to the water's edge through the bluffs.

Clay, sand, and stone bluffs—sometimes as high as 250 feet—along the West Beach are a serious hazard to us beach walkers if the tide comes up and traps us beneath them. So pay close attention to your tide tables and be ready to retreat to high ground. (An intermediate point, a low spot on this cliff-full coast, is the boat ramp at Hastie Lake Road.) If you choose not to hike this section of beach, you will have 2.1 miles of road travel via the West Beach Road through fields and developments to Libbey Road, then .7 mile west on Libbey Road out to Libby Beach Park. However, the low-tide beach sands, with their miles of waves and birds and their views of Smith Island, the Olympics, etc., should not be missed if you can time it safely.

From Libbey Peach Park continue down the low-tide beach .2 mile to a picnic area at Fort Ebey State Park. (Look for the path up the bluff to the picnic area and fill your canteens at the modern rest rooms there.) You may also spend the night at the fee-camping area in this park, which even has coin-operated hot showers. But for hikers a better idea would be to carry as much water as you can down the beach to the DNR's Point Partridge bluff-top, walk-in campsites. To get to the waterless DNR campsites from the picnic area, you can walk the low-tide beach all the way to Cedar Gulch's stairway up the bluff (beyond Point Partridge). Or you could hike along the top of the bluffs, dodging the prickly gorse planted here long ago by the Army as a substitute for barbed wire. Bicyclists could travel there entirely by road from Libbey Beach, Libbey Road, Valley Road, and Floral Circle (1.8 miles).

From Libbey Beach Park to Cedar Gulch is 1.9 miles by low-tide beach. By going this way—getting water at the picnic area, camping at the primitive bluff-top sites, and continuing down the beach or undeveloped

Whidbey Island (West Shore)

bluffs to Ebey's Landing, then low-tide beach to the Keystone Ferry—you will experience the same feelings for this incredible area that Captain George Vancouver or other early explorers must have felt. Of course, you won't see any of the rich Indian culture that they knew, but the seals, birds, views, winds, smells, and sounds will be as similar to the primeval environment as possible.

From Cedar Gulch only 6.4 more miles on the beach bring us to the Keystone Ferry Landing at Admiralty Head. This part of the PNWT passes Perego's Lagoon—there is a lovely trail on the bluffs above it—Ebey's Landing, and the bluffs beyond to Fort Casey State Park. Much of this route was preserved by Congress in 1978 as the Ebey's Landing National Historic Reserve. This commemorates a famous incident in Northwest history, the 1857 beheading of Col. Isaac Ebey by Haida Indians after one of their chiefs had been killed by an American warship. Tread carefully here, for there are native plants—cacti, believe it or not—that make Perego's Lagoon extra special and indicate this microclimate's unexpected aridity. Because a violent 1983 storm breached the lagoon's protective dune, the bluff-hugging route is necessary except at low tide.

Look for snarled lookout trees, high above the shore, where you may see a bald eagle scanning the waves for his dinner. Enjoy grassy, cultivated Ebey's Prairie—so alive with redwing blackbirds and sparrows in summer and so buffeted by gales in winter.

Bicyclists here will have to pedal east on Libbey Road to rejoin Highway 20. (Our Scenic Heights Road bicycle alternate from Deception Pass rejoins 20 along here, too, from Oak Harbor.) Cycle southeast on the Penn Cove Road past Kennedy's Lagoon to Cemetery Road. Visit the old pioneer blockhouse at the Ebey's Prairie cemetery. Then follow Ebey's Landing Road around through the rich farmland to the coast and southeast along the bluffs. Bicycle Engle Road south to the ferry.

Fort Casey State Park, in addition to its interesting 1890s coastal gun emplacements, provides camping, restrooms, showers and drinking water. A restaurant is nearby.

After the sandy bluffs of the last few miles, Admiralty Head opens out as a sandy, cobbled, log-strewn spit, an appendage of Whidbey Island extending out into Admiralty Inlet and Puget Sound.

The Keystone Ferry crosses to Port Townsend year round.

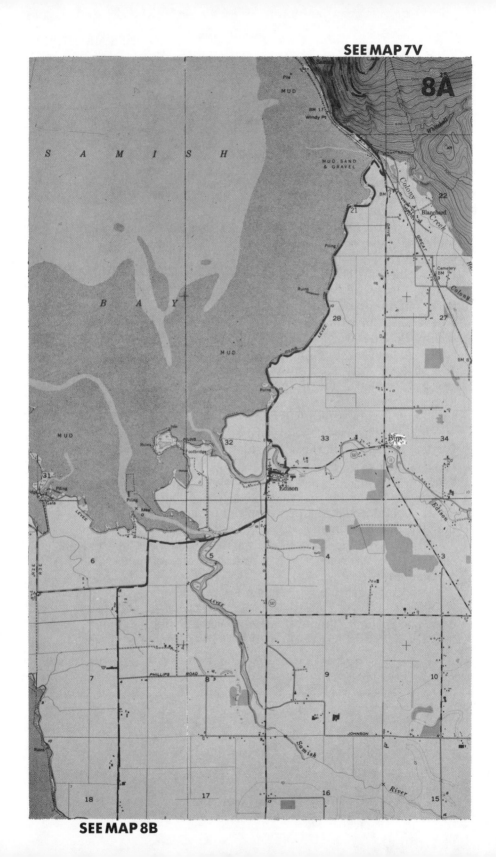

8A

SEE MAP 7V

S A M I S H

BAY

MUD

MUD

Pile
MUD

BM 17
Windy Pt

MUD, SAND
& GRAVEL

Colony Creek

Blanchard

Cemetery
BM

21

22

28

27

BM 8

32

33

Edison

34

31

Ruins

Footbridge

Piling

Edison

6

5

4

3

7

PHILLIPS ROAD

8

9

10

JOHNSON

Samish River

18

17

16

15

8B

SEE MAP 8C

LA CONNER 3 MI.

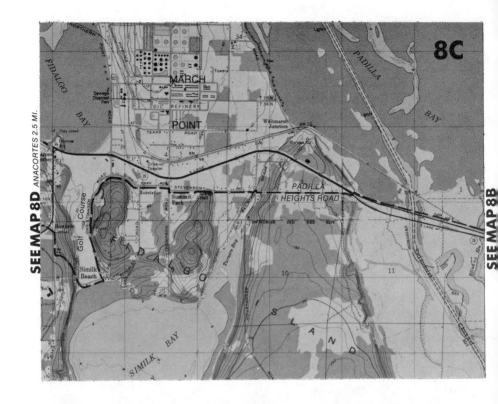

SEE MAP 8D ANACORTES 2.5 MI.

8C

SEE MAP 8B

SEE MAP 8C

8D

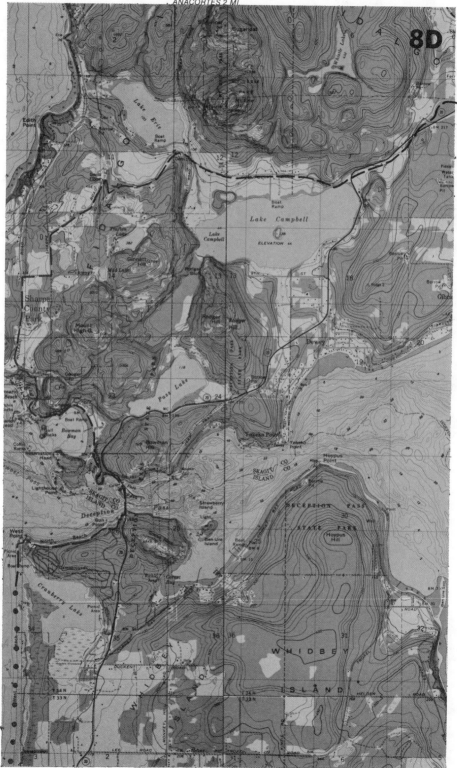

8E

CRESCENT

HARBOR

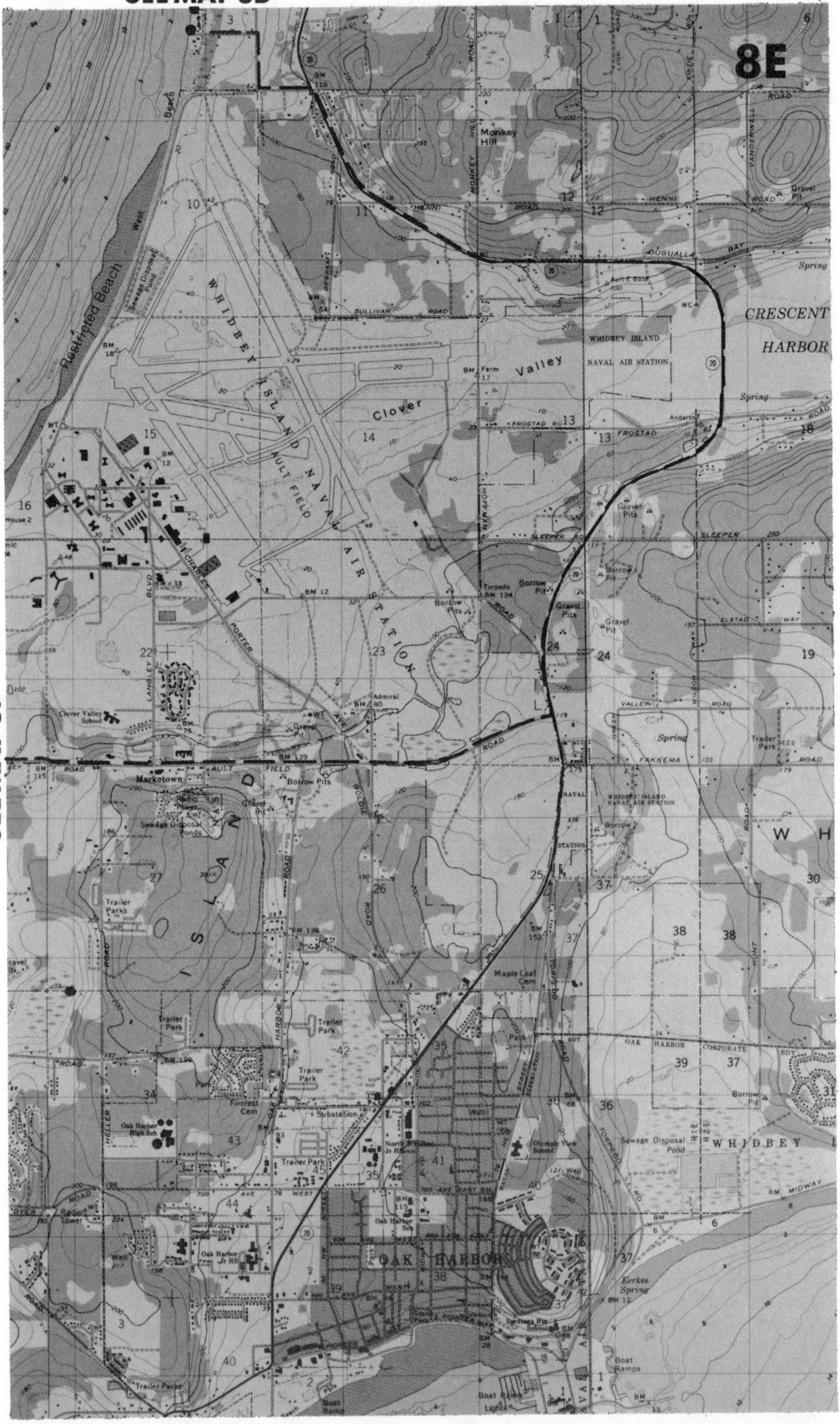

OAK HARBOR

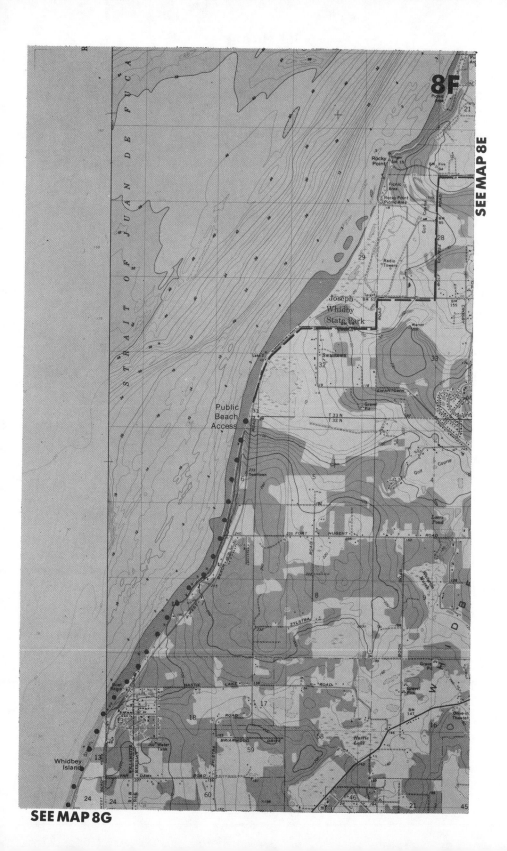

SEE MAP 8E

STRAIT OF JUAN DE FUCA

Rocky Point

Picnic Area

Rocky Point Picnic Area

Golf Course

Radio Towers

28

29

Joseph Whidby State Park

Swantown

32

33

Public Beach Access

T 33 N
T 32 N

5

4

Golf Course

FORT NUGENT

8

ZYLSTRA

17

HASTIE LAKE

ROAD

18

BRIARWOOD DRIVE

59

58

Hastie Lake

16

Whidbey Island

13

24

60

45

21

46

SEE MAP 8G

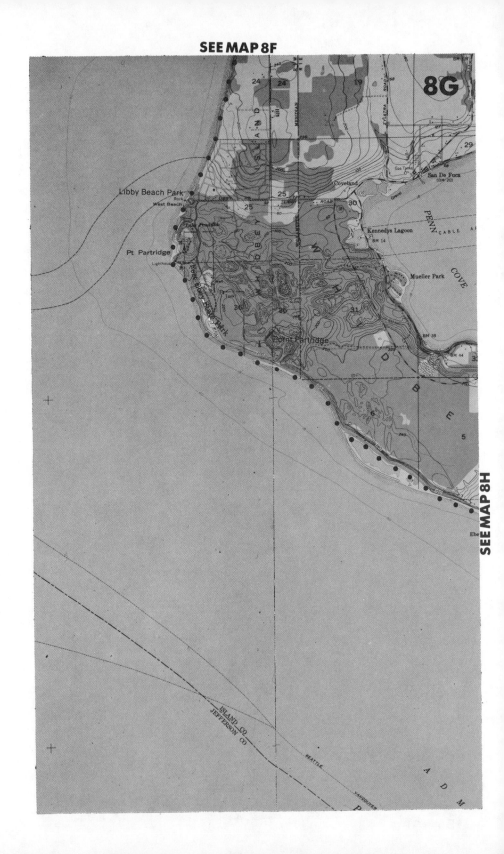

SEE MAP 8G

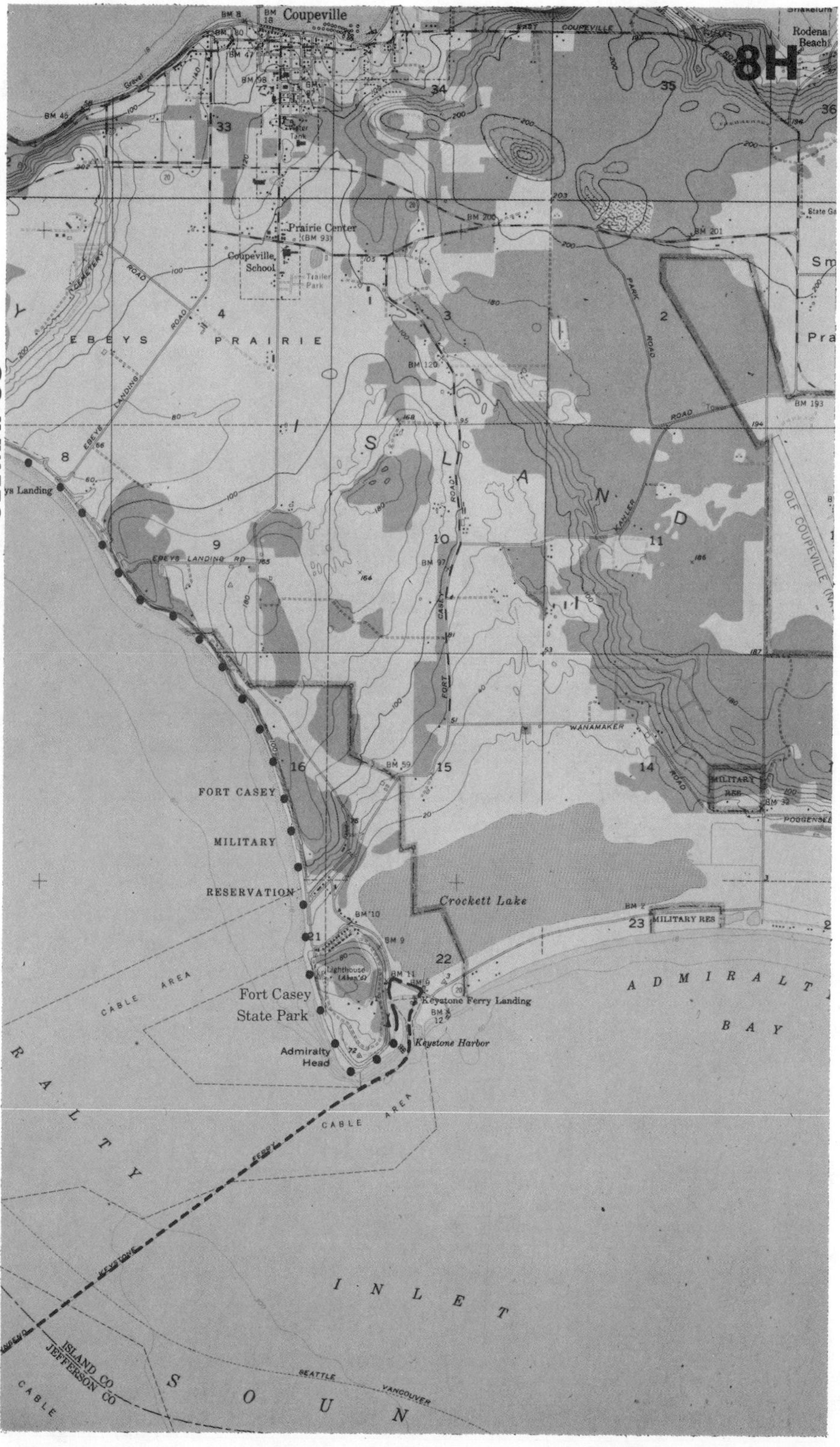

PORT TOWNSEND 1 MI.

THE OLYMPIC MOUNTAINS

(Keystone Ferry to Bogachiel State Park)

|| **9**

Mt. Carrie from Hurricane Ridge

INTRODUCTION

The Olympic Peninsula is the last major geographic portion of the Pacific Northwest Trail. It is like an enormous afterthought spliced onto the state of Washington. The mainstays of the peninsula are logging and tourism, with the area in the Olympic Mountains "rain shadow" an increasingly popular retirement area, especially near the town of Sequim. Whereas the rain-forest Pacific Ocean coast receives up to 200 inches annual rainfall, the northeast lee of the Olympic Mountains is semi-arid.

Beyond Port Townsend's quaint streets, the PNWT lingers along the shorelines of the Quimper Peninsula before crossing a series of hills to the Dungeness River and the Gray Wolf River. For a while all thought of sea water is forgotten as the route follows rivers and creeks and ridges toward the glacier-decked peaks at the center of the peninsula's spiral galaxy of great valleys. Halfway across, the PNWT drops steeply into one of the finest of these, the Elwha River Valley. Then, after hot springs, remote passes, and alpine spectacles, the Trail follows the wild Bogachiel River west out of Olympic National Park. From there the wilderness ocean beach of our next chapter is only a short rain-forest hike west.

The Olympic Peninsula is truly unique. It has its own brand of herbivores, the Roosevelt elk, and it boasts rare native plants along the PNWT's high-elevation scree slopes. Its marine life includes the mammals everyone wants to see, such as river otters and killer whales, and the creatures everyone wants to eat, such as the famous Dungeness crab.

PROBLEMS

We do not have a truly satisfactory route down the Quimper Peninsula and into the Olympic Mountains. We hope someday to replace most of this road walking with a real trail. (Any volunteers?)

Drinking water can be a problem along the high trails if you are not careful. Plan ahead and carry all the water you'll need and more. Sure, it rains a lot here, but you may be wet outside and thirsty inside.

There are no official campsites on Hurricane Ridge and Hurricane Hill, places heavily visited by summer auto traffic. Plan carefully where you are going to camp. backcountry permits are not required for Olympic National Forest. But in Olympic National Park, Backcountry use permits are required for all overnight backcountry use and are obtained free at all ranger stations and at some self-registration trailheads.

SUPPLIES

Snack-type food is sold on the Keystone Ferry. (The ferry ride itself costs $1.45 for a backpacker and $2.00 for a bicyclist.)

Port Townsend (98368), Sequim (98382), Port Angeles (98362), and Forks (98331) provide full PNWT-type services. In addition, you may send cache boxes ahead to yourself c/o Don and Bill Sullivan, Discovery Bay Grocery, 7760 Highway 101, Port Townsend, WA 98368. (Junction of Highways 101 and 20.) The Hurricane Ridge Visitors Center will *not* accept your box. But the concessionaires in the center do sell meals and junk food. There is a pay phone (206/452-9191) at the Elwha Ranger Station.

DECLINATION   22° E

USGS TOPOGRAPHIC MAPS

Port Townsend, North		Elwha	
Port Townsend, South		Mount Carrie	
Center		Bogachiel Peak	
Uncas		Slide Peak	
Tyler Peak	15'	Spruce Mountain	15'
Mt. Angeles	15'	Forks	15'
Hurricane Hill			

MILEAGES   (total 129.9)

		Total
Ferry slip at Port Townsend	0.0	0.0
Discovery Road via Seattle and North Coast tracks	4.3	4.3
Discovery Bay via Discovery Road	2.9	7.2

Railroad tracks just beyond Adelma Beach	.8	8.0
West Uncas Road (at foot of Discovery Bay)	6.0	14.0
Salmon Creek Road (80) via West Uncas Road	1.0	15.0
Spur 5 Road (721)	3.0	18.0
Snow Creek Road (965)	1.5	19.5
Louella Work Camp/Guard Station (1550) via Jimmycomelately Creek Road	5.0	24.5
Dungeness Forks Campground (850)	2.0	26.5
Gray Wolf River Trail No. 834 (950)	1.2	27.7
Twomile Camp (1100)	2.0	29.7
Cliff Camp (1300)	1.1	30.8
Camp Tony (1600)	1.7	32.5
Slab Camp (2500) via Slab Camp Creek Trail	2.4	34.9
Deer Park (5411)	6.1	41.0
Elk Mountain (6550)	5.5	46.5
Obstruction Point (6150)	2.1	48.6
Waterhole Picnic Area (5000)	4.5	53.1
Hurricane Ridge Visitors Center (5250)	3.9	57.0
Fire Road (5000)	.8	57.8
Whiskey Bend (1150)	8.0	65.8
Altair Campground (300)	5.0	70.8
Lake Mills Dam (605)	1.2	72.0
Observation Point	2.5	74.5
Happy Lake Ridge Trail (1750)	.8	75.3
Olympic Hot Springs (2061)	3.2	78.5
Appleton Pass (5000)	5.2	83.7
Soleduck River (3100)	2.6	86.3
Seven Mile Camp (3150)	.5	86.8
High Divide (5050)	3.1	89.9
Bogachiel Peak/Hoh Lake turn-off (5150)	2.1	92.0
Deer Lake (3150)	4.2	96.2
Mink Lake Trail junction (4130) via Little (Low) Divide	3.6	99.8
Slide Pass (3600)	2.7	102.5
21 Mile (2214)	1.5	104.0
Hyak Shelter Site (1400)	3.2	107.2
15 Mile Shelter (1000)	3.0	110.2
Flapjack Shelter Site (645) and Bogachiel-Hoh Trail	4.1	114.3

River crossing to largest Pacific silver fir (780)	2.1	116.4
Bogachiel Shelter (445) and Indian Pass Trail	2.1	118.5
Park Boundary (400)	4.1	122.6
Bogachiel Road 2943 (360)	2.0	124.6
Bogachiel State Park and U.S. 101 (203)	5.3	129.9

ROUTE DESCRIPTION

In the 1870s many Olympia Peninsula boosters thought that Port Townsend would become the major city of Washington Territory. By the time of statehood in 1888, that hope had been dashed; Olympia became the capital and Seattle quickly outpaced every rival. Port Townsend slumbered on into the twentieth century, shipping out lumber, grain, coal, and fish. It is now a busy, progressive town and, by virtue of its splendid bluff overlooking Admiralty Inlet and its well-preserved Victorian architecture, a "must" for PNWT aficionados. Plan to surrender to the town's spell and stay awhile. Wash that laundry. Restore those feet. Ease those aches.

Several types of lodging are available. North of town at Fort Worden you can keep to your trusty tent at the State Park campground. Or you can sample American Youth Hostel life (206/385-0655). Even better are the in-town bed-and-breakfasts in gingerbread houses. Inquire at the Chamber of Commerce, 2437 Sims Way (206/385-2722). Also, ask the chamber for information about the following attractions: the museum, the post office (in the old customs house), the commandant's house at Fort Worden complete with period furnishings, clock tower tours and splendid views at the Courthouse, the fire bell tower, and the Rothschild House's 1860s period furnishings.

Private land currently limits route possibilities on the way south, so the PNWT now follows rails and roads to the bottom end of Discovery Bay. An alternate route for the hard-core hiker is the all-beach route (low tide) west from Fort Worden, a thirsty, no drinking water trek. That way does have the potential for good views of Protection Island, a new (1982) National Wildlife Refuge with about 90 species of Puget Sound nesting birds (including rhinoceros auklets).

Fill your canteens with water at Port Townsend, and choose a grocery store. Port Townsend has several, including the large Safeway located at Haine Place on the main highway at the south edge of town. Downtown there are two bakeries, an ice cream parlor, and a classic old tavern with an Old West bar. The new (1984) ferry slip is south of the main Water Street business district.

PNWT hikers and bicyclists and horsemen go south along Water Street all the way to the marina at the south end of town, passing many boatyards and small businesses. Near the railroad ferry wharf, begin to walk the Seattle and North Coast Railroad's right-of-way. A dirt road parallels the tracks and shore most of the way to the Crown Zellerbach paper mill at Glen Cove. Trains are infrequent, and the tracks squeezed between sandy bluffs and the shore are a good birding and rubbernecking place.

Close to the paper mill's rail entrance, you can follow a motorcycle trail uphill to a potential campsite (waterless) atop the sandy bluffs. This is not an official site, but an informal motorcycle-scramble course heavily used by bikers. Still, the view is an unbeatable PNWT combination of smokestacks and watery, island-studded horizons.

After 4.3 miles the railroad tracks reach the overpass of Discovery Road. (Don't mistake this overpass for the earlier Highway 20 overpass.) Climb up the left bank and go left (south) 2.9 miles down this quiet, rural road to the Chevy Chase Golf Course at Discovery Bay.

Turn left at a beautiful, white former inn and pass the Discovery Bay Camp Meeting on your way to the residential community of Adelma Beach (.75 mile). This bluff-top road has a prospect south (with clear-weather views of the Olympics) and western views of the Miller Peninsula's Cry Baby Hill.

At Adelma Beach do not turn right downhill through houses on Lower Adelma Beach Road. Do turn right .1 mile later, immediately before the railroad tracks at a sawmill, and follow a paved road 1 mile to a dead end at private property, where you cross about 50 feet over onto the railroad right-of-way again.

Why not, you ask, take good old State Highway 20 all the way from Port Townsend to the foot of Discovery Bay—especially since it is more direct? Do not try it! This road is a major, *high speed* arterial—often with no shoulders at all. The railway and Discovery Road are not perfect, but at least they give the PNWT pilgrim more flavor of the country with less danger.

From Adelma Beach continue south all the way to Port Discovery on the railroad grade. Don't be tempted to dig up any of the millions of clams on the beaches here because they are private property and are jealously guarded by observers on the other side of Discovery Bay at Mill Point. And at the scattering of houses known as Woodman's, do not be tempted to make the 1-mile side trip to Anderson Lake State Park; it has neither camping nor drinking water. Continue south down the Quimper Peninsula, enjoying the changing prospects of the bay and thinking of the Olympic high country ahead.

If you have sent a food cache box ahead, pick it up from Don and Bill Sullivan at their Discovery Bay Grocery. Ask them about tenting possibilities in the immediate vicinity.

From the Discovery Bay Grocery we have a 15-mile walk to reach Gray Wolf Trail No. 834. The Gray Wolf River is composed primarily of its main branch, originating near Gray Wolf Pass, and Cameron Creek and Grand Creek. This powerful stream itself is the main tributary of the Dungeness River. The two join near where we first meet them and flow north past Sequim to just east of New Dungeness Bay's Dungeness Spit. This Douglas fir, fern, and salmon gateway to the mountains is a classic PNWT experience and one quite different from the rain-forest valleys on the other side of the peninsula. The Gray Wolf and Dungeness Rivers are often semi-arid during the prime hiking season. Sequim's annual precipitation averages 19 inches, quite a difference from the 200 inches not far away at the summit of Mount Olympus.

There are two problems with our eastern Olympics route. First, that 15-mile access route is all on heavy-duty logging roads rather than pathways. Our Association will try to remedy this trail gap, but for now it's road pounding for you. Second, the river's volatile water levels eventually sweep away even the finest backwoods bridges, leaving us, so to speak, up the crick. Because the condition of these wooden crossings may change suddenly, we recommend that you inquire in advance about your possible need to take a detour. (Quilcene Ranger Station, Quilcene, WA 98376; 206/765-3368.)

Although there are actually several good automobile approaches to the Gray Wolf River trailhead and to the PNWT west of there, our Practical Route is the most direct for a person on foot. Go south from the Discovery Bay Grocery 1 mile on the West Uncas Road. This road hugs the west side of the farm valley that contains both Salmon Creek and Snow Creek. After leaving placid Discovery Bay, our next contact with salt water will be the mercurial reaches of the open Pacific.

Our route westward will parallel Salmon Creek. Then, after crossing it on the West Uncas Road, look immediately for a homestead between the creek and the high-voltage power lines. The Salmon Creek Road does not look like much—just a dirt driveway leading back into the woods past the few buildings. Follow this former logging road, at first travelling near the power lines and then edging left under them to a locked gate in the alder woods. Continue west and around a clearcut to a junction with a new logging-road spur coming up from farther south on the Uncas Road. Continue west on this improved road to the far side of the next clearcut; there turn right onto the woodsy, little-travelled original road. This part loops north around a forested hump. Afterward we resume our westward direction toward a new bridge crossing of Salmon Creek. Shortly after the bridge, turn left into the alders up another remnant portion of the original road, this time all the way to an unmarked junction with the comparable-looking Spur 5 Road 2905. Turn left and continue uphill to another clearcut and beyond to a signed junction with Snow Creek Road 2907 (965). Throughout this area, water supply is not a problem.

Walking .7 mile beyond, we make a right turn onto the Snow Creek Road that puts us at a pass between the Salmon Creek drainage and the drainage of a tributary of Jimmycomelately Creek. (The road we are following is called the Snow Creek Road because it does connect with Snow Creek much farther south.) We descend this tributary to Road 2925, which we take up the broad, homesteaded valley of Jimmycomelately Creek—a total of 5 miles to the unmarked site of the former Louella Guard Station (1550).

Shortly before the Louella Work Camp, the Palo Alto Road joins us from Sequim in the north. (If you are interested in history, the Sequim

Bicentennial Committee's *Dungeness: The Lure Of A River* is a good reference.) Not far beyond the Louella Work Camp, turn south on Road 2958 and follow it down to the river at the Dungeness Forks Campground. This is a no-fee, Forest Service car campground with a water pump and an extremely small shelter (actually a covered, three-sided notice board).

From the campground climb to Road 2927. Turn right and descend to a bridge across the river and to Trail No. 834 immediately beyond. There is a campsite on the south side of the bridge. Just 2 miles up the trail we reach Twomile Camp, in the forest at the river's edge. On the way, this newly built trail section climbs through charming cedar and fir woods to a clearcut with tantalizing views up the valley. Beyond Twomile Camp the valley widens, and the trail follows a ferny, up-and-down route near the river 1.1 miles to Cliff Camp (1300).

The valley walls beyond Cliff Camp are so abrupt and narrow that the trail must cross to the south side of the river to avoid a high, sheer wall of fascinating conglomerate rock. Beyond the sturdy bridge the trail climbs high above the river, and in 1.7 miles we reach the excellent shelter at Camp Tony (1600). In salmon spawning season, look for thousands of the migrating fish and for their rotting carcasses.

At Camp Tony the side trail down to the river begins next to the upstream wall of the shelter. A short walk brings us to the new 4-foot-diameter log that was winched into place for this crossing in September 1983. The 900-foot elevation gain on pretty but unspectacular Slab Camp Creek Trail No. 838 takes 2.4 wooded miles.

When you reach Road 2926, look across it to your left for Trail No. 846. Because there is no reliable water on the 4.9-mile climb west from here to Deer Park, you should tank up either down on Slab Camp Creek or off our route northeast along the road at Canyon Creek. Although trail No. 846 is steep and offers neither camping nor reliable water, its semi-open environment is a heady change from the valley bottoms. We climb quickly from 2500' at the trail junction to 5411' at Deer Park, crossing from Olympic National Forest into Olympic National Park. This trail is where the Olympic Mountains, the San Juans, Mt. Baker, Glacier Peak, and Puget Sound all begin to come into focus.

Once we arrive at Deer Park, we are at last upon the heights of the Olympic Mountains. (This, like most alpine areas in the park, is a stove-only zone.) A short side road is available to take us to the summit of Blue Mountain (6007). The Deer Park Road also provides good automobile access to Port Angeles, about 20 miles north. A national park ranger is stationed at the Deer Park car campground all summer; backcountry use permits are available here. Because of no water ahead, be sure to fill your canteens on the road at the ranger cabin spring, where there is also a garage/shelter and the next trailhead.

The 7.6-mile trail to Obstruction Point is an extremely scenic ridge path. This trail is not only open-slope, unobstructed vistas but also the highest part of our PNWT through the park. Our up-and-down route takes us over Green Mountain (5622), Maiden Peak (6434), and the east end of

Hurricane Ridge (highest at 6550' on Elk Mountain). A height of 6550' may not seem very high in relation to many other sections of the PNWT, but tree line in the Olympic Mountains is lower than in, say, the Rockies, the Selkirks, and the Cascades. The West Peak of Mount Olympus, highest point in the park, is only 7965'. What these mountains lack in raw elevation they more than make up for in alpine scenery, wildlife, and flowers. Mountain goats, for instance, are so tame that they are considered pests by park management, who are trying to relocate them all out of the park.

People are easily fooled by these mountains' relatively gentle appearance and altitude. Trail conditions here can be very dangerous because of the weather's unpredictability and severity. Ridgetop visibility on even a sunny day can quickly shrink to zero during sudden whiteouts. Drenching rain and/or sleet, of course, is a constant possibility in an area subject to record precipitation. Hypothermia conditions are always just around the corner.

On this waterless, exposed trail between Deer Park and Obstruction Point, low-impact, hypothermia-wary trekkers should plan carefully where to camp. Camping is not allowed within a mile of Obstruction Point. This route has a number of potential places for dry camping. One is Maiden Lake and another is Roaring Winds. Maiden Lake is stagnant by late July, and Roaring Winds is waterless except for seasonal snowfields. End-to-enders may very well be doing snow camping here, which expands one's water and site possibilities if one is adequately prepared.

Don't forget, too, that the steep east face of Obstruction Point is often solid ice in early summer until the park staffers dig out the trail. In that case, you could bypass this part by going down into Badger Valley and then up to Grand Lake and up East Ridge, an 8.3-mile side trip. Dangerous weather is another reason to think about dropping a thousand feet down into lush, green Badger Valley (no badgers, plenty of marmots) about 5 miles west from Deer Park. The Badger Valley Trail passes good water and many campsites down in the timbered bottoms. And farther south, in Grand Valley, there are several attractive lakes. You could even make a loop from them back to the Gray Wolf River via Grand Pass and Cameron Creek. Another alternate route to consider is the connection between Three Forks on the Gray Wolf River and Deer Park, a 4.5-mile trail that has one water source en route and would give you more time on the river. As always, we invite you to regard the main line PNWT as a white-colored thread in a fabric of potential routes.

During snowy years the Deer Park–Obstruction Point trail may be open only from mid-July to Labor Day. In case of a bad storm, get down off the exposed ridge or, better yet, do not venture west from Deer Park without signs of favorable weather conditions.

In the 1950s this trail had been scheduled for conversion to an extension of the Hurricane Ridge Road. However, the unstable slopes at Obstruction Point literally blocked that scheme. Our Association favors closing the Obstruction Point road to automobiles and leaving it to the foot-powered set and to park shuttle buses. In any case, the scenery from this road is spectacular—the Lillian River Valley; McCartney Peak (6784); and, of course, glacier-white Mount Carrie and Mount Olympus.

Despite its high summer visitation and its lack of water and developed campsites, Hurricane Ridge is a PNWT highlight. To enjoy its grand scenery, go northwest 4.5 miles from Obstruction Point to the Waterhole Picnic Area (5000) below Eagle Point (6247). Camping is no longer permitted here, nor is the waterhole reliable. The road crosses wildflower meadows studded with scenic copses of subalpine firs. The farther we continue, the more amazing the views of the deep Lillian and Elwha Valleys become and the more primeval glacier-clad Mount Carrie and Mount Olympus seem. But to all this must now be added a third element—northern seascapes, beyond Port Angeles, of the Strait of Juan de Fuca and of B.C.'s provincial capital, Victoria, on Vancouver Island.

Continue northwest 3.9 miles to the Hurricane Ridge Visitors Center. Halfway, we pass Steeple Rock (5567) which, when we look back, does look like a church tower.

The 18-mile Mount Angeles Road connects the Visitors Center with the Heart O' The Hills Olympic National Park headquarters and with Port Angeles. (No bus service except for tour buses.) The visitors center is great for modern restrooms, telephones, and for its limited, but non-freeze-dried, food. You may wish to make a side trip up the paved trail to the old lookout site atop Hurricane Hill (5757) to enjoy some of the best views in the park. Unfortunately, no hiker/horseman camping facilities have been provided anywhere on the ridge. However, Olympic National Park does not restrict backcountry travelers to limited campsites; use common sense to find a low-impact spot.

Go .8 scenic meadow-ridge mile on the asphalt, dodging vehicles of all sizes, until you reach the old fire-protection road, now the 8-mile Wolf Creek trail, down the Elwha River. The first water on the Wolf Creek Trail is 1.9 miles down; the trail's width is usually wide enough to accommodate camping. As you descend the long road-type switchbacks to Whiskey Bend, note the lower Elwha River Valley's mix of dark old growth and lighter, fire-produced second growth.

The name Whiskey Bend commemorates the bottle of booze given to the Civilian Conservation Corps's highest-mileage road locator in the Depression-era contest to decide the route of this old road. But it's water, not liquor, you'll find if you take the ¼-mile side trail from the Whiskey Bend Road to the campground where the Elwha River joins Lake Mills. Be sure to turn the corner up the creek to see the waterfall at the head of Lake Mills.

From Lake Mills the Ideal Route goes up trailless Cat Creek to the fabulous High Divide country. Back on Hurricane Ridge, we could see this next destination across the Elwha River Valley. The High Divide is a very rugged alpine ridge, which separates the Elwha River, Hoh River, and Soleduck River watersheds. To reach it by our Ideal Route, we must cross the Elwha River near the campground to the west bank of Lake Mills. Short of making a raft or finding a friendly boatman, the only ways over are to walk about 3 miles upstream to the Long Ridge Trail bridge and bushwhack back or to go around the lake by road and bushwhack south from Observation Point. Anyway, once we are at the south end of Lake Mills, the Ideal Route is a brush-bucking, windfall-wrestling siwash 8 miles up to the High Divide. We begin at Lake Mills' 600' elevation and climb steadily to 4350' at a col west of Cat Peak. Although this bushwhack is quite feasible and in many ways extremely attractive, it should not be attempted unless you are prepared for much difficult slogging. But if you do follow Cat Creek, you will experience some of the peninsula's deepest wilderness in arriving at its most spectacular ridgetop trail. Cat Creek drains the glaciers and late snowpacks of Mount Carrie, Mount Fitzhenry, and the unnamed ridge to the west. Many creeks feed its turbulent waters, and wildlife abounds in its woods, sandbars, meadows, and mountains. Dwarfed by the neighboring Elwha and Hoh River Valleys, Cat Creek is nevertheless one of the PNWT's greatest wilderness streams.

Our Practical Route leaves Whiskey Bend via the 5-mile Lake Mills Road to the Altaire (fee) Campground. From its pleasant setting amidst cottonwoods, maples, and alders, we turn upstream on the old Olympic Hot Springs Road 1.2 miles to the Lake Mills Dam (605). At Observation Point we have a very good view of the upper and lower parts of the Elwha Valley, including snowy Mount Fitzhenry. The road is closed to vehicles at Cougar Creek, 1.5 miles below the hot springs. There is a small creek and an outhouse at this popular roadhead.

The Olympic Hot Springs once were an elaborate concession of cabins, pools, and piped waters. Today we have a nice campground (picnic tables, rest rooms, piped water, and bear-proof food-suspension cable) on the north side of Boulder Creek and the sulphur-smelling springs scattered over the hillside on the south side. Cross the bridge and look for the hot-water pools informally created by earlier bathers.

From the Boulder Creek Campground (2061) we climb in 5.2 miles to 5000' at Appleton Pass. There is plenty of water along this route, except at the pass itself. Camping is good at both the hot springs and the pass and at several places in between, such as Upper Boulder Creek Falls and where the trail first emerges from the deep woods into the brushy creek and basin country. However, the Park Service has posted the following sign at the pass to make people think twice about camping in this area:

Warning—Severe Bear Problems, Boulder Campground
to Appleton Pass.
Bears have reached and removed food and camping gear that was hung in and between trees. Some was hung 20 feet high.
If you camp in the Appleton Pass area, you will very likely lose property and there is a possibility of personal injury!!!

The first 4.5 miles to the pass are in hemlock, cedar, and Douglas fir woods as the trail crosses the creek twice and intercepts numerous smaller brooks. Finally, after switchbacking into alpine meadows and basins, we reach good views of Mount Olympus and of the High Divide. Oyster Lake is a scenic pool in meadows atop this ridge·

From Appleton Pass our next destination—the High Divide—is not as near as it seems. We must first descend 2.6 miles through dense Douglas-fir forest to the Soleduck River (3100). From there the PNWT climbs .5 mile to Seven Mile Camp and switchbacks 3.1 more miles to the High Divide, passing plenty of water and campsites (but no shelters). The Park Service encourages people to spread out and not to camp at Heart Lake in the center of the upper basin. This area is sometimes a very popular weekend destination.

Anyway, there is no need for you to join the crowds if you do not want to. Even in an area of heavy visitor use, there are ways to find relative solitude. For instance, in the Seven Lakes Basin area you could camp a bit out of the way at Clear Lake, Long Lake, or Morganroth Lake (but not Lunch Lake). At Deer Lake try the side valley behind the small hill where the creek enters the lake near the ranger's tent. Also, from our initial point on the Soleduck River, you could go downstream 5.1 miles to the beautiful narrow canyon of Soleduck Falls, then 1.5 miles farther to the Sol Duc Hot Springs resort and a refreshing soak. This spa is a great place to dry out and clean up after weeks on the PNWT. There are cabins, small store, swimming pool, ranger station, phones, and meals. From the resort it is only 4.3 miles via the Mink Lake Trail to the Little Divide and the main-line PNWT. Another variant would be to turn south at the Soleduck Falls on the 3.1-mile Deer Lake Trail to the Little Divide junction at Deer Lake. This deep-woods route is a safe-from-storms choice when the high country is socked in and the subalpine firs are holding on for dear life.

Neither words nor photographs are adequate to portray the beauties of the High Divide Trail. Where our Practical Route joins the High Divide above the meadows of Heart Lake and then turns west past the glacier-scoured Seven Lakes Basin, we are at the scenic focal point of the Olympics (5050). If you have time and good visibility, go *east* on the High Divide Trail to enjoy its Hoh Valley/Mount Olympus views. In 2 miles you will reach Cat Basin above Cat Creek Valley. (A .3-mile way trail connects with the creek.) Continue 2 miles farther on the High Divide Trail to the trailless ridge at the south end of Cat Peak, where our Ideal Route emerges from a side valley of Cat Creek. Camping and water are very limited on the last 2 miles of this trail. But here we enjoy unexcelled views of Mount Olympus. Plus, for end-to-enders we now have the thrill of looking out the Hoh River Valley to the no-longer-distant Pacific Ocean!

From the Soleduck River junction above Heart Lake, the PNWT follows the High Divide's open meadows west. Expect stunning views not only of Mount Olympus (due south) but also of the deep, U-shaped, green trough of the Hoh River Valley. Almost equally lovely is the lake country north of us. (Keep your eyes peeled for summering elk herds.)

One of the best places to take in all this beauty is the former lookout-tower site atop Bogachiel Peak (5464). A short side trail leads up to the summit from the U-shaped pass where the High Divide, Canyon Creek-Hoh Trail, and the Bogachiel Trail meet. This viewpoint is one of those PNWT favorites where many days of walking can be seen all at once. And if you have brought up water and a strong tent, you are possibly in for an epic ocean sunset.

Despite unimaginative names like Lake No. 8 and No Name Lake, the dozen or so ponds of the highly glaciated Seven Lakes Basin attract legions of fishermen and campers. The basin was misnamed and miscounted by its discoverer, Chris Morganroth, since immortalized by the name Morganroth Lake.

From Bogachiel Peak the immense bulk of Mount Olympus seems to shimmer very near at hand. If you wish to touch its Blue Glacier, a Herculean side trip would drop you down 6.5 miles to the Hoh River for a further 7.1-mile climb to the foot of the ice field.

From the trail junction at a saddle immediately below Bogachiel Peak, we go northwest away from the Hoh River Valley and around the head-waters of the main-fork Bogachiel River (parallel to the Hoh) on the Little (Low) Divide. Our route follows the ridge northwest between the upper Bogachiel and the Seven Lakes Basin. In .9 mile of superb scenery the Bogachiel Trail reaches a way trail down into the Seven Lakes Basin. (Round Lake is .8 mile this way.) However, our route continues along the ridge for another 3.3 miles to Deer Lake, mostly in the meadows of the upper Bogachiel Basin but eventually descending into the forest near Deer Lake.

Deer Lake is on the north side of the ridge between the Soleduck and Bogachiel Valleys. (There is no shelter here now.) Because the trail made a detour off the ridge to reach the lake, we must now climb back up. The trail up to the Little (Low) Divide starts at a boardwalk at the boggy south end of Deer Lake. This 3.6-mile, meadows/subalpine-fir-forest Bogachiel Trail offers no reliable on-trail water. And Bogachiel Lake is too far below the path to be a convenient source. However, a short, downhill side trip north on the Mink Lake Trail would bring you to a creek, which drains an ice-cold tarn.

The alpine meadows of Knob 4304' look out on forest-ringed Blackwood Lake and the whole magnificent Upper Bogachiel Valley. After our long climb from Deer Lake, the trail breaks out of the forest at Knob 4304' for more Mount Olympus views. Then we zigzag down the narrow ridge and leave it at forested Slide Pass (3600).

Whereas the High Divide north of the Hoh River ranges in elevation from between 5000' and 6000', the Low Divide between the Bogachiel and the Soleduck is only 3500' to 4100' high. Furthermore, at Slide Pass the PNWT turns northwest between Misery Peak and Slide Peak into the head-waters of the North Fork Bogachiel River. In other words, instead of continuing to follow the ridge north of the river's main branch, the trail loops around north to settle into the North Fork Valley. At this point a very interesting cross-country hop would take us 6 miles from Slide Pass's silver-fir and hemlock woods along this trailless, 3500' high exten-sion of the Little Divide, over Sugarloaf Mountain (3365), and down to the 15 Mile Shelter footbridge near the junction of the river's North and main forks.

That ridgehop would make an excellent circuit hike with the PNWT's next superb valley section, 7 miles of the remotest rain forest in the park. To reach this special environment, we drop down 5 miles from Slide Pass (3600) to the site of the late, lamented Hyak Shelter (1400). A good campsite along this heavily forested stretch is at 21 Mile Shelter (2214), where our trail finally levels out into the valley bottom. The Hyak Shelter is an excellent campsite at the edge of a beautiful riverside meadow, where we can see up out of the great trees to the ridges beyond.

From Hyak prepare for a lazy day moseying the 7.1 miles down to the Flapjack Shelter site. This is prime rain-forest valley bottom which, unlike the Hoh River Valley, has not been developed. Admittedly, this valley is not as total a rain forest as the Hoh, Queets, and Quinault valleys because it has a greater proportion of Douglas fir and silver fir than they do and fewer mature colonnades of trees that have grown from "nurse logs." However, the Bogachiel's lush growth and enormous Sitka spruce certainly do spell rain forest. Its park-like retreats must seem ideal enough to the elk, who keep them open with winter and spring browsing. No other long-distance trail has anything comparable.

Near the 15 Mile Shelter site, we cross a footbridge to the North Fork's north bank. Giant Douglas firs dominate the bench here near a delightful waterfall. Our trail continues via the north shore and soon reaches the place where the Bogachiel's main branch and North Fork join. We follow this single, mightier river oceanward.

The distance is only 8.3 miles from the site of the former Flapjack Shelter to the park boundary. (There is a good swimming hole ¼ mile upriver from the Flapjack site, near a cliff on the south side of the river.) The trail's easy, slight ups and downs are initially in old-growth forest. From the Bogachiel Shelter (and ranger station) it is 4.2 miles to the park boundary.

Near the park boundary we encounter mossy stumps. Part of this area had been logged years ago, and in 1983 the old logging-road route was partially changed to include a new trail section up to a new extension of Bogachiel Road 2943. From the park boundary to this road totals 2 miles. Then, after 5.3 miles of road walking, we finally reach Bogachiel State Park and U.S. 101.

Bogachiel State Park (203) has $5.50 car campsites, $3 walk-in campsites, and 25-cent showers. A public phone is available just across the river bridge at the Bogachiel Resort store. Public transportation is not available to the nearby town of Forks.

Mt. Angeles from Hurricane Hill

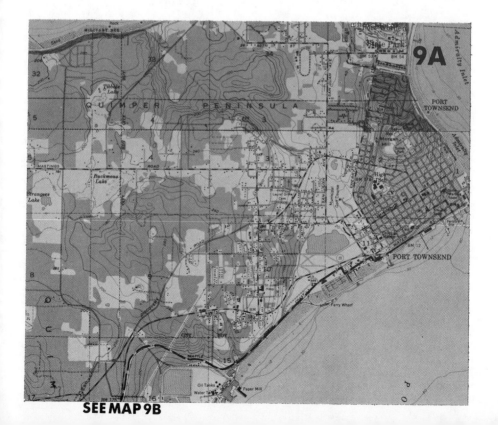

SEE MAP 9B

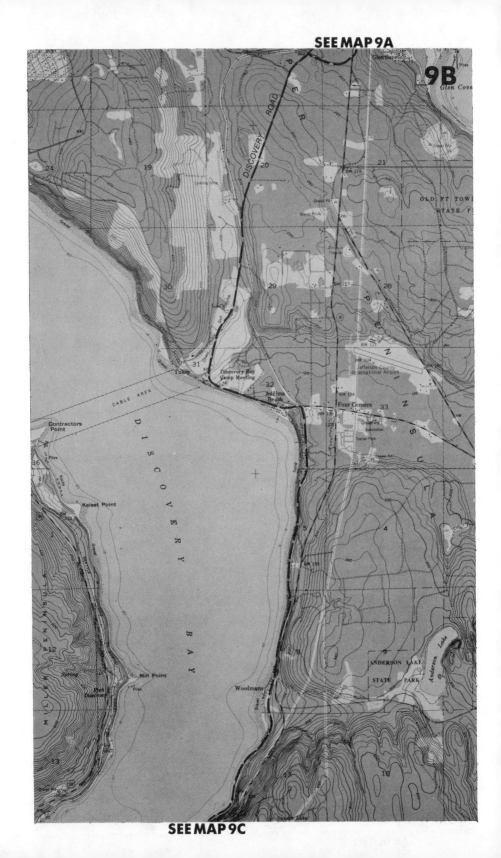

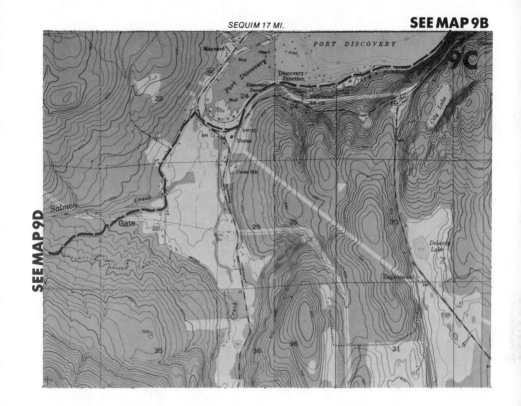

SEE MAP 9D

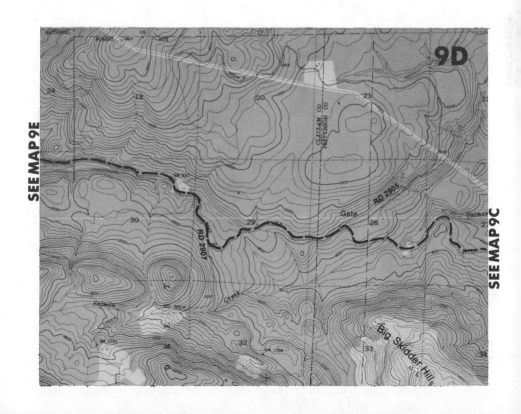

SEE MAP 9E

SEE MAP 9C

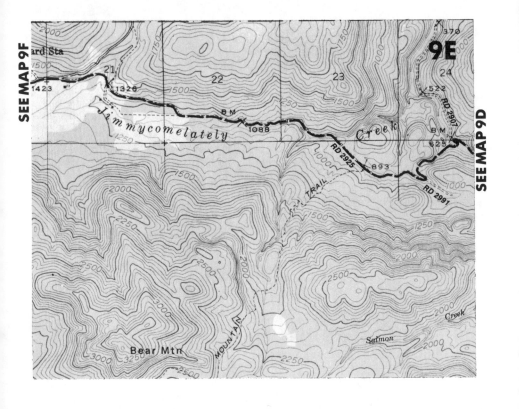

SEE MAP 9F

9E

SEE MAP 9D

ard Sta

21

22

23

24

1423

1320

BM
1088

Jammycomelately

Creek

522

RD 2907

BM
625

893

RD 2925

RD 2931

TRAIL

Bear Mtn

MOUNTAIN

Salmon

Creek

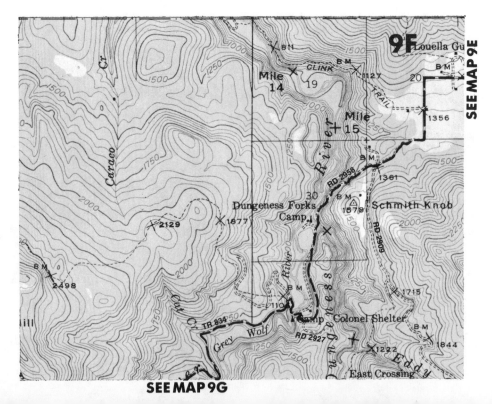

9F Louella Gu

SEE MAP 9E

Cr

BM

BM

20

BM

Mile
14

19

CLINK

1127

TRAIL

1356

Mile
15

Caraco

River

BM

1361

30

RD 2958

Dungeness Forks
Camp

1578

Schmith Knob

RD 2909

2129

1677

BM
2498

1715

Cut Cr

Dungeness

BM

TR 834

110

Camp
Colonel Shelter

BM

ill

Grey Wolf

RD 2927

1844

1222

River

Eddy

East Crossing

SEE MAP 9G

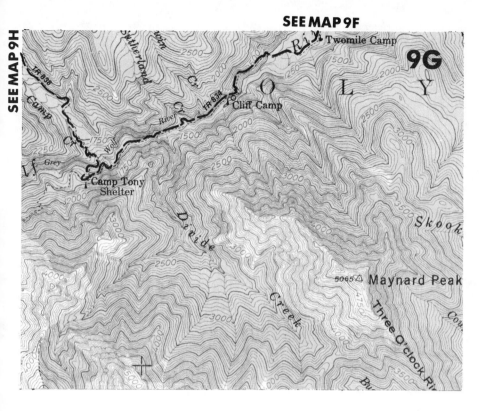

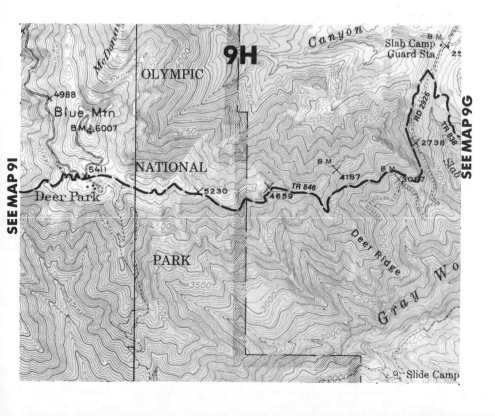

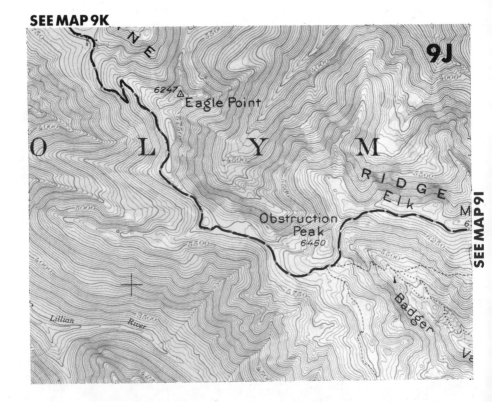

SEE MAP 9H

9I

3750
3500
3500
5000
4250
4500
3750
3500
5250
5500
5250
5622
Green
Mtn
*Maiden
Lake*
Maiden Peak
△6434
4750
4500

P   I   C

5000
3750
4250
3250

Roaring Winds

ountain
764

SEE MAP 9J

Creek
Grand
3500
3500
3250
4500
4500

SEE MAP 9K

9J

3500
3500
1000
3500
5500
△6247
Eagle Point

O   L   Y   M

RIDGE
Elk
M
5000
4500
4000
3500
Obstruction
Peak
6450
5750
5500
6250
6

SEE MAP 9I

Badger
Ve
Lillian
River
3500
4000

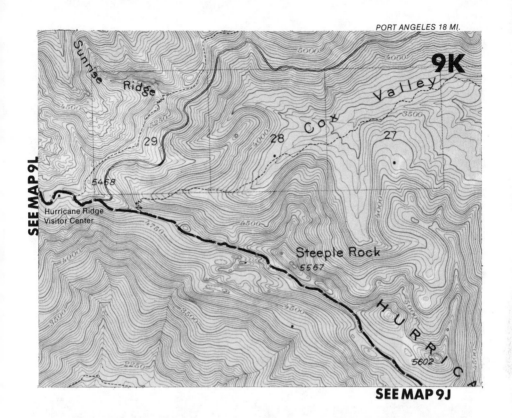

9K

Sunrise Ridge

Cox Valley

29   28   27

5468

Hurricane Ridge
Visitor Center

Steeple Rock
5567

HURRICA

5602

SEE MAP 9L

SEE MAP 9J

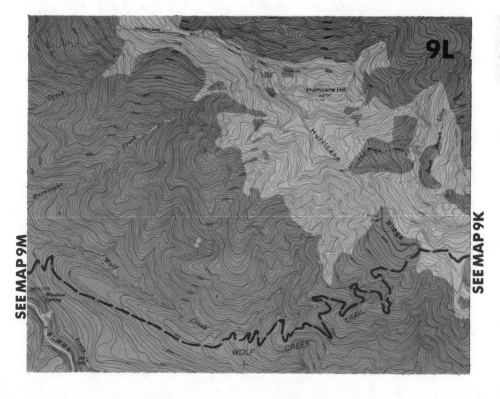

9L

Hurricane Hill

Creek

Wolf

WOLF CREEK

TRAIL

SEE MAP 9M

SEE MAP 9K

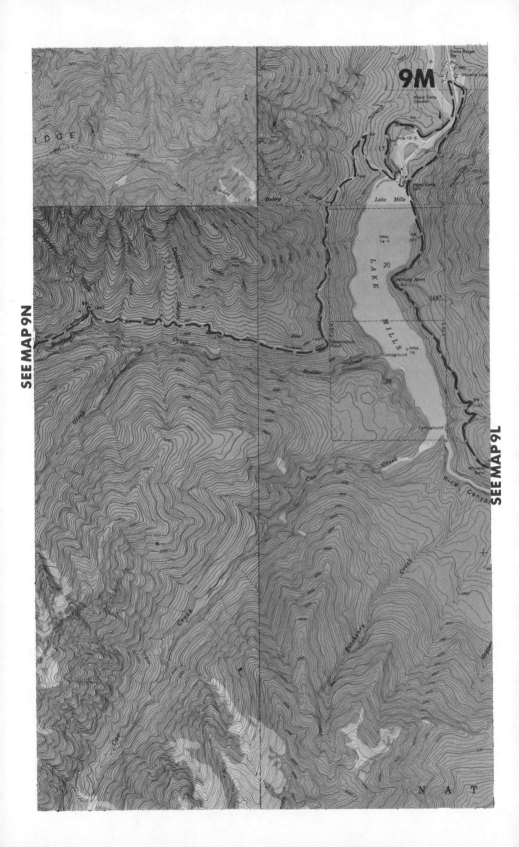

SEE MAP 9N

SEE MAP 9L

SEE MAP 9M

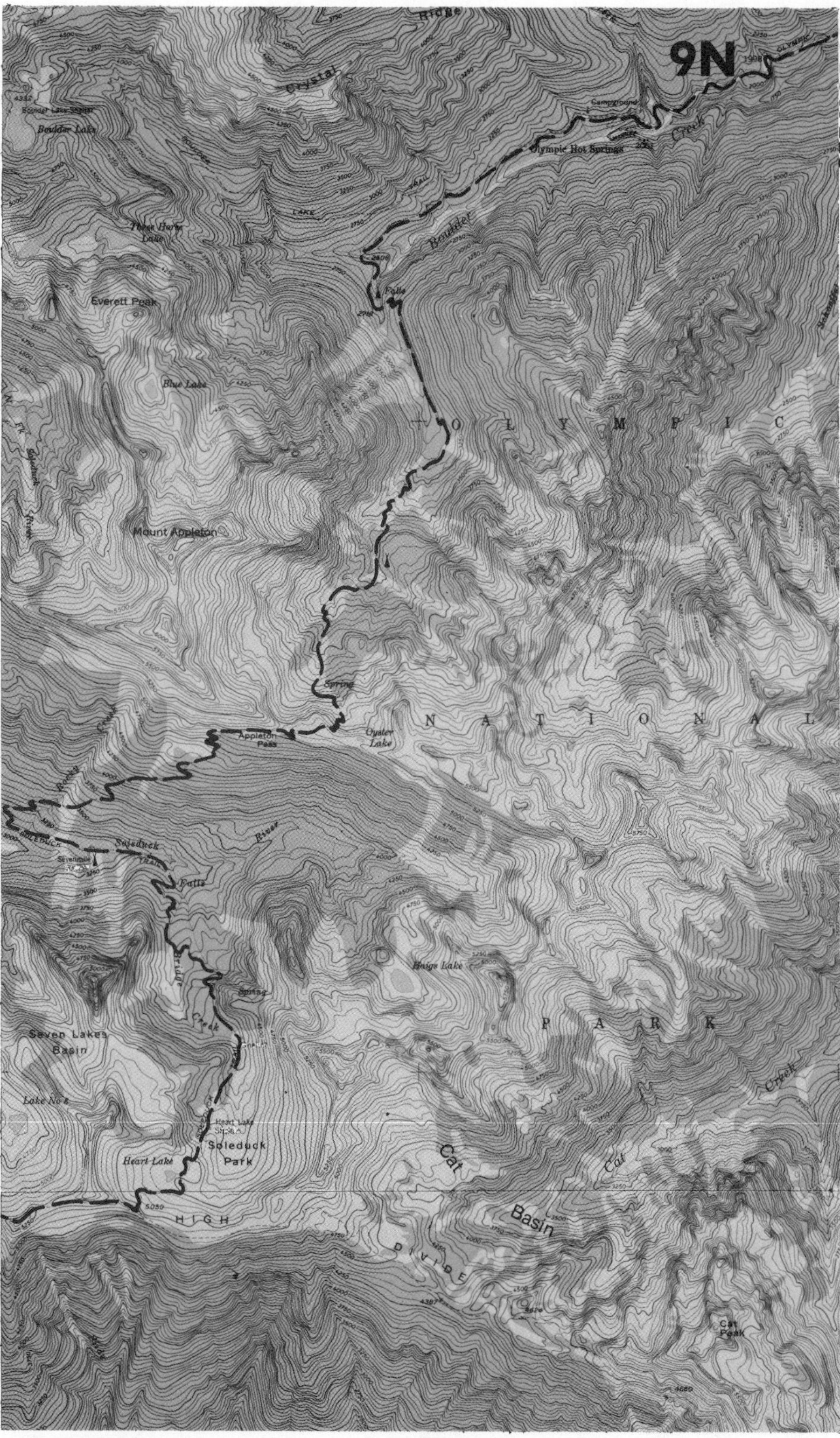

SOLEDUCK RANGER STATION 7 MI.

SEE MAP 9O

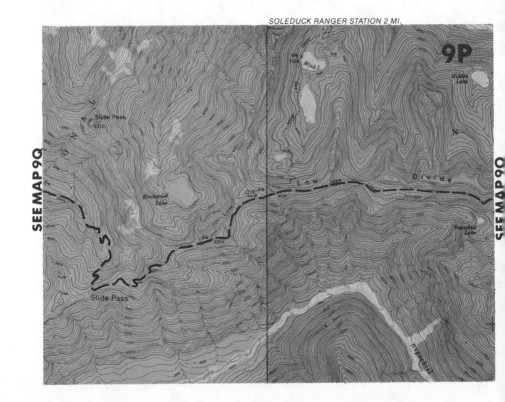

SEE MAP 9P

90

Soleduck River

Canyon Creek

Deer Lake

Deer Lake Shelter

P A R K

Soleduck Lake

Long L.

Clear Lake

Morganroth Lake

Seven Lakes

Round Lake

Lunch Lake

Basin

No Name Lake

SEE MAP 9N

Bogachiel River

Bogachiel Peak

High Divide

Hoh Lake

9P

Mink L.

Hidden Lake

SEE MAP 9Q

Slide Peak

N

Blackwood Lake

Low Divide

Divide

CUTOFF

Bogachiel Lake

SEE MAP 9O

Slide Pass

Bogachiel

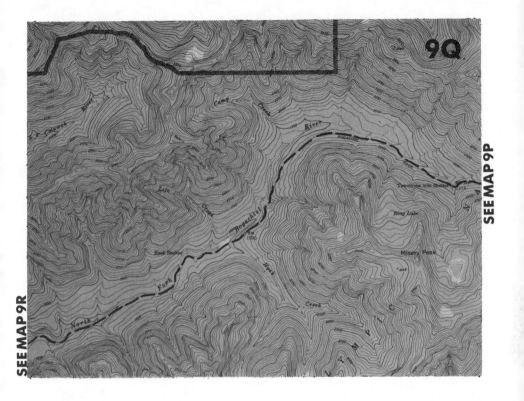

SEE MAP 9P

SEE MAP 9R

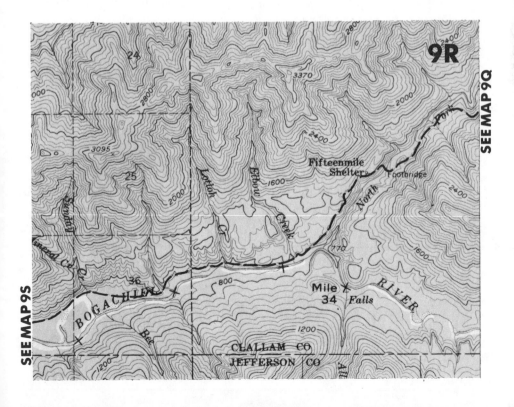

SEE MAP 9Q

SEE MAP 9S

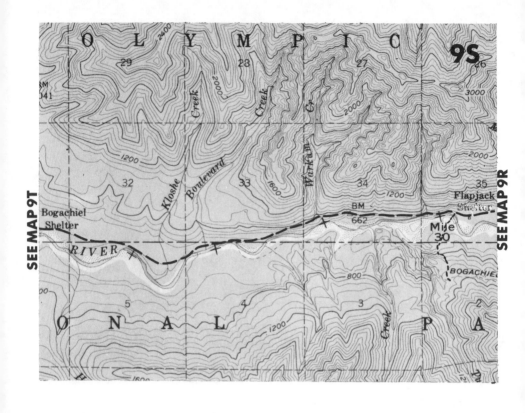

SEE MAP 9T
SEE MAP 9R

9S

OLYMPIC

29   28   27   26

BM
041

32   33   34   35

Kloshe Boulevard   Warm Cr   Flapjack Shelter

Bogachiel Shelter   BM 662   Mile 30

RIVER   800   BOGACHIEL

O   N   A   L   PA

5   4   3   2

1200   1600

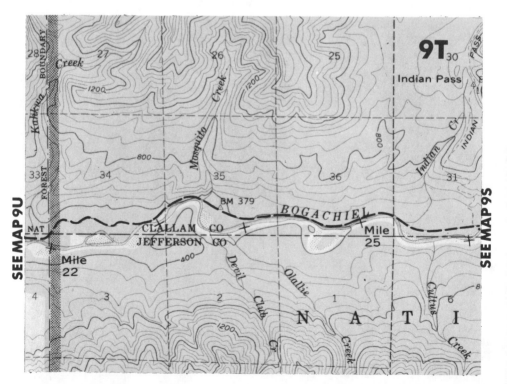

SEE MAP 9U
SEE MAP 9S

9T   30

28   27   26   25   PASS

Creek   1200   Indian Pass

Kalaloch   Mosquito Creek   800   Indian Cr   INDIAN

FOREST BOUNDARY   33   34   35   36   31

800

NAT   BM 379   BOGACHIEL   Mile 25

CLALLAM CO   Mile 22
JEFFERSON CO

4   3   2   1   6

400   Devil Club Cr   Olallie Creek   Cultus Creek

1200   N   A   T   I

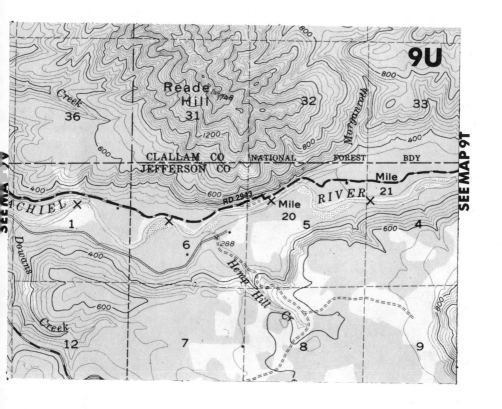

SEE MAP 9T

Reade
Hill
1788

36

Creek

31

32

33

1200

800

800

400

600

CLALLAM CO   NATIONAL   FOREST   BDY
JEFFERSON CO

400

ACHIEL

600

RD 2943

R I V E R

Mile
21

Mile
20

Dowans

1

6

1288

5

4

600

400

600

Hemp Hill Cr.

12

Creek

7

8

9

800

FORKS 4 MI.

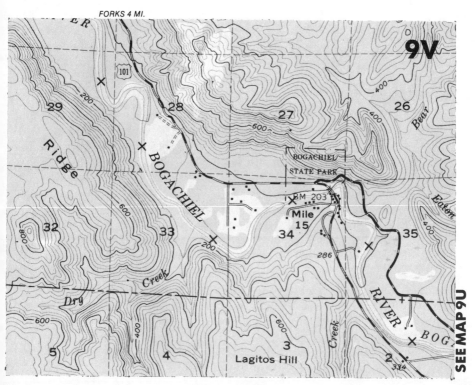

R   E   R

101

200

400

29

28

27

26

Bear

600

Ridge

BOGACHIEL

BOGACHIEL
STATE PARK

BM 203

Eaton

32

33

Mile
15

34

35

800

200

286

400

600

Creek

Dry

600

400

600

RIVER

5

4

3

Creek

BOG.

2

Lagitos Hill

334

SEE MAP 9U

PACIFIC OCEAN WILDERNESS BEACH
(Goodman Creek to Cape Alava)

‖ **10**

Olympic National Park Beach

INTRODUCTION

This section has no mountainous elevation changes, but a careful observer will be struck by the complexity of its land/water environment. The coast's total effect upon the hiker is one of constant surprise and enticement. The full horizons of the endless sea draw us on.

Everywhere there is something of interest. Beside us the cliffs each greet us with their own characters. Some have the rocky solidity of geologic time. Others are sand, clay, and pebbles—erodable stuff from which alders and other trees tumble to the beach. Everywhere the ceaseless play of natural forces is at work before us—in the adaptation of shell shapes to their different environments, in the types of sand and rock we walk upon, and in the wildlife, both above and below water. Here, too, a PNWT hiker quickly becomes a beachcomber, an opportunist of Japanese glass-ball fishing floats, of notes in bottles, and of the beach's endless treasure trove of flotsam and jetsam. Here, too, grow memories: the first sound of the ocean's roar, a rainbow arched across the whole primeval coast, the high-pitched cries of an osprey, the driftwood smoke of your evening campfire, and the intense fern green of the rain forest.

PROBLEMS

Remember that a wilderness beach is not completely safe simply because it's at sea level. You can get into trouble fast. In fact, the first thing to appreciate is that sea level varies a lot—four times a day. Carry a watch and a tide chart with you. Some headlands *cannot* be rounded at high tide. Don't be caught with your back up against the cliffs. (Certain headlands must always be crossed by inland trails.)

"Water, water, everywhere, nor any drop to drink." You may get that impression when you see the tealike color of the area's creeks and rivers. But don't worry, because the color is only harmless tannic acid, which has leached through the rain forest's vegetation and humus. Beware, however, of the reportedly polluted water at Cape Alava, Scott Creek, and possibly elsewhere.

This is not Disneyland, and those cute critters can ruin your trip if they get into your food supply. At night beware of skunks, mice, raccoons, etc. And because certain campsites may have experienced recent bear problems, you should be especially cautious about bruins; ask Park Service folks and other hikers.

Although this area is famous for its rain, you may hit the sunshine jackpot and eagerly begin working on a tan. Be careful. Direct sun and water and sand-reflected rays can quickly cause debilitating sunburn. Be sure to bring a good sunscreen.

If you do learn from hard experience why this is called a *rain* forest, nothing is lost if your raingear, tent, and sleeping bag are up to the challenge. But conditions here can endanger you unexpectedly. Especially cold, blowing rain. Remember that the air temperature needn't be below freezing for hypothermia to set in. Dress appropriately. Use the layer method.

Transportation. Public buses run to neither Bogachiel State Park nor Ozette Lake Ranger Station.

SUPPLIES

The following have post offices and general stores: Forks (98331); La Push (98350); Beaver (98305); and Neah Bay (98357). You cannot arrange food drops at Bogachiel State Park. However, for food purchases there is a very small general store at the Bogachiel Resort nearby. You can send a food cache box to Ozette Lake Ranger Station, Box 39A, Clallam Bay, WA 98326.

DECLINATION   23° E

USGS TOPOGRAPHIC MAPS

Forks	15'
La Push	15'
Ozette Lake	15'

MILEAGES   (total 37.2)

		Total
Bogachiel State Park (203)	0.0	0.0
Road 2400 Dead End (320)	6.1	6.1
Trailhead to beach (200)	1.9	8.0
Beach	1.8	9.8
Toleak Point	.8	10.6
Strawberry Point	1.2	11.8
Giants Graveyard Point	1.3	13.1
Scott's Bluff Point	.5	13.6
Taylor Point Trail	.6	14.2
Third Beach via Taylor Point Trail	1.2	15.4
La Push Road	1.1	16.5
La Push	2.2	18.7
Point No. 1	1.5	20.2
Cape Johnson	1.5	21.7
Point No. 2	2.0	23.7
Cedar Creek	1.8	25.5
Point No. 3	.2	25.7
Norwegian Memorial	.5	26.2
Point No. 4 (at south end of Yellow Banks)	6.0	32.2
Sand Point	2.0	34.2
Cape Alava	3.0	37.2

ROUTE DESCRIPTION

The PNWT in this chapter is so short and the hiking so easy that you could certainly walk it in three days if you wished. But once you have reached the coast from the Bogachiel River, the wise thing to do is to linger over these short miles. Sip their marvels like a connoisseur savors a fine wine. You can pack more looking into 5 miles here than on almost any other section of the Pacific Northwest Trail.

Getting to the wilderness beach is our first goal. The Practical Route follows logging roads from U.S. 101 a bit southwest of Bogachiel State Park. Lagitos Hill (1200) and the surrounding area belong to the state Department of Natural Resources. These lands are managed for timber production to provide money for the state's schools, and they are a maze of clearcuts and logging roads. We follow logging roads to the boundary of Olympic National Park's wilderness beach strip.

Continue south from Bogachiel State Park and across the Bogachiel River bridge. Continue .8 mile along U.S. 101 to a right turn onto DNR Road G2000.

This road winds 3 miles up Lagitos Hill, past a quarry and through clearcuts to a junction with Road G2400, where we turn left. (Sometimes these dirt roads are dangerous because of high-speed logging traffic.)

Follow Road G2400 southwesterly as it crosses into the valley of Goodman Creek. There are several spur-road turnoffs along the way, but stick to the main route, which dead-ends in 2.3 miles. One widely distributed DNR map shows Road G2400 continuing west all the way to Road 3000, the main coast-paralleling trunk road between La Push and the Hoh River. However, that is totally incorrect. When you reach the dead end, you will see clearcuts in all directions and an enormous, brush-filled ravine/gully ahead of you.

Bushwhack .3 mile across this gully; there is a small creek in the bottom. Climb to the logging road at the clearcut on the other side. Walk along this Road G2530 for .1 mile, at first going south, then west, until it reaches a larger dirt road, which is Road 3200. (The latter could be considered a sort of continuation of Road G2400, which we were on originally.) Road 3200 arrives in 1 downhill mile at Road 3000.

We have thus come down Goodman Creek Valley on logging roads rather than the overgrown and/or clearcut old fishing trail along the creek. Turn left on Road 3000. We very soon cross the Goodman Creek bridge, and immediately beyond it we veer right onto Road 3300—a total of .1 mile.

Now go .1 mile on Road 3300 to a spot where three roads diverge quite close together. Do not take the first right you come to, but do follow the second one 100 feet later. (This spot is where the main Road 3300 is curving left uphill.) Now follow this unnamed spur road down a narrowing corridor of brush alders to the trailhead at the dead end.

This trailhead is not signed, and the trail is a very informal affair; so much so that horseback travellers should not attempt to follow it at all. A better stock route to the ocean is to continue south on Road 3000 and intersect the Hoh River Road. The ocean beach itself is not recommended for horses because of its rocky sections and its difficult headland crossings.

A bad-weather alternate for approaching the ocean would be to walk 5 miles to Forks, resupply yourself there, and then go 2 miles north to the La Push Road. That will take you to the junction where the Soleduck River and the Bogachiel River join to form the Quillayute River. Then go 5 miles west on the Mora Ocean Beach Road to Rialto Beach.

In so many ways hiking is a metaphor for life. And taking the easy road is never likely to produce the greatest rewards. The national park's Goodman Creek route not only avoids the cars but also introduces us to a 9.2-mile stretch of extremely beautiful, wild coastline, which the Forks/Mora Road misses.

From the end of the alder-brush road, our faint Goodman Creek trail descends in about 100 feet to a creek crossing. Then we wind through heavy brush northwest about .3 mile to an abandoned logging road. Turn left and follow this road west .3 mile through big alders, passing an opening to a clearcut and crossing two washouts. The road seems to fork and/or dead-end 50 yards after the second washout. Turn left there up an inconspicuous, but definite, trail. Follow this trail .2 mile uphill and southwest to the U.S. Park boundary. The trail becomes much more distinct as we enter old-growth forest.

Soon we reach the drainage that we will follow to the ocean. The trail emerges from the forest onto the beach immediately north of this creek and 150 yards south of the large, close-in, wooded seastack, which itself defines the little bay south of Goodman Creek.

To the south we see Hoh Head and (straight out to sea) large, flat-topped Alexander Island. Closer in we see a seastack (island) shaped like an off-center arrowhead. And to the north the impassable peninsula of Goodman Creek.

Pilgrim, we have arrived! Stick your toes in the ocean and marvel at the total beauty of this amazing Pacific Northwest Trail.

Goodman Creek is tidal at this point, and you may arrive to find its wide sand and gravel bars exposed by the slowly receding waters of its curved channel. Mists are likely to be hovering over the creek's borders of Douglas fir, Sitka spruce, western hemlock, and western red cedar. Of course, you may find the flow reversed as the level rises under pressure from the not-so-distant sea. Stand on an overhanging river bank and look for schools of fish in these greenish depths and for chattering kingfishers in the air above.

The trail around the impassable tidal mouth and cliffs of Goodman Creek is marked by a large, multicolored "target." Follow the trail inland and ford the creek at a large gravel/sand bar.

Beyond Falls Creek's small but pretty waterfall, we climb a hill on a very good trail through the coast's typical lush vegetation. We see some of the largest western red cedars in the world and, at the other extreme, epiphytes, ferns, salal, huckleberries, willows, devil's club, and salmon-berry. We walk only .8 mile in this dense forest before the sounds of the coast rise to greet us. Just .5 mile north of the creek's mouth we break out of the deep green world of cedar and fern into the deep blue of the Pacific Ocean. The instant when you first hear the breaking waves, scolding gulls, and Japan-brought winds is one of the most adrenalin-stirring moments on America's finest trail.

Our first approach to the wilderness beach is down the sand, clay, rock, and gravel cliff that extends for almost this entire coast. Sometimes this rampart is just a big driftwood-stacked dune. Elsewhere, we go for miles beside cliffs as high as 200'. Occasionally, our beach route runs out of passable margin between cliff and tide, and we must climb over a headland on a ferny trail.

A surprise for Olympic beach strangers is the irregular way time has sheared away so much of the continent. Jagged remnants remain scattered everywhere. For instance, a short distance offshore from where we clamber down that first time from the Falls Creek Trail, there is a tall, stony islet, a typical example of what is poetically called a seastack. A column of harder rock. An evader of the doom that has already carried away all of the original land around it. Grasses, trees, salal, and flowers give its vertical sides an incongruous green cap. Seabirds swirl in incredible numbers around many such sanctuaries, and their cries add to our sense of primordial peace and beauty.

Goodman Creek is funneled into the ocean by narrow rock walls, the reason why the trail crosses well inland at Falls Creek. However, once you have reached the beach, you may wish to explore the tide pools and rocks at Goodman Creek's outlet.

We begin our coast walk on a rough-grained sand beach, which shimmers westward .8 mile to Toleak Point. Jackson Creek's brown water joins the sea near the point, and from here on the sand is resort quality. At the creek there is an A-frame shelter, mainly a respite for storms, when no one would mind its rats and rents. Not far away is an interestingly pierced, flat-topped seastack. A new marine view opens up beyond the reefs, seastacks and sands of Toleak Point. From here we can suddenly see all the way north to Teahwhit Head.

Strawberry Point is northwest across a 1.2-mile sandy, crescent beach. Like Toleak Point, it is easily rounded. In 1.3 more Robinson Crusoe miles we pass another point, this one nameless and opposite the reefs and seastacks known as Giants Graveyard. Here, for the first time, we must watch our tide tables to go around the obstruction at low tide.

Yet another ½-mile brings us to Scott's Bluff, a sheer cliff, which we must climb over. The trail begins near the Scott Creek shelter. Do not try to save time by going around on the ocean side! (Also, Scott Creek is known to have infected some campers with giardia!)

A short, crescent beach brings us in .6 mile to Taylor Point, a major obstacle; the mandatory trail across it is 1.2 miles long. Locate its entrance by a round, orange and black marker, and follow the path through the forest. The meanders, footlogs, and great trees of this trail are fun, and the inland detour enables us to approach the ocean anew.

Third Beach is a popular tourist destination from the La Push Road, but the waters of Strawberry Bay daily cleanse the strand clear of visitors' traces. The Taylor Point trail hits Third Beach near some giant boulders and a cliffside waterfall. We then amble .5 sandy miles to a stairway trail up to the road. This trail now begins at the site of the former Third Beach Shelter, where there is a creek and a good campsite.

Lacking an Ideal Route to 1.5-mile-long Second Beach, we are forced onto the road—unless we want to try our luck against the salal jungle of the trailless interior. Warning: salal is a springy, almost malevolent, evergreen bush more ornery than almost anything else on the Pacific Northwest Trail.

In 1.1 miles we reach the La Push Road, a paved route between the Soleduck/Bogachiel forks of the Quillayute River. We follow this road 2.2 miles to the Quileute Indian Reservation and the town of La Push, which has a grocery store, post office, Coast Guard Station, and marina. There are several resorts, including La Push Ocean Park (206/374-5267), which has camping and cabins. Many of the fishing boats whose lights you see at night are La Push-based. Stop by the docks to listen to the latest scuttlebutt about the weather or about who is catching what. And don't be shy about asking the Indians and fishermen for a ride across the wide mouth of the Quillayute River. You may not want to venture out to sea past former Indian fortress James Island, as they do. But if you cannot persuade or pay someone to ferry you, it's an 11-mile walk.

Camping is not permitted on Rialto Beach itself, but the national park does have a car campground (fee) inland at Mora. Also, at the end of the road just behind Rialto Beach, there is a very convenient and modern restroom.

Rialto Beach is notable for immense quantities of driftwood. And not just quaint little sticks, either. Of the enormous trees that grow along mile upon mile of Calawah, Bogachiel, Soleduck, and Quillayute riverbanks, some inevitably are washed out to sea, only to be deposited like giant beached whales here. Their polished, bleached carcasses often make great impromptu shelters.

Our next and last destination on the Pacific Northwest Trail is Cape Alava, the westernmost point of the California-Oregon-Washington coast. This 18.5-mile coast walk is exceptionally wild and remote, though one can sometimes hear loggers' saws from a mile inland behind the park boundary. Sea lions, seals, whales, river otters, bald eagles, ospreys, bears, skunks, and a host of sea life add to the elemental excitement of light, sound, smell, form, and color. Our ears grow accustomed to the waves roaring advance and sibilant withdrawal, perhaps across smooth sand, perhaps a rattling retreat across pebbles. For a while we may tune out the breakers, riffles, and swells entirely and catch instead the odd notes of the long-billed, black oyster catchers or the hard, scuttling sounds of the fiddler crabs. But before long the ocean's powerful bass notes will thunder across the beach, and the timpani of its wavelets will remind us of what a great privilege it is to be alive at this time and place.

A mile north of the roadhead we cross Ellen Creek. This is just beyond the no-camping zone and is a suitably scenic stopping place, with dozens of rocks offshore. (Here again, the creek's tealike color does not necessarily mean that it is bad to drink.) We continue north past appropriately named Cake Rock, which is more than a mile out to sea. Close at hand, between the trees and the surf, we pass a romantic buttress, very easily rounded at low tide and esily traversed at higher tides through a sea-gouged opening.

Soon after we've become mesmerized by the beautiful sandy beaches and the constantly changing scenery, the trance is broken by a headland, sometimes called Point No. 1, which can be rounded at low tide or climbed over. This is the first of five promontories in the Cape Johnson complex. We encounter long stretches of flat tidal plain, actually upright sedimentary layers rubbed smooth by eons of wave-worked erosion. Walking this grooved, wave-cut terrace is not as easy as its flatness would suggest. Crabclaw kelp grows everywhere; footing on the wet, slick, kelpy rocks is uncertain. Black or brown "tar" rocks are especially slippery. Step carefully. Look carefully, too. In addition to the obvious purple or orange starfish and the fiddler crabs, small tidepools are full of easily missed lives. Also, be sure to walk out to some of the rocky fissures in this odd land- seascape, and listen for the barks and flipper claps of basking sea lions. Their great, overstuffed, blubbery bodies are deceptively awkward. Once in the water, they can move very quickly. But more likely they will watch you for a while, like periscopes, and clamber back onto their barnacled lounges when you have departed up the beach.

From Chilean Memorial stay close to the cliff. There is usually a gravelly upper-beach route to follow to avoid the worst, slipperiest rocks. When we are finally beyond the Cape's slow, rocky going, the strand broadens out into a paradise of fine sand, hard near the water's edge for idyllic walking and shifting, dunelike high up the berm. The breakers roll in straight and free; we are in a beachcomber's Eden. In 2 miles we can climb over Point No. 2 on another one of the old World War II Coast Guard trails, recently improved by the U.S. Park Service.

This point is a perfect lookout from which to enjoy the rolling Pacific. Wind-wracked conifers atop this 200' high proto-island provide shelter from the winds and offer shade (if you are lucky enough to have sun). Enjoy the antics of seals below in the kelp beds. And train your binoculars on fortess-like Jagged Island. There whirling, soaring, crying sea birds create an ageless spectacle of boundless energy. Their purposeful orbits symbolize the clockwork cycles of tides, sun, moon, and life that govern the coast.

Jagged Island is part of the 117-acre Quillayute Needles National Wildlife Refuge, part of the Washington Islands Wilderness. This magnificent sanctuary covers a total distance of more than 30 miles. Its reefs and rocks are home to nesting seabirds, including: glaucous-winged western gulls, glaucous-winged gulls, western gulls, double-crested cormorants, pelagic cormorants, Brandt's cormorants, pigeon guillemots, black oyster catchers, common murres, tufted puffins, fork-tailed petrels, Leach's petrels, rhinoceros auklets, and Cassin's auklets. During fall and spring migration the refuge's total bird population sometimes totals one million. In addition, there are sea lions, fur seals, Pacific harbor porpoises, harbor seals, piked whales, gray whales, Pacific right whales, humpbacked whales, and sea and river otters. Public access and use are not permitted because of the sensitivity of these creatures to human disturbance and because of the hazards of landing on the islands.

At the end of the Needles area we pass a minor point, from which eagles can sometimes be seen in the trees of close-in seastacks. Cedar Creek, where there is a shelter and an idyllic campsite, is 1.8 miles up the coast from Point No. 2. We pass a good campsite .2 mile farther on, at Point No. 3.

The Norwegian Memorial is a granite obelisk in memory of eighteen sailors of the three-masted bark Prince Arthur, wrecked here in January 1903 and one of the many ships lost on this dangerous coast. It is also a popular camping spot (and shelter) .5 mile south at a creek, where the Allens Bay Trail from Ozette joins Kayostla Beach. There is a good boat-access campground on the lake. This is a dead-end trail unless you have a boat on the lake.

At Norwegian Memorial we leave the sands for a long spell of shipwreck country. This is rock walking. Careful stepping is necessary from one slippery cannonball-sized ankle-sprainer to the next. Plan to do this slow section at low tide, when you will have the greatest opportunity to complete it all at once. Carry water, too, because there is none until the point that marks the south entrance to Yellow Banks Bay. From Norwegian Memorial to this Point No. 4 totals 6 miles. This rocky, kelpy, creekless environment may be beautiful, but you will certainly be happy to sag off the rocks onto the sands at Yellow Banks.

The crumbling, overgrown clay cliffs at Yellow Banks have water and good camping. To go beyond this bay, we must wait for low tide. Then Point No. 5 is easily negotiated, partly through a cave in the fallen headland's jumbled boulders.

Sand Point, a gentle, wide arc of lovely beach 2 miles north, is an excellent camp spot—but beware of possible trouble. Bears! Also, it would not hurt to boil or otherwise treat local water because of the great flood of visitors who make the Ozette Ranger Station/Sand Point/Cape Alava loop.

A little knob at the tip of Sand Point provides a good view of the PNWT's last 3 miles to Cape Alava and the Ozette Indian Reservation. There are no more Ozette Indians, but some petroglyphs are easily found 1.5 miles up the beach. One design looks like a whale, a reminder that the original inhabitants were not mere cheechakos like us but skilled hunters of seals, whales, and other food. They gathered berries, roots, and mollusks and wove intricate patterns in cedar bark and spruce-root fibers.

The 1970s archaeological excavations of the slide-ravaged, Cape Alava prehistoric village revealed thousands of details about a civilization forever lost to us. (The Makah Indian tribe has stationed a watchman/docent at the site and provides the public with an artifact museum at Neah Bay.) At this westernmost point, our tale ends with Ozette prehistory as it began with Kootenai prehistory on the Continental Divide. Along the way you will have gauged and felt enough of contemporary America and seen enough matchless scenery to enrich your life forever.

At Cape Alava there is no more land ahead, no more trail to walk. Only the 3.3-mile boardwalk inland to the Lake Ozette Road and ranger station. But we invite you to join with us in developing and protecting the Pacific Northwest Trail. Walking it once is only the first part of the Trail's meaning and pleasure. Saving it for others is the real challenge.

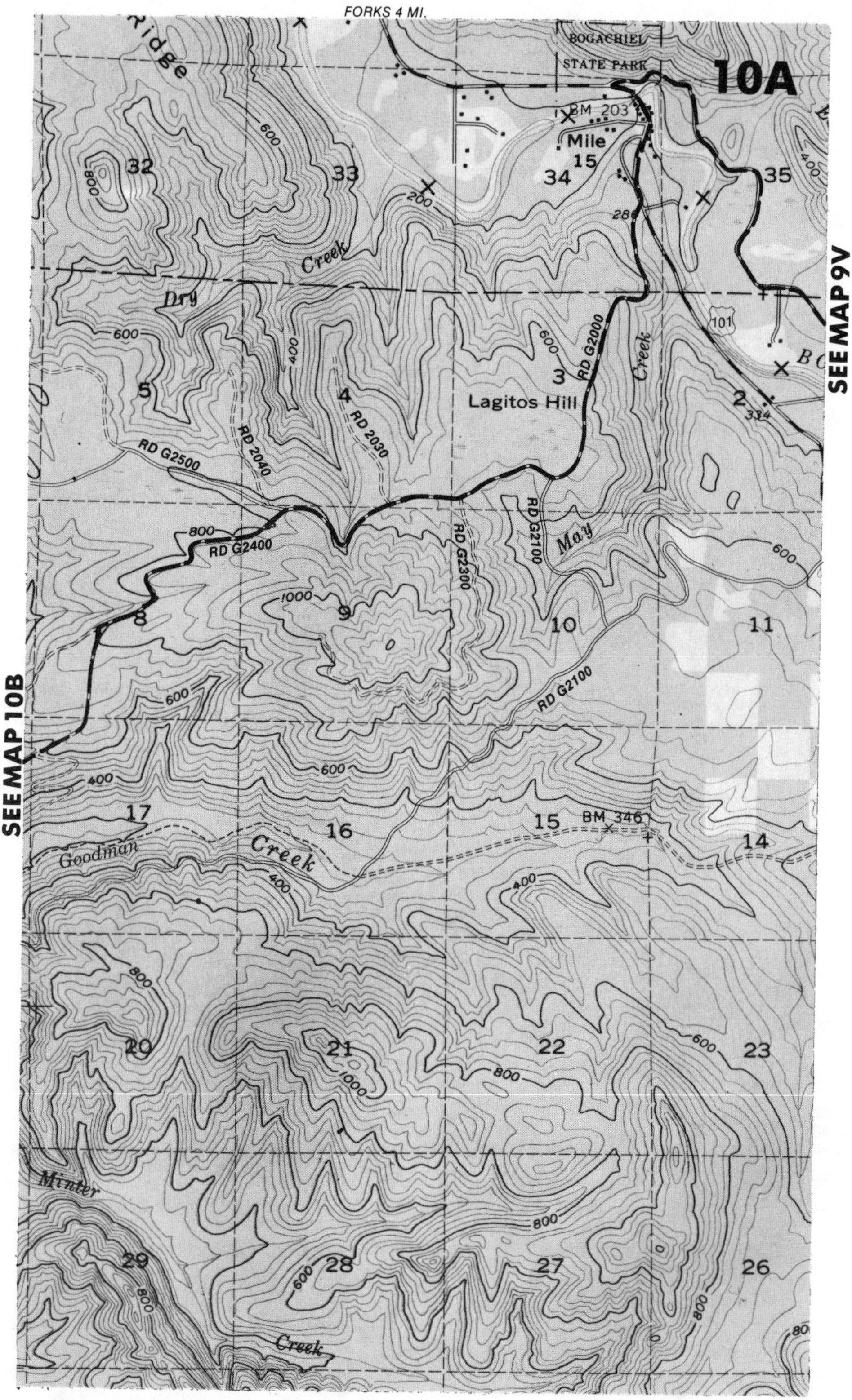

BOGACHIEL
STATE PARK

SEE MAP 9V

SEE MAP 10B

Ridge

32

33

Creek

Dry

600

5

4

RD 2030

RD G2500

RD 2040

RD G2400

800

1000

8

9

600

400

17

Goodman

Creek

16

400

800

20

21

1000

Minter

29

28

600

Creek

BM 203

Mile
15

34

200

280

3

RD G2000

Lagitos Hill

Creek

600

RD G2100

RD G2300

May

Creek

10

RD G2100

600

15

BM 346

400

22

800

27

800

35

400

101

2

334

B

11

600

14

600

23

26

80

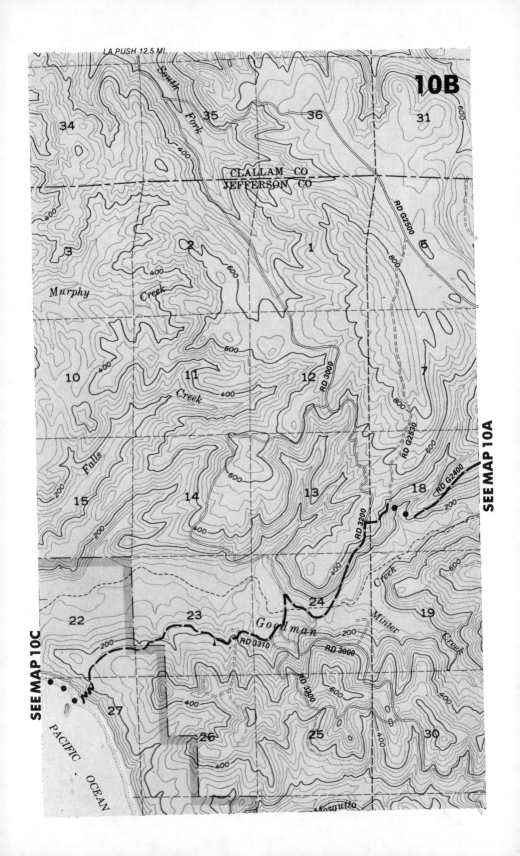

LA PUSH 12.5 MI.

34

35

36

31

South Fork

CLALLAM CO
JEFFERSON CO

3

2

1

6

RD G2500

Murphy

Creek

400

600

400

10

11

12

7

Creek

400

RD 3000

800

RD G2550

Falls

15

14

13

18

RD G2400

600

600

200

RD 3200

SEE MAP 10A

Creek

600

22

23

24

Minter

19

Goodman

RD 3310

RD 3000

200

Creek

SEE MAP 10C

400

600

27

26

25

30

RD 3300

PACIFIC

OCEAN

400

400

Mosquito

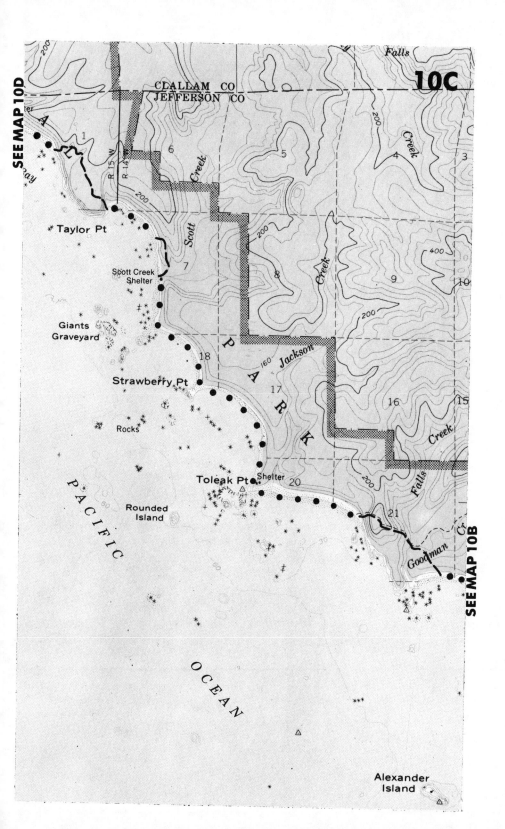

SEE MAP 10D

SEE MAP 10B

Falls

CLALLAM CO
JEFFERSON CO

Creek

1

6

5

4

3

R 15 W

R 14 W

200

200

Scott Creek

Taylor Pt

7

200

8

Creek

9

10

400

Scott Creek
Shelter

Giants
Graveyard

P

A

200

Jackson

160

18

Strawberry Pt

17

16

15

R

Rocks

Creek

Toleak Pt

Shelter

20

21

Falls

Goodman Cr

Rounded
Island

200

PACIFIC

OCEAN

Alexander
Island

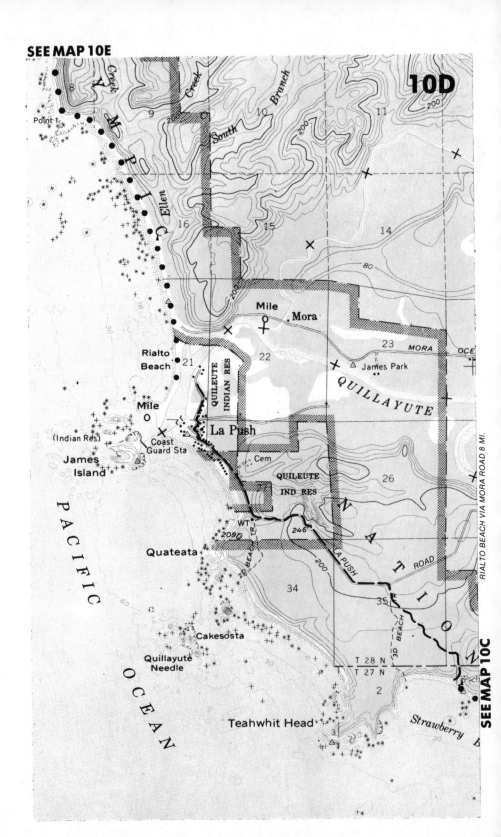

Point 1

Creek

Creek

South Branch

9

10

11

200

200

200

MPIC

Ellen

16

15

14

80

200

Mile
Mora

Rialto
Beach

21

22

23

MORA

OCE

James Park

QUILLAYUTE

Mile
0

(Indian Res)

Coast
Guard Sta

La Push

James
Island

Cem

QUILEUTE
INDIAN RES

QUILEUTE
IND RES

26

WT
209

246

Quateata

20 BEACH TR.

LA PUSH

200

ROAD

PACIFIC

34

35

3D BEACH

Cakesosta

Quillayute
Needle

T 28 N
T 27 N

2

OCEAN

Teahwhit Head

Strawberry

3

RIALTO BEACH VIA MORA ROAD 8 MI.

SEE MAP 10C

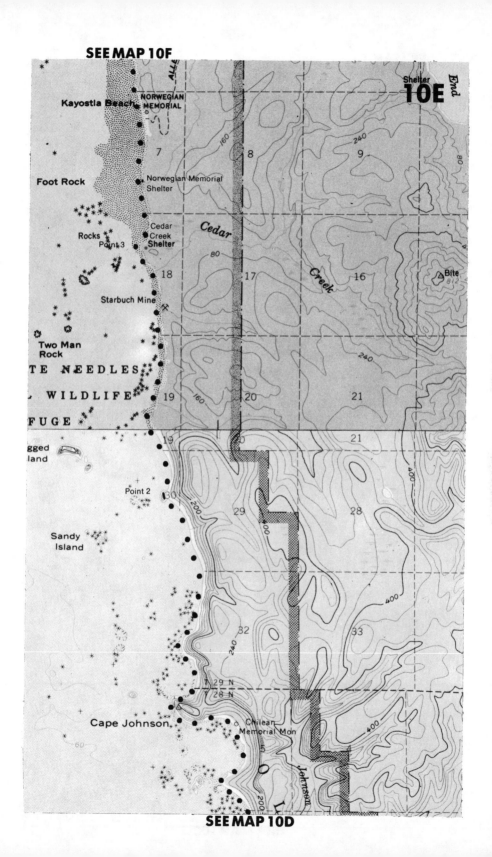

NORWEGIAN
MEMORIAL

Kayostla Beach

Shelter
10E

End

7

8

9

160

240

80

Foot Rock

Norwegian Memorial
Shelter

Cedar

Rocks

Point 3

Cedar
Creek
Shelter

Creek

18

17

16

Bite
812

80

Starbuch Mine

Two Man
Rock

240

TE NEEDLES

WILDLIFE

19

20

21

160

FUGE

19

21

400

gged
land

Point 2

30

29

28

200

400

Sandy
Island

32

33

240

400

400

29 N

28 N

Cape Johnson

Chilean
Memorial Mon

400

60

Johnson

200

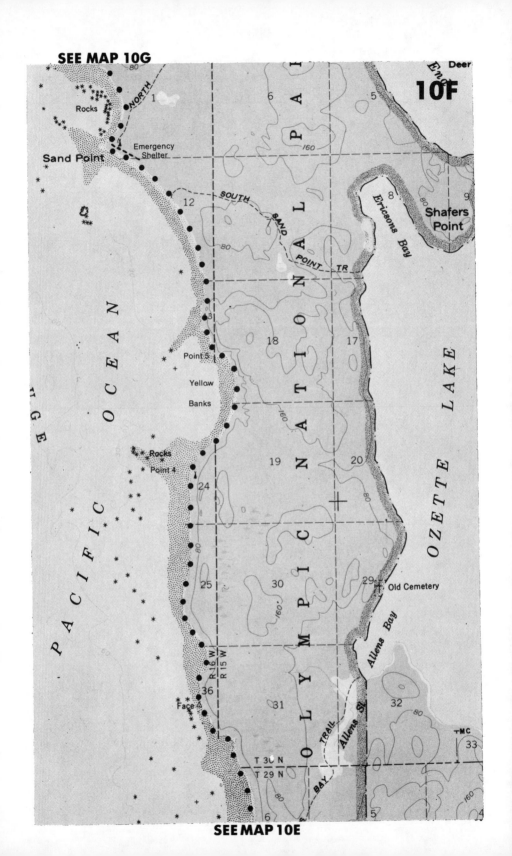

10F

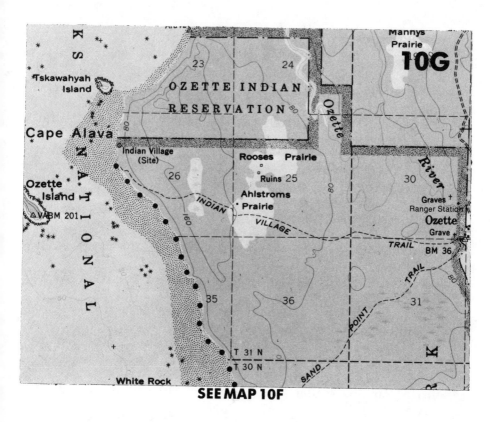

BIBLIOGRAPHY

Alt, David D. and Hyndman. *Rocks, Ice & Water: The Geology of Waterton-Glacier Park.* Missoula, MT: Mountain Press, 1973.

Arno, Stephen F., and Hammerly, Ramona P. *Northwest Trees.* Seattle: The Mountaineers, 1977.

Bancroft, Hubert Howe. *History of Washington, Idaho, and Montana.* 1845-1889. The History Company, San Francisco 1890.

Blood, Donald A. *Rocky Mountain Wildlife.* Saanichton, B.C.: Hancock House Publishers, Ltd., 1976.

Brown, Vinson. *Peoples of the Sea Wind: The Native Americans of the Pacific Coast.* New York: Collier Books, 1977.

Cantwell, Robert. *The Hidden Northwest.* Philadelphia: J. B. Lippincott Co., 1972.

Clark, Norman. *Washington: A Bicentennial History.* New York: W. W. Norton & Co., Inc., 1976.

Clevinger, Woodrow R. "Southern Appalachian Highlanders in Western Washington." *Pacific Northwest Quarterly.*

Cook, Jimmie Jean. *"A particular friend, Penn's Cove": A History of the Settlers, Claims and Buildings of Central Whidbey Island.* Coupeville, WA: Island County Historical Society, 1973.

Dasmann, Ray, and Yocum, Charles. *Pacific Coastal Wildlife Region.* Healdsburg, CA: Naturegraph Co., n.d.

Dodge, Elizabeth H. *Island County, A World Beater.* Seattle: Frayn Printing Co., 1968.

Doig, Ivan. *Winter Brothers.* New York: Harcourt Brace Jovanovich, 1980.

El Hunt, Ruby. *Lost Mines and Treasures of the Pacific Northwest.* Portland, OR: Binfords & Mort, 1960.

Farrow, Moira. *Nobody Here But Us: Pioneers of the North.* Vancouver, B.C.: J. J. Douglas Ltd., 1975.

Federal Writer's Project. *Washington: A Guide to the Evergreen State.* Binfords and Mort, Portland, OR, 1950.

Fleming, June. *Staying Found.* New York: Vintage Books.

Fletcher, Colin. *The New Complete Walker.* New York: Knopf, 1974.

Fries, Mary A. *Wildflowers of Mount Rainier and the Cascades.* Seattle: The Mountaineers, 1970.

Garner, Janet. "Along the Pacific Northwest Trail." Backpacker Vol. 7, No. 4 (Aug./Sept. 1979), pp. 30-35, 76-78.

Gildart, Robert C. *Meet the Mammals of Waterton-Glacier International Peace Park.* Kalispell, MT: Thomas Printing, Inc., 1975.

Haard, Richard and Karen. *Poisonous & Hallucinogenic Mushrooms.* Brackendale & Seattle: Cloudburst Press, 1975.

Haley, Delphine. *Sleek & Savage: North America's Weasel Family.* Seattle: Pacific Search Press, 1975.

Hancock, David. *Adventure With Eagles.* Saanichton, B.C.: The Wildlife Conservation Centre, 1970.

Hanna, Warren L. *The Grizzlies of Glacier.* Missoula: Mountain Press Publishing Co., 1978.

Harris, Stephen L. *Fire and Ice, The Cascade Volcanoes.* Seattle: The Mountaineers, 1976.

Haskin, Leslie L. *Wild Flowers of the Pacific Coast.* Portland, OR: Binfords and Mort, 1967.

Hawley, Robert Emmett. *Squee Mus or Pioneer Days on the Nooksack.*

Heckman, Hazel. *Island Year.* Seattle: University of Washington Press, 1972.

Hult, Ruby El. *Untamed Olympics.* Binfords and Mort, Portland, OR, 1971.

Hult, Ruby El. *Lost Mines and Treasures of the Pacific Northwest.* Binfords and Mort, Portland, OR, 1974.

Hunt, Herbert, and Kaylor, Floyd C. *Washington West of the Cascades.* Chicago: S. J. Clarke Publishing Co., 1917.

Hunt, Herbert, and Kaylor, Floyd C. *Jimmy Come Lately, History of Clallam County.*

Kellogg, George Albert. *A History of Whidbey's Island.* Island County Farm Bureau News. 1933-1934 Oak Harbor.

Kirk, Ruth. *Exploring the Olympic Peninsula.* Seattle: University of Washington Press, 1967.

Kirk, Ruth, and Daugherty, Richard D. *Exploring Washington Archaeology.* Seattle: University of Washington Press, 1978.

Kirk, Ruth, and Namkung, Johsel. *The Olympic Rain Forest.* Seattle: University of Washington Press, 1966.

Kozloff, Eugene N. *Plants and Animals of the Pacific Northwest.* Seattle: University of Washington Press, 1976.

Lakin, Ruth. *Kettle River Country: Early Days Along the Kettle River.* Colville, WA: Statesman-Examiner, Inc., 1976.

Larrison, Earl. *Birds of the Pacific Northwest.* Moscow: University Press of Idaho, 1981.

Larrison Earl J., and Sonnenberg, Zella M. *Washington Birds: Their Location and Identification.* Seattle: Seattle Audubon Society, 1968.

Larrison, Earl J. et al, *Washington Wildflowers.* Seattle: The Seattle Audubon Society, 1974.

Larrison, Earl and Johnson. *Mammals of Idaho.* Moscow: University Press of Idaho, 1981.

Leissler, Frederick. *Roads and Trails of Olympic National Park.* Seattle: University of Washington Press, 1976.

Lewis, Emanuel R. *Seacoast Fortifications of the United States: An Introductory History.* Washington D.C.: Smithsonian Institution Press, 1970.

Manning, Harvey. *Backpacking One Step At A Time.* rev. ed. Seattle: Recreational Equipment, Inc.

Manning, Harvey. *Footsore: Walks and Hikes Around Puget Sound.* 4 vols. Seattle: The Mountaineers, 1978, 1982.

Martin, Paul J. *Port Angeles, Washington: A History.* Port Angeles, WA: Peninsula Publishing Co., 1983.

McDonald, Lucile. *Coast Country.*

McKee, Bates. *Cascadia: The Geologic Evolution of the Pacific Northwest.* New York: McGraw-Hill, 1972.

Meany, Edmond S. *History of the State of Washington.* Macmillan Co., New York, 1924.

Mitchell, Dick. *Mountaineering First Aid.* Seattle: The Mountaineers, 1972.

Molson-Chesaw-Knob Hill Comunities. *Okanogan Highland Echoes.* 6th edition. Xerox bound copy, 1974.

National Collection of Fine Arts. *Art of the Pacific Northwest: From the 1930s to the Present.* Washington, D.C.: Smithsonian Institution Press, 1974.

Nicholson, George. *Vancouver Island's West Coast, 1762-1962.* Vancouver, B.C.: George Nicholson's Books, 1965.

Northport Over Forty Club. *Northport Pioneers: Echoes of the Past from the Upper Columbia Country.* Colville, WA: Statesman-Examiner, Inc., 1981.

Olson, Joan and Gene. *Washington Times and Trails.* Grants Pass, OR: Windyridge Press, 1970.

Parratt, Lloyd, P. *Birds of Glacier National Park.* Kalispell, MT: Thomas Printing, Inc., 1964.

Phillips, James W. *Washington State Place Names.* Seattle: University of Washington Press, 1976.

Pitzer, Paul. *Building the Skagit.* Portland, Oregon: The Galley Press, 1978.

Powell, Jay, and Jensen, Vickie. *Quileute: An Introduction To the Indians of La Push.* Seattle: University of Washington Press, 1976.

Ratliff, Donald E. *Map, Compass and Campfire.* Portland, Oregon: Binfords and Mort, 1964.

Rodney, William. *Kootenai Brown, His Life and Times.* Sidney, B.C.: Gray's Publishing, Ltd., 1969.

Ross, Lorraine Wilcox. *Port Angeles, U.S.A.*

Roth, Lottie Roeder. *History of Whatcom County.*

Rue, Walter. *Weather of the Pacific Coast: Washington, Oregon, British Columbia.* Seattle: The Writing Works, 1978.

Ruhle, George C. *The Ruhle Handbook: Roads and Trails Waterton-Glacier National Parks.* Minneapolis, Minnesota: John W. Fornery, 1976.

Sampson, Martin J. *Indians of Skagit County.* Mount Vernon, WA: Skagit County Historical Society, 1972.

Schneider, Bill. *Where the Grizzly Walks.* Missoula, MT: Mountain Press, 1977.

Schwartz, Susan. *Cascade Companion.* Seattle: Pacific Search Books, 1976.

Scofield, W. M. *Washington's Historical Markers.* Portland, OR: The Touchstone Press, 1967.

Sequim Bicentennial History Book Comittee. *Dungeness: The Lure of a River.* Port Angeles, WA: Olympic Printers, 1976.

Shaw, George C. *The Chinook Jargon and How to Use It.* Seattle: Rainier Printing Co., 1909, reproduction 1965 by the Shorrey Book Store, Seattle, WA.

Shea, Marie C. *Early Flathead and Tobacco Plains:* A Narrative History of Northwestern Montana. Eureka, MT: Marie Cuffe Shea, 1977.

Simpson, Claude & Catherine. *North of the Narrows: Men and Women of the Upper Priest Lake Country, Idaho.* Moscow, ID: University Press of Idaho, 1981.

Speidel, Bill. *The Wet Side of the Mountains: or Prowling Western Washington.* Seattle: Nettle Creek Publishing Co., 1974.

Stewart, Hilary. *Indian Fishing: Early Methods on the Northwest Coast.* Seattle: University of Washington Press, 1977.

Swan, James G. *The Northwest Coast: or, Three Years' Residence in Washington Territory.* Seattle: University of Washington Press, 1972.

Tabor, Rowland W. *Guide to the Geology of Olympic National Park.* Seattle: University of Washington Press, 1975.

Uebelacker, Morris. *Cultural Resource Overview of Tonasket Planning Unit.* Okanogan, WA: Okanogan National Forest, 1978.

Verne, Ray. University of Washington Publication in Anthropology. *The San Poil & The Nespelem Salishan People of North Eastern Washington.* 1932.

Wauconda & Surrounding Area Historical Committee. *Trails & Tales of the Early Day Settlers of Northeast Okanogan County.* Colville, WA: Statesman-Examiner, Inc., 1982.

White, Richard. *Land Use, Environment, and Social Change: The Shaping of Island County, Washington.* Seattle: University of Washington Press, 1980.

Wilkerson, James A. *Medicine for Mountaineering.* 2nd Edition. Seattle: The Mountaineers, 1975.

Williams, L. R. *Our Pacific County With Pride in Heritage, History of Jefferson County.*

Willis, Margaret. Ed. *Chechacos All: The Pioneering of Skagit.* Mount Vernon, WA: Skagit County Historical Society, 1973.

Wood, Robert L. *Wilderness Trails of Olympic National Park.* Seattle: The Mountaineers, 1968.

Woodcock, George. *Peoples of the Coast: The Indians of the Pacific Northwest.* Bloomington, IN: Indiana University Press, 1977.

Woods, Erin and Bill. *Bicycling The Backroads Around Puget Sound.* Seattle: The Mountaineers, 1972.

Wright, William H. *The Grizzly Bear.* Lincoln Nebraska: University of Nebraska, 1977.

INDEX

Abbotts Flats 34-36, 39
Abercrombie Mountain 93-94
Ace Creek Trail 66
Acme 183
Adelma Beach 224
Admiralty Head 211
Agassiz Glacier 33
Akamina Highway 36
Akamina Pass 36
Alpine Ridge Trail 65
Altaire Campground 229
Amphitheater Mountain 154
Anacortes 203, 206-207
Anderson Lake State Park 224
Angeles Road, Mt. 228
Ann, Lake 180
Antoine Creek 136
Antoine Creek Trail 135
Apex Mountain 154
Apex Pass 154
Appalachian Trail 4
Appleton Pass 229
Armstrong Meadows 90
Arnold Peak 153
Artist Point 180
Ashnola River 155
Austin Pass 180

Badger Valley 227
Baker Highway, Mt. 179
Baker Hotsprings 180
Baker Lake, MT 59
Baker Lake 181
Baker Lake Resort 181
Baker Lodge, Mt. 179
Baker, Mt. 180-181
Bald Mountain 155
Ball Lakes 86
Barker Brown Cabin 155
Bauerman Ridge 153
Bay View Ridge 205
Bear Creek Road 184
Bear Skull Shelter 159
Beaver 247

Beaver Creek 90
Beaver Pass 177
Beef Pasture Cabin 138
Beehive Lake 89
Bellingham 174
Bethlehem Hill 67
Big Beaver Creek 177
Big Sheep Creek 114
Big Sheep Creek Campground 115
Big Therriault Lake 41
Blackwood Lake 231
Blanchard 203, 205
Blue Mountain 226
Blue Lake 137, 182
Bluebird Basin 42
Bluebird Creek 42
Bogachiel River, North Fork 231
Bogachiel Peak 230
Bogachiel Shelter 232
Bogachiel State Park 232
Bonaparte Lake Boy Scout Camp 134
Bonaparte Lake 134
Bonaparte, Mt. 131, 135
Bonners Ferry, ID 57, 82
Boulder Creek 60, 116, 227
Boulder Creek Campground 181, 229
Boulder Creek Road 60
Boulder Lakes 61
Boulder Mountain 61
Boulder–Deer Creek Road 117
Boulder Glacier 33
Boulder Pass 33, 35
Boulder Pass Trail 35
Boundary Camp 179
Boundary Dam 93
Boundary Mountain 34
Boundary Trail 153, 155-156
Bow 203, 205
Bowman Creek 32
Bowman Lake 32
Bowman Lake Trail 33
Brown Pass 32-33
Brush Lake 66-67
Bunker Creek 63, 156
Bunker Hill 63, 156
Bussard Creek 66
Bussard Mountain 66

Cain Lake 183
Cake Rock 252
Campbell Lake 207
Camp Kiser 181
Camp Nine Road 66
Camp Tony 226
Canuck Pass 65
Canuck Peak 65
Canyon Creek, North Fork 159
Canyon Creek Valley 158
Cape Alava 254
Caribou Hill 90
Cascade Crest 157
Castle Pass 157
Castle Fork 158
Carrie, Mt. 229
Cat Basin 230
Cat Creek 228-229
Cathedral Creek 54
Cathedral Peak 154
Cavanaugh Creek 183
Cedar Creek 253
Cedar Gulch 210
Challenger Glacier 178
Chilean Memorial 253
Chilliwack River 178
Chopaka Creek 138
Chopaka Lake 138
Chopaka Mountain 138
Chopaka Road 138
Chuchuwanteen River 157
Chuckanut Drive 186, 204
Chuckanut Mountain 184
Clackamas Mountain 133-134
Clarence Creek Road 40
Cleft Creek Trail 39
Cleft Rock Mountain 39
Cleft Rock Mountain Trail 36
Cleveland, Mt. 32
Cleveland Creek 32
Cliff Camp 226
Climatic Conditions 17
Clover Valley 209
Coal Creek 37
Coal Ridge 37
Cold Spring Campground 138
Colony Creek 204
Columbia Mountain Lookout 118
Columbia River 95, 81, 114
Continental Divide 32

Coolin 82, 88
Cooney Peak 64
Copeland Bridge 67, 84
Copper Ridge 179
Coupeville 203, 208
Cranberry Lake 208
Crawford State Park 93
Crowell Ridge 92
Cyclone Peak 37

Danquist Trail 67
Davis Mountain 64
Dead Lake 157
Deadman Creek 90
Dean Creek 156
Deception Pass 159, 207-208
Deemer Creek 92
Deep Creek Valley 94
Deer Creek Road 65
Deer Creek Summit 116
Deer Lake 231
Deer Park 226
Devil's Creek Gorge 160
Devil's Junction Campsite 160
Devil's Dome 159
Devil's Pass 159
Devil's Stairway 158
Diablo Lake Resort 174
Discovery Bay 221, 224
Discovery Road 224
Dock Butte 182
Dodge Summit 61
Dome Camp 153
Dugalla Bay 209
Duff Spring 135
Dungeness Forks Campground 226
Dyes Ranch 182

Eagle Point 228
East Bank Trail 160
East Deer Creek 116
East Glacier 31
East Shore Road 88
Eastport, ID 57, 65
Ebey's Landing 208, 211
Ebey's Landing National Historic
  Reserve 211
Ebey's Prairie 211

Edison 205
Elbow Lake 115
Ellen Creek 252
Elwa Valley 229
Erie, Mt. 207
Eureka, MT 42, 57, 59
Ewing Peak 64

Falls Creek 250-251
Fidalgo Bay 207
Fidalgo Island 206
15 Mile Shelter 232
Fire Camp Shelter Ford 179
Fireplace Camp 153
Fish Lakes 62
Fisher Peak 85
Fitzhenry, Mt. 229
Flagstaff Mountain 115
Flapjack Shelter 232
Flathead River, North Fork 33
Flume Creek Road 94
Forks 221, 232, 247
Fort Casey State Park 211
Fort Ebey State Park 210
Fort Worden 223
Foundation Creek 40
Frances, Lake 32
Francher's Dam 136
Franklin D. Roosevelt Lake 114
French Creek 63
Frosty Creek 157
Frosty Lake 157
Frosty Pass 157

Galton Ridge 39
Gardner Cave 93
Gardner Point 34
Garver Mountain 64
Garver Mountain Trail 64
Giants Graveyard 251
Gibralter Ridge 39
Glacier National Park 31, 33, 35
Goat Haunt Ranger Station 32
Goat Lakes 158
Goodenough Peak 152
Goodenough Park 152
Goodman Creek 249-251
Goodman Creek Trail 249

Granite Creek, West Fork 133
Grave Creek 40
Grave Creek Road 39
Graybeal Shelter 178
Green Mountain 226
Gun Point 208

Haig Mountain 153
Hall School 66
Hannegan Pass 179
Harrison Camp 156-157
Harrison Lake 89
Havillah 136
Hay Creek 36
Hay Creek Road 37
Heart Lake 230
Henry Lakes, Mt. 62
Henry, Mt. 62
Hidden Hand Pass 160
Hoh River 231
Hole In The Wall 33
Hole In The Wall Campsite 33
Hole In The Wall Falls 33
Holman Pass 158
Holman Peak 158
Hooknose Mountain 93-94
Hopkins Pass 158
Hopkins Lake 158
Hopkins Pass 158
Horseshoe Pass 153
Huntsberger Lake 38
Hurricane Ridge 221, 228
Hurricane Ridge Visitor Center 228
Hurricane Hill 228
Hurricane Ridge Road 227
Hyak Shelter 232

Indian Creek 117
Indian Creek Store 88
Indian Slough 206
Inland Empire 80
Iowa Heights 183

Jack Mountain 159
Jackson Creek 257
Jagged Island 253
Janet, Lake 32

Jimmycomelately Creek 225
Joe Mills Mountain 152
Joseph Whidbey State Park 209
Jungle Creek 64, 116

Kayostla Beach 253
Kent Lake 86-87
Kent Peak 87
Kettle Crest Trail 117
Kettle Range 112, 114
Kettle River 114
Keystone Ferry 211, 221
Kintla Creek 34
Kintla Lake 34
Kintla Lake Trail 35
Kishinena Creek 34-36
Kloatch Mountain 88
Koocanusa Lake 59-60
Koocanusa Bridge 59-60
Kootenai River 56, 84
Kounkel Pass 65

La Conner 206
La Push 247, 251
Lagitos Hill 248
Lakeview Ridge 158
Larry Reed Camp 61
Larson's Bridge 102
Lead Pencil Mountain 115
Leadpoint 94, 96
Lembert Mountain 118
Leola Creek 92
Leona, Mt. 117
Lewis Creek Road 38-39
Lewis, Mt. 38
Libby Beach Park 209
Libby, MT 60
Lily Lake Incline Trail 184, 186
Lime Lake 92
Lion's Head 86
Little Beaver Creek 177
Little Boulder Creek, South Fork 116
Little (Low) Divide 231
Little Sheep Creek 114
Little Snowy Top 91
Little Therriault Lake 42
Lizard Lake 184
Lock Cabin, Mt. 38

Locke Lookout 38
Lone Brook Canyon 35
Lone Lakes Trail 35
Lone Wolf Camp 153
Long Canyon Creek 84-85
Long Canyon Pass 84
Long Trail 4
Loomis 132, 150
Louden Lake 153
Louella Guard Station 225
Lower Cathedral Lake 154
Lyman Pass 181-182, 185

Maiden Lake 227
Maiden Peak 226
Makah Indian Tribe 254
Manning Park Lodge 157
Marblemount Store 174
Marble Mountain Lookout 116
Marmot Mountain 64
Martina Creek 155
May Creek 160
Metaline Falls, WA 82, 93-94
Midnight Mountain 118
Midnight Spring 118
Mill Creek 136
Mills, Lake 228-229
Mink Lake Trail 231
Mirror Lake 183
Moran's Beach 209
Morovits Campground 181
Morovits Stamp Mill 180
Mosquito Bay 88
Mosquito Bay Campground 89-90
Mountain Home Camp 158
Moyie River 66
Myrtle Lake 86
Myrtle Peak 86

Navigation Campground 90
Neah Bay 247
Neff Spring 118
Nokio Creek 39
Nooksack Ridge 179
Nooksack River, North Fork 179
Nooksack River, South Fork 181
Nooksack River Road, South Fork 182
Noonday Spring 116

North Beach 208
North Butte 184
North Cascades National Park 174
North Fork Road 39
Northwest Peak 64
Northwest Peak Scenic Area 64
Northport, WA 82, 95, 113
Norwegian Memorial 253
Nulle Road 184

Oak Harbor 203, 208
Obstruction Point 227
Okanogan Highlands 131, 136
Okanogan River Valley 137
Olallie Creek 152
Old Toroda 134
Olson Creek 32
Olympic Hot Springs 229
Olympic National Park 221
Olympic Peninsula 220
Olympus, Mt. 231, 233
Orient 113, 116
Oroville 132, 137
Orser Creek 66
Osoyoos 137
Osoyoos Lake 137
Othorp Lake 59
Oyster Lake 229
Ozette Indian Reservation 254
Ozette Ranger Station 247

Pacific Crest Trail 4, 156, 158
Pacific Northwest Trail Association 3
Park 183
Padilla Bay 205-206
Padilla Bay Interpretive Center 205
Padilla Heights Road 206
Park Creek Campground 181
Parker Creek 84-85
Parson Smith Tree 157
Pasayten 149
Pasayten Landing Field 157
Pasayten River 156
Pasayten River, East Fork 156
Peak Creek 87
Pend Oreille Bridge 94
Pend Oreille River 93
Penn Cove 208

Pepoon Canyon 115
Perego's Lagoon 211
Pete Creek 64
Picket Range 179
Pierce Creek 177
Pierre Creek 115
Pierre Lake 115
Pinkham Creek 59
Pinkham Wye 59
Plowboy Campground 90
Point No. 1 252
Point No. 2 253
Point No. 3 253
Point No. 4 254
Point No. 5 254
Point Partridge 210
Polebridge 34, 36
Port Angeles 221, 226
Port Townsend 221, 223
Porthill, ID 57, 82
Powder Mountain 158
Prairie 185
Priest Lake 88
Private Property 23
Ptarmigan Ridge 180
Pumpkin Mountain Camp 177
Purcell Mountains 57
Pyramid Lake 85
Pyramid Pass 85
Pyramid Peak 85

Quartz Lake 155
Quartz Mountain 155
Quilcene Ranger Station 225
Quileute Indian Reservation 251
Quillayute Needles National Wildlife
    Refuge 253
Quillayute River 249, 252
Quimper Peninsula 221, 224

Rainbow Creek 180
Rainbow Point 160
Red Meadow Campground 38
Red Rock Canyon Highway 35
Red Tide 203
Remmel Mountain 154
Republic 113, 119
Rialto Beach 252
Roaring Winds 227

Rock Candy Mountain 65
Rock Mountain 153
Rock Pass 158
Rocky Creek 181
Roland Point 160
Rosario Beach 207
Rose Ranch 115
Ross Dam 176
Ross Lake 160
Ross Lake Resort 150, 160, 174, 176
Ross Lake National Recreation Area 174
Ruby Creek 160
Ruby Creek Road 90
Ruby Ridge Trail 65
Russian Ridge 93
Russin Spring 86-87
Ruth Mountain 179
Ryan Cabin 117
Ryan Hill 117

Salmo Mountain 92
Salmo-Priest 91
Salmon Creek 225
Samish Bay 184, 204-205
Samish, Lake Road 184
Samish Overlook Trail 184
Samish River Bridge 205
San Juan Islands 207
Sand Point 254
Sand Ridge 155
Sanspoil River 119
Saxon 183
Saxon Bridge 183
Scotts Creek Bluff 251
Scotts Creek Shelter 251
Seemo Pass 39
Selkirk Crest 81
Sequim 220-221
Seven Lakes Basin 231
Sharpe County Park 207
Shedroof Divide Trail 91
Sheep Mountain 155
Sherman Pass 119
Shorty Creek 38
Silver Fir Campground 179
Similk Bay 207
Similk Beach 207
Similkameen River Bridge 137
Skagit Range 179
Skookum Hatchery 183

Sky Pilot Pass 159
Sleepy Hollow 115
Slab Camp Creek 226
Slide Pass 232
Slide Peak 231
Smith Creek Road 84
Snowshoe Cabin 152
Snowy Top 91
Snyder Guard Station 66
Soda Creek, North Fork 157
Soleduck Falls 230
Soleduck Hot Springs 230
Soleduck River 230
Solo Joe Creek Road 62
Soundview Logging Camp 182
South Kootenay Pass 35
South Kootenay Pass Trail 35
Spanish Camp 154
Spread Creek Road 64-65
Springsteen Lake 182
Squaw Bay 88
Squaw Creek 88
Squawman Lookout 88
St. Clair Creek 42
St. Clair Creek City Park 59
St. Clair Peak 40
Stahl Peak 41
Standard Lake 89
Starvation Creek 34
Steeple Rock 228
Stillwell Shelter 177
Strawberry Bay 251
Strawberry Point 251
Summit Lake 136
Sunset Beach 209
Sutherland Road 184
Sweat Creek 133
Sweat Creek Campground 119, 133
Swift Creek 180
Swinomish Channel 206

Tapto Camp 178
Taylor Point 251
Taylor Ridge 117
Ten Lakes Scenic Area 39
Therriault Creek 41
Therriault Pass 41
Third Beach 251
Thirsty Mountain 60

Thomas-Seton Mount 39-40
Thorofare 89-90
Thunderbird Point 32
Tilly Mine 66
Timberwolf Creek 155
Toleak Point 251
Trail Creek 36, 39
Trapper Creek 90
Tuchuck Campground 39
Tungsten Creek 154
Tungsten Mine 154
Turk Creek 86
Turner Creek Falls 62
Twin Lakes Trail 35
Twin Rocks Shelter 178
Twin Sisters Mountain 181
21 Mile Shelter 232
Twomile Camp 226
Two Mouth Lakes 87

Upper Cathedral Lake 154
Upper Ford Guard Station 63
Upper Kintla Lake 34
Upper Priest Lake 89
Upper Priest Lake Scenic Area 81, 89
Upper Priest Lake Trail 90
Upper Waterton Lake 32
U.S. Cabin Camp 179

Vancouver Island 207
Vinal Creek 62
Vinal Lake Road 62

Wagon Track Camp 153
Wam, Mt. 40

Wam Lookout, Mt. 39
Wanlick Creek 181
Wanlick Creek Trail 181
Wanlick Pass 181
Waper Ridge 63
Washington Monument 182
Watch Creek 92
Waterhole Picnic Area 228
Waterton Lakes National Park 31
Waterton Park, Alberta 31-32
Waterton River 32
Webb Mountain 60
West Point 208
West Side Road 84
Whale Lake 38
What Spring 134
Whatcom Pass 178
Whidbey Island 208
Whidbey Island Naval Air Station 203, 208-209
Whiskey Bend 228
Whistle Lake 207
Whitefish, MT 37
Wickersham 183
Wigwams 88
Windy Peak 153
Winkum Creek Road 64
Winthrop, Mt. 157
Wolf Creek Trail 228
Woody Pass 158

Yaak, MT 57, 63
Yaak River Road, West Fork 63
Yakinikak Creek 38
Yellow Banks Bay 254
Yon Dodge Cabin 159

TRAIL NOTES